BEYOND VIRTUE ETHICS

Recent Titles from the Moral Traditions Series

David Cloutier, Andrea Vicini, SJ, and Darlene Weaver, Editors

The Structures of Virtue and Vice
Daniel J. Daly

Consumer Ethics in a Global Economy
Daniel Finn

The Aesthetics of Solidarity: Our Lady of Guadalupe and American Democracy
Nichole M. Flores

Radical Sufficiency: Work, Livelihood, and a US Catholic Economic Ethic
Christine Firer Hinze

Humanity in Crisis
David Hollenbach, SJ

Tragic Dilemmas in Christian Ethics
Kate Jackson-Meyer

The Fullness of Free Time: Leisure and Recreation in the Moral Life
Connor Kelly

Beyond Biology: Rethinking Parenthood in the Catholic Tradition
Jacob M. Kohlhaas

Reimagining Human Rights: Religion and the Common Good
William O'Neill, SJ

Reenvisioning Sexual Ethics: A Feminist Christian Account
Karen Peterson-Iyer

Tomorrow's Troubles: Risk, Anxiety, and Prudence in an Age of Algorithmic Governance
Paul Scherz

Wealth, Virtue, and Moral Luck: Christian Ethics in an Age of Inequality
Kate Ward

Beyond Virtue Ethics

A CONTEMPORARY ETHIC OF ANCIENT SPIRITUAL STRUGGLE

STEPHEN M. MEAWAD

GEORGETOWN UNIVERSITY PRESS / WASHINGTON, DC

Library of Congress Cataloging-in-Publication Data

Names: Meawad, Stephen M., author.
Title: Beyond virtue ethics : a contemporary ethic of ancient spiritual struggle / Stephen M. Meawad.
Description: Washington, DC : Georgetown University Press, 2023. | Includes bibliographical references and index.
Identifiers: LCCN 2022008388 (print) | LCCN 2022008389 (ebook) | ISBN 9781647123116 (hardcover) | ISBN 9781647123123 (paperback) | ISBN 9781647123130 (ebook)
Subjects: LCSH: Christian ethics—Catholic authors. | Spiritual life—Catholic Church. | Ethics. | Virtues. | Virtue.
Classification: LCC BJ1249 .M295 2023 (print) | LCC BJ1249 (ebook) | DDC 241/.042—dc23/eng/20221107
LC record available at https://lccn.loc.gov/2022008388
LC ebook record available at https://lccn.loc.gov/2022008389

24 23 9 8 7 6 5 4 3 2 First printing

Printed in the United States of America

Portions of chapter 4 were previously published as "Sexuality, Angelification, and Divine Indwelling: A Contemporary Ethic of Early Christian Asceticism" in *Modern Theology*.

Portions of chapter 5 were previously published as "Virtue Ethics, Scripture, and Early Christianity: Patristic Sacred Reading as a Transformative Struggle of Perpetual Ascent" in *Studio Patristica*.

Cover design by Nathan Putens
Interior design by BookComp, Inc.

God-seeking strugglers, you are nearer to God than you know,
and your ignorance of this fact inflames the labor that
frees your grasp from all which is contrary to God.
ἐπεκτείνου και ἀνάγου!

CONTENTS

Acknowledgments ix

PART I: SITUATING THE ETHICS

Introduction 3

1 Which Virtue Ethics? Which Problems? 26

PART II: DEVELOPING THE ETHICS

2 A Case for Spiritual Struggle 71

3 Onward and Upward: The Perpetual Godwardness of Spiritual Struggle 99

PART III: APPLYING THE ETHICS

4 Asceticism as Godward Spiritual Struggle Applied to the Body 135

5 Sacred Reading as Godward Spiritual Struggle Applied to Scripture 167

6 Embodied Ethics and Inevitable Tensions 193

Bibliography 201

Index 217

About the Author 229

ACKNOWLEDGMENTS

This book is an amalgamation of wisdom, insight, dedication, and love that on too many scores are not my own. My familiarity with Christian spirituality, especially that of Orthodoxy, incorporates the decades of the deep sagacity I have witnessed in the many examples of intellectual saints or sanctified intellectuals who are witnesses to the transformative luminosity described in this book. My intimation of Christian spirituality is a product of these interactions, both explicitly, in spiritual guides and teachers, and implicitly, sometimes even at a distance in a paradoxically vociferous silence. As these enlightened women and men would have it in their modesty, I name none, though they serve as the heart and soul of this monograph.

In its first iterations, this book began as a dissertation under the guidance of Darlene Weaver, who has seen this work through all its stages and continues to offer a wealth of insights and to be an invaluable academic mentor to a budding scholar. I am grateful also to Elizabeth Cochran and Bogdan Bucur, who provided important feedback as readers in the manuscript's initial stages, and to Radu Bordeianu, for his support in many ways through my doctoral studies, often beyond the call of duty.

I thank the many colleagues and scholars who have provided services, including resource acquisition (especially Ramez Mikhail, now Father Arsenius), help with the many translations herein, and critical but gracious feedback, without which the completion of this book would not have been possible. I am grateful to the editors of the Moral Traditions Series at Georgetown University Press—David Cloutier, Andrea Vicini, and Darlene Weaver—for seeing this book through a helpful editorial process, and to James Keenan, for recommending me to the Press upon his interest in and reading of the manuscript. On this front, I would be remiss not to mention the readers at the Press, who despite their anonymity, deserve recognition for strengthening this book a great deal through their constructive feedback.

My family, too extensive to list here, has been instrumental at every turn. My parents, Maher and Wafa, have inculcated in me a deep love for God through their own. My older brother, Andrew, has served as an example and support all throughout. Among many things, he is always ready, in accord with the blessed Apostle's words, to rejoice in my rejoicing and to share in my sorrow. My wife, Veronica, has been my backbone, bearing me patiently and encouraging me daily in this process, especially whenever this labor of love would inadvertently and without warning transfigure into an arduous task. Through her, I am constantly becoming a better person through the revelation of my many shortcomings; not because she points them out, but because of the union God has designed in the mystery of matrimony. I carry this ever-unfolding (and in some ways salvific) process into the content of this book. To her, my incalculable debt can be paid only by boundless love, which only God can provide.

I take up the task of writing not primarily for vocational or occupational purposes but instead out of a deep conviction that the thoughts presented herein, though deficient, are foundational to exacting true and good change in this world. I thank, then, my children, Sophia and Theodore, who provide the thrust for this work. This book is as much a letter to their future selves (and maybe their future siblings) to take up a posture of Godward spiritual struggle as it is an attempt at mending—even ever so slightly—a humanity fallen and risen, and hungry for fulfillment.

Finally, I thank my God, in whom, for whom, and through whom I have written these pages as a submissive practice of Godward spiritual struggle.

PART I

Situating the Ethics

Introduction

> Belief in God, or in many gods, prevented the free development of moral reasoning. Disbelief in God, openly admitted by a majority, is a recent event, not yet completed. Because this event is so recent, Non-Religious Ethics is at a very early stage. We cannot yet predict whether, as in Mathematics, we will all reach agreement. Since we cannot know how Ethics will develop, it is not irrational to have high hopes.
>
> —Derek Parfit, *Reasons and Persons*

Nearly a century and a half after Nietzsche's declaration that "*Gott ist tot*," the insight behind the German philosopher's prophetic proclamation continues to unfold.[1] "*Gott bleibt tot*," and with the death of God comes the rise of the human, the one responsible for the construction of God, as postmodern deconstructionism might have it:[2]

> Indeed, we philosophers and "free spirits," as by a new dawn, feel illuminated by the news that the "old [*alte*] God is dead"; thereby, our hearts overflow with gratitude, astonishment, presentiment, and expectation. At last, the horizon appears to us again open, even if not bright; finally, our ships may put out to sail once again, at every peril. Every risk of the discerner [*Erkennenden*] is allowed again; the sea, our sea, is open again. Perhaps, such an "open sea" has never before existed.[3]

Humans, then, are free from the bonds that would prevent exploration of the uncharted sea of rational creativity. Thoughts and opinions—and the actions, decisions, and lifestyles derived therefrom—know no limit except those of the rational mind and encompassing societal structures. Possibilities are as diverse and numerous as are human beings. This Nietzschean shift has affected human deliberations widely and has manifested itself potently within the field of ethics, encumbered contemporarily by a conspicuous pluriformity of opinion that seems insurmountable.[4] With regard to the current state of ethics, this book laments the confusion and disagreement that have come to characterize the field, suggesting instead concepts that might come as interruptions to the prevalent lines of inquiry characteristic of modern ethics.

The starting point for this project is Jonathan Sanford's discerning critique of modern moral philosophy's disorientation:

> The level of disagreement about basic issues in moral philosophy is staggering. There is no shortage of evidence on this point: simply open any anthology or handbook of moral philosophy and read through the table of contents. Sentimentalism is pitted against deontology, both of which are pitted against utilitarianism, all of which are contrasted with divine command theory, which is again contrasted with contractarianism, which are all again opposed to virtue ethics, and so on. Add to this the striking contrast between the sorts of inquiries that ancient and medieval philosophers pursued and those pursued by philosophers today, and the picture of the state of ethics is even more complex. There simply are no questions settled once and for all in contemporary moral philosophy. Still more unsettling, there is not even basic agreement about what it is that a philosopher engaged in ethical inquiry ought to be doing.[5]

This is not what any moral philosopher wishes upon her field; diversity of opinion should be celebrated when that diversity can stake even the mildest claim in working toward a unitive front, albeit one that concomitantly celebrates distinction. The optimistic promise expressed toward nonreligious ethics in this introductory chapter's epigraph by Derek Parfit might have been cast in too vast a valley; with the Kantian autonomous mind and the Nietzschean unbound ship sailing the "open sea" comes unbridled potential with little direction. Does God's death—to continue the Nietzschean allusion and to lend Sanford's account credence—bring about the death of ethics, at least in its foundationless (in)ability to decipher between claims to right and wrong, good and bad? Bleak as this account may be, it seems to run along the same current that propelled contemporary virtue ethics. In efforts to rescue ethics from the stalemates and dissensions that decorated the field, with optimism, virtue ethicists heeded G. E. M. Anscombe's perceptive insight that modern moral philosophy required significant redress, so much that it should altogether redefine its purpose or at the very least redirect its focused efforts. Yet, in doing so, contemporary virtue ethicists fell into much the same patterns as did the deluge of post-Enlightenment moral theories that preceded virtue ethics' modern resurgence.

"Modern virtue ethics," as Sanford admits, "has become something soothing, edifying and familiar. It has grown up in the polluted atmosphere of contemporary expectations (assumptions, presuppositions, confusions, distractions) and naturally enough has quickly become tarnished by them."[6] What called for a forceful separation was in fact welcomed by a relaxed shift of terms from rules, principles, and obligations (deontology); actions and outcomes (consequentialism); and dilemmas and conundrums (quandary ethics) to a scientific parsing of virtues and character; the conceptual framework remained.[7] Virtue ethics failed to escape the factious currents in modern moral philosophy, rightly accused of failing to escape relativistic consequentialist ideologies.[8] Faction might not always point to inadequacy, but as it relates to virtue ethics, diversity of thought is telling of a more fundamental dissonance.

Does this vast disagreement find root in a prima facie assertion, a first principle, that if uncovered functions as a uniting force? Put another way, is there a fundamental disagreement from which spring the boundless, divisive perspectives responsible for political, social, ethical, and religious chasms? Claiming to locate the culprit, or even claiming that there is a single culprit, is as bold as it is unpromising, and yet contenders present themselves based on their comprehensive existential natures. Answers to questions about philosophy, theology, sociology, psychology, and anthropology, to name a few, might direct the quest for a narrower consensus among possible first principles. Going through the task of locating this uniting front is an arduous, if not virtually impossible, task, beyond the scope of this book. At the same time, questions of anthropology strike me as the most promising areas of inquiry that, if agreed upon, can begin addressing the lamentable discord in contemporary ethics.

As a catalyst in the virtue ethics movement, Anscombe's appeal to a "philosophy of psychology" might more fittingly have been to a philosophical *anthropology*. Anscombe warns against developing a moral philosophy without first having an adequate philosophy of psychology: "It is not profitable for us at present to do moral philosophy; that should be laid aside at any rate until we have an adequate philosophy of psychology, in which we are consciously lacking."[9] Sanford interprets Anscombe to mean that we must develop a more robust philosophical *anthropology*, a reasonable reading of Anscombe, considering her emphasis on understanding the human person before making claims as to what that person ought to be doing.[10] Constantine Sandis also agrees that an unintended and unforeseen consequence of Anscombe's "divisive" article in 1958 was the creation of a new branch of "'moral psychology' as an independent and increasingly empirical 'branch' of ethics whose interest in questions of motivation, agency, and responsibility have largely neglected investigations into the good and the right."[11] This much is echoed in Alasdair MacIntyre's observation that ethics collapses when telic human nature is separated from the current state of human nature and from the bridge between the current and the telic. Each of the three (the current, the telic, and the bridge between the two) requires the other two, yet modern moral philosophy has abandoned the telic; it has not sufficiently answered (or even asked) what the end of human nature is.[12] To this end, Demetrios Harper rightly summarizes Alasdair MacIntyre and Bernard Williams's critique of Western ethics' oversight: "The question of ethics hinges on the question of nature."[13] Harper further nuances this observation, taking form in Kant and brought to fruition in Nietzsche, identifying a shift in the definition of human nature "away from the notion of nature as a living reality to nature as a mechanical process."[14] Not without warrant, I do proceed boldly in emphasizing the task of anthropology as a promissory shift for ethics generally and for virtue ethics specifically, if their hopes are ever to evade the cyclical impasses of its various conclusions.

Bernard Williams pulls some of modern moral philosophy's questions ("What is our duty? . . . How may we be good? . . . How can we be happy?"[15]) back to Socrates's question ("How should one live?"[16]). Yet ethicists might need to pull the question back even further, more fundamentally asking (and hopefully answering) questions regarding the nature of human beings, how they came to be, what parts constitute their whole or comprise their flourishing, and what might constitute their telic purposes.[17] In the interim, we should not be imprudently misled to believe that we have the tools to answer more nuanced questions, the ones to which ethicists often rashly leap because of their seemingly more urgent relevance: What actions ought I to take? What justifications can I make for my actions? What sorts of relationships am I to have with the animal world, with the material world, the rest of humanity, as a spouse, a parent, a colleague, a stranger, a friend? How am I to use my mental faculties for the betterment of humanity? Am I to cultivate ecological consciousness? Am I to be politically and socially engaged in my present contextual location? What values am I to promote? What virtues am I to pursue?

It should not come as a surprise that these secondary questions often take the limelight; they are all of great consequence and deserve their due attention, appearing as foundational concerns indeed. Yet we would be unreasonable to assume that we could ever reach agreement on these secondary matters when our starting points are fundamentally discordant. Do not the majority of answers given these secondhand questions carry presuppositions from their prima facie antecedents? I think it honest and effective, then, to address some of the anthropological presuppositions that direct the ethics I present in this book.

Humans do not always behave in the manner they should. In fact, we possess a unique capacity even to desire those things that are not good for our flourishing. At the same time, we often realize within ourselves a capacity toward that which we deem good. We often want to reach outside ourselves symbiotically toward others. We fail, we flourish; we err, we succeed; we experience moments of clarity, we collapse under complex confusion. We experience a pendular reality, oscillating between desiring that which is good for us and that which is bad for us—that is, that which is in accord with human nature and that which is discordant with that nature's flourishing.[18] We act contrary to our desires, and we desire contrary to our knowledge. This reality is characterized in Christian—especially in Orthodox Christian—anthropology as the fallen and risen nature of humanity. It is, on one hand, a nature that carries within it the death and decay chosen freely when humanity separated itself from the source of life Himself. It is, on the other hand, through the sacramental initiation into the ecclesial Body of Christ, risen in the risen Christ, the Mediator between humanity and the divine, who (1) *redeemed* humanity through the Incarnation, Crucifixion, and Resurrection; (2) *redeems* humanity through human participation in divine grace by the indwelling of the Holy Spirit; and (3) *will redeem* humanity in His Second Coming from the heavens for the final judgment. Within this lens, the reality of the tension experienced by humans is one that is always already-there-not-yet on this side of the eschaton. As such, humans possess the clairvoyant potentiality to use their collective faculties in the pursuit of truth and reality, and yet must always do so with caution, acknowledging the limitations inherent in such an endeavor. All human faculties must be engaged in this pursuit, and yet all human faculties will fall short of comprehensive knowledge.

The simple theological premise undergirding this anthropological observation is that humans are fallen and at the same time are risen. For this reason, the framework out of which arises the Orthodox Christian Patristic lens of this project is fundamentally opposed to the Enlightenment project that honors reason as the sole arbiter in determinations of good and evil, right and wrong. Reason is good, helpful, and necessary but requires the complementary functions of all other modes of human experience in order to appropriately (and still insufficiently) access truth: "Christian reason must plumb to the depths and heights of all created phenomena and must most be concerned with the nature of the God-created souls intended to return to

Him."[19] One potential promise of this book, then, is a starting point different from the Catholic and Protestant approaches to virtue ethics that might fall within either of these categories (too much or too little trust in human capabilities). Humans are neither entirely morally depraved nor are they entirely perfected.[20]

With this anthropological ambivalence, it is a challenge to discuss human nature in this book with precision. God, the Good Himself, is the perfect fulfillment of human nature and the guiding principle of this ethic. Increasing unity with God *is* growth in goodness, which in turn is natural to humans. However, that human nature is at the same time fallen implies that what at times may seem "natural" to humans is in fact contrary to human nature. Any number of vices—anger, pride, lust, and selfishness, among others—can become disguised under this pretense. It is this part of human nature—the part that at times miscalculates or improperly assesses what is natural to itself—that requires transformation. For this reason, though this book tends toward the language of transformation, it is with an eye to the fallenness that is currently integral to human nature. This project acknowledges a tension between the innate goodness of human nature, the fallenness of that nature, the restoration of this nature in Jesus Christ's economy of salvation, the initial steps of transformation a person undergoes on Earth through grace-enabled struggle, and the eschatological perpetuity of this transformation in the afterlife. It is with this Orthodox Christian understanding and within this predicament that the concepts developed in this book are placed.

More specifically, the two most central components of this book—spiritual struggle and perpetual progress (ἐπέκτασις) or ascent (ἀναγωγή)—are not being developed in relation to ethics for the purposes of providing evidence for my prima facie assumptions. First principles are just that—the starting points with which we must be transparent. The evidence is, in some sense, in the types of actions encouraged and the formed and transformed people and communities created when these first principles and their immediate corollaries are incarnated. My emphasis here is that ethicists often seem to be arguing "final steps"—what decisions should I take; what actions should I make; what kind of person am I to become—without an appeal to their starting points. We should not then be surprised at the ethical stalemates that ensue. My other anthropological assumption, not unique to Orthodox Christianity dogmatically (though potentially by way of emphasis), is that humans are created in the image and likeness of God, as the Genesis account maintains, and that the end or telos of humanity is the perpetual realization of this God-likeness; God is the fulfillment of human nature.[21] What this means is that the form that actions, decisions, virtues, and other ethical considerations take is revealed when placed within the purview of unity with God. In chapters 4 and 5, I will demonstrate how this Godward orientation transforms concrete practices.

Three interrelated elements of my thesis will unfold simultaneously as I develop my narrative in this book: (1) Christians can and should envision ethics as a subset of, or entirely subsumed in, the spiritual life, because modern moral philosophy tends to amputate rules, obligations, actions, consequences, and even virtuous formation from the source—that is, God—that grants these concepts moral grounding and relevance; (2) Orthodox Christianity, grounded in an early Church ethos, serves as a helpful starting point in envisioning this ethic as one of "Godward spiritual struggle"; and (3) applying this framework to any practice directly dictates the form of that practice, taps into the transformative depths of that practice, and transforms a person in a manner consonant with the "good life" in God that evades many of the problems within the field of ethics.

Given that I spend two chapters detailing the elements that constitute an ethics of Godward spiritual struggle, I only define them directly and very briefly here before further reference to them. Spiritual struggle refers to the exertion of effort in all conceivable dimensions of human existence—including the physical, emotional, psychological, intellectual, and spiritual—with intent to attain a semblance of, knowledge of, and intimacy with Jesus Christ in community, for God, and for others. *Epektasis,* as it will be developed, is a term intended to capture the progressive quality of the perpetual, struggle-filled ἀναγωγή to God. It is a term that principally implies orienting to God for ontological transformation in an eternal life that begins now and continues eschatologically or anagogically.[22] It is the persistent upward trajectory of a person's pursuit of God, enabled by God's gracious condescension (συγκατάβαση) and enlivened by spiritual struggle (ἀγωνίζομαι), resulting in a newfound, though ever-unfolding, assimilation to Him.

This book, then, is interdisciplinary in nature, piecing together ethics, spirituality, and systematic theology (and, in chapters 4 and 5, asceticism and Scripture); as such, I do not claim authority on all fronts. In continuing the candor demonstrated in exposing the starting points assumed in this book, I write as an Orthodox Christian ethicist deeply concerned with modern instantiations of ancient Christian spirituality. The Patristic corpus allows me to develop categories integral to my thesis, and though I do not claim myself to be a Patristic scholar, it is from within the Orthodox tradition that I find the Fathers especially convincing, because Patristic scholarship "does require at least a very high degree of trust in the experience of the Fathers and the church of Christ within which patristic theology developed. Someone knowingly alienating himself from the patristic context, or aloof from the 'patristic faith,' cannot be a patristic scholar."[23] The primary lens I utilize is that of the "ethics" of Orthodox Christians, embodied and articulated both contemporarily and historically, responding in part positively to John Haldane's concern that "in recent decades moral philosophy has in some part lost its way and become disconnected from lived experience."[24] Contemporarily, Orthodox Christian spirituality, which might replace or subsume the concept of ethics proper, finds its expression most fully in Patristic resources, especially those of the first three centuries, before Constantine's famous edict that granted freedom to practice Christianity. For this reason, I rely on these ancient Christian resources in developing as accurately as I can two concepts that express the "ethics" (if there ever were one) of Orthodox Christians. In the next section, I address the difficulties of appropriating these resources in a modern context.

I both utilize and subvert contemporary virtue ethics to situate this spirituality within scholarly discourse. The considerations within virtue ethics (and even deontology and consequentialism) are not put aside but emerge as logical and inevitable consequences of the spiritual life. Robert C. Roberts accurately describes the "ancient virtue ethical goal" as one of "forming souls in excellence."[25] At the same time, the spiritual life mitigates certain issues within normative ethical theories, the most relevant of which is virtue ethics. After laying this groundwork, I demonstrate how these concepts, as direct corollaries of the anthropological assumptions noted above, might manifest themselves in concrete practices, namely, in asceticism and sacred reading. These practices serve as two examples of the "ethical" model in this project, which is in actuality a *spiritual* model that determines actions, attitudes, decisions, virtues, character, and all other concepts typical of ethics proper. If spirituality might be understood as the proximity of a human being's spiritual existence to its spiritual Creator, then it is the pursuit of this proximity that provides answers to the "final steps" typical of ethical discussions.

Though I start with Sanford's critique, this book does not take up his recommendation for a truly Aristotelian project, as all other attempts have fallen short of taking on the full gamut of his categories and assumptions. Instead, I contend that part of the recovery of a classical Christian view of virtue ethics, unencumbered by modern sentiments, is accomplished through an appeal to the Golden Era of Patristics, especially those of the first three centuries of Christianity.[26] To appeal to the early Church Fathers is one way to make sense of a culture that did not see itself as "doing virtue ethics" but as understanding virtue as the embodiment and perpetual fulfillment of an already-teleological framework. Instead of deciding between right and wrong actions; deciphering is-versus-ought formulas; cracking perplexing, uncouth, and improbable conundrums; weighing the risks and benefits of decisions and their consequences; or even developing a philosophically convincing account of virtue theory or a comprehensive list of enduring virtues, it is incumbent on moral philosophers first to provide answers to the fundamental questions that if agreed upon would allow for more cohesion and reaching a consensus in an otherwise disjointed field.

The deeper task of ethics is accomplished either by recasting ethics as but one piece of the unified fabric of human experience that defines the good life or by assuming a premodern lens that altogether disposes of ethics categorically. The latter, the self-effacing task of theories of virtue in the face of modern moral philosophy, is the approach taken by unconventional or marginal virtue ethicists, including Anscombe and MacIntyre, to use Sanford's helpful categories.

At times, this book will strike the reader as part of the marginal efforts in virtue ethics—that is, an effort that does not see itself as working within virtue ethics but as increasingly skeptical and critical of the currents within the field: "Marginal contemporary virtue ethicists . . . seek to revive premodern ethical concerns and criteria for judgment in a way made relevant within our contemporary context."[27] This marginality will manifest itself in at least two ways throughout this book, especially in its constructive elements addressed in chapters 2 through 5. First, the early Christian Fathers, steeped in ancient Greek philosophy, knew of no functional use for "ethics" as used in its modern sense, and thus they provide a model for the "virtue ethics" to which Anscombe and MacIntyre beckon.[28] Categorically, then, this project is one of unconventional or marginal virtue ethics in its critical view of modern moral philosophy. It is an abrupt insertion of concepts and categories foreign to modern moral philosophy instantiated in the concrete, embodied spiritual practices characteristic of Orthodox Christian praxis. It appeals to the premodern Patristic framework embodied in the Orthodox Christian spiritual ethos. Second, this book subverts virtue as an end to the good life, placing virtue instead as a by-product of the good life reenvisioned in the struggle-laden pursuit of unity with God.

At other times, this book may strike the reader as consonant with mainstream or conventional virtue ethics, specifically in its response to the criticisms posed against the elevation of character and virtue against rules, obligations, actions, and consequences. In charting an ethics that is untraditional vis-à-vis modern moral philosophical conventions, I find it helpful, at the risk of reverting entirely to conventional methods of doing ethics, to elaborate on how this project does mitigate certain complexities within conventional virtue ethics—a task to which I turn explicitly in chapter 1.

FROM ANCIENT TO MODERN: CREATING SPACE FOR THE CHURCH FATHERS

Before proceeding, it is needful at this point to articulate, at least briefly, a defense of my reliance on the Patristic corpus—a "genre" overflowing with a wisdom and spiritual acumen that risk extinction, as evidenced paradoxically, though not surprisingly, by contemporary antipathy. The thread of contemporary critiques waged against the early Fathers is a necessary corollary of the broader fabric of postmodernism, and a description of the latter suffices in articulating the former. The thrust of my defense, then, might be expressed most effectively in a challenge, unpopular in academe,[29] of some of the guiding principles of postmodernity, including, among other descriptions, its rejection of grand narratives; its confused (and contradictorily universalized) repudiation of universal worldviews; its dismissal of objectivity as it relates to matters of anthropology, rationality, and truth; and in more recent times, its abandonment of history itself as a reliable guide for future directions.[30] Yet, given the immensity of this task and the limited scope of this project, a more direct defense of the Fathers might be offered effectively by pointing to a few lamentable anachronisms superimposed on this otherwise invaluable, though obviously fallible, corpus.

Arguments placed against a heavy reliance on the Patristic corpus, in principle, might discredit the Fathers' voices as oppressive, elitist, and patriarchal, as implied in its appellation. The Fathers, as the opposition would have it, quieted the voices that soon fell to the fringes, marginalized by a body seeking a hierarchy, or kyriarchy, tyrannical and hungry for imperious power.[31] This view is complicated by, and largely finds its origins in, the discovery of the Nag Hammadi manuscripts discovered in 1945, which challenged the portrayal of the early Church as largely univocal in perspective, revealing instead a diversity in early Christian thought.[32] These charges are warranted and highly uncontested, as noted in Morwenna Ludlow's observation that only "a few have argued that the dominant position [in the early Church] is in fact not misogynistic at all."[33] I do not claim to dismantle or dismiss these charges; nor do I wish to defend any blatant offenses attributed to this era. I only wish to create space for the spiritual formation embodied by many in this time by interpreting their contexts from within their own ancient Christian perspective, that is, with consideration to the very priorities that gave rise to patristic texts and not to anachronisms retrojected onto early Christian thinkers.

In my brief examination here, I will not appeal to a mode of analysis that "transcends" historical particularity but that considers concepts and evidence that have either morphed or are altogether nonfunctional in modern critical theory.[34] It is worth noting that this transcendence of historical particularity appealed to—for example, in ressourcement theology[35]—is often not what it seems, that is, ignoring "what actually happened" within the cultural, social, and contextual dimensions out of which texts arise.[36] For a particular historical context, certain concepts held positions of prominence against those held within a modern historian's purview; this disconnect is often the very source of anachronistic studies. It may appear, then, that at times this book ignores historical particularity; but on the contrary, it attempts to give priority to those very notions that were most important to the early Fathers, at times over and against modern sentiments. What seems to emerge when one allows oneself to enter into the history of the early Fathers is in fact an ecclesial culture that, though not always innocent of the social errors of its day, was moved by interests much different than those pointed out as problematic in our time. To situate these lenses, I suggest three brief concepts—truth, servitude, and eschatology, which were relatively ubiquitous among the monastic-episcopal leadership—to make a brief case for applying a premodern lens in modern times that has often been either gleaned over or intentionally discarded.

First, the picture drawn of early Christian leaders, as expressing oppressive views of a power-stricken majority and silencing minority views, is an unfair assumption based largely in the discussion of truth and heresy. Putting aside the distasteful ring these concepts might have for the modern ear, the fact that truth and heresy, right and wrong, were conceptually relevant, need not imply that an insistence categorically on a certain truth was at the same time a claim to power. This conflation requires a leap; it is possible for power and truth, even as absolute, to be decoupled. The narrative in an ancient Christian self-understanding, and in the understanding of the centuries to follow, was of a truth that is at its core transformational. Often, the silenced or marginalized voices were the ones that ultimately prevailed, not by the imposition of power—and this is the key difference—but in their pursuit of a truth that is not only rational but also lived, virtuous, communally verified, just, and experienced incarnationally in concert with the divine revelation just a few generations prior. It is primarily through the collective attestation to the transformational capacity of a truth by *all* believers in that community that claims were accepted and adopted. Even the imposition of power could not render a truth acceptable, especially as evidenced by the overwhelming number of Christian martyrs in those first four centuries deemed the era of Golden Patristics. Those martyrs propagated the Christian life, and the lethal power forced on them was ultimately ineffective in changing that conviction.[37] Constantine's edict could do no more to save Christianity than did the sacrificial blood of the martyrs from whose seed sprouted the faith.[38]

One would be remiss to speak of truth in Christianity and ignore the illustrious Saint Athanasius the Apostolic, whose defense of the truth in the fourth century led to the development of the creedal statements (not to mention his significant impact on Scriptural codification) affirmed by nearly all of Christendom until this day. Not all historians will agree with my portrayal of Athanasius here;[39] but from within his own context, submerged in Alexandrian spirituality, a more forbearing picture emerges.[40] As a champion of the truth, Athanasius's views were in fact the minority opinion. He was sentenced to exile five times, from which a famous saying of his earned him the sobriquet "contra mundum."[41] If the accusations of the affinity of truth claims to power dominance were accurate, one would expect that the Scriptural canon and the Nicaean-Constantinopolitan Creed—both finding their origins in Athanasius to some degree—would be examples par excellence of tyrannical enforcement in the name of dogmatic orthodoxy. On the contrary, his emphasis was one of truth validated primarily through the experience of the risen Christ. To be sure, Saint Athanasius's journey was one of struggle throughout, not the least of which included his years of discipleship under the father of monasticism, Saint Antony, from whom Athanasius came to understand the intimate and inextricable connection between *orthodoxia* and *orthopraxia*. This very spiritual struggle, springing from the fountain of early Christian ascetics, is the paradigm shift unpacked in this book. Truth was pursued through renunciation, poverty, and humility—not power, status, or authority. One need not take more than a quick glance at the stories of the majority of popes selected in the See of Alexandria to be convinced of the actual "power" dynamics in place: these ascetics have often been documented to flee from the honor and responsibility of the papacy, preferring instead to remain in their simple monastic lives pursuing unity with God.[42] Right worship, right belief, and right actions were part of a cohesive whole, the experience of which served as the pressing force that animated the Alexandrian's defense of fundamental Christian truth.

This same See of Alexandria has seen a great deal of oppression and persecution throughout the ages, whether under the guise of Christianity or of Islam, but have not been documented to stake the justification of their claims in their oppression—a negative example of the decoupling of truth from power.[43] Absolute claims—theological, praxical, and spiritual—again were repeatedly tested and verified, first, and most importantly, in the experience of the resurrected Christ in the communities that embodied those claims, and then in the texts that documented (and continuously formed and informed) these experiences. This lens—one that emphasizes matters of truth experienced, embodied, and disseminated—is far from the one often placed on the Patristic era or their spiritual heirs. That in postmodern times this sentiment of truth and "absolutism" might not resonate well does not imply that it was not in fact the very impetus for early Patristic spiritual endeavors, ultimately in the pursuit of unity with God. As such, the search for accurate theological expressions should not be dismissed as "the most punishingly patriarchal practice"[44] when judging the validity of appealing to these resources for modern inspiration or guidance.

Second, a parallel line of argument can be placed alongside important instances of power dynamics at the heart of ancient Christian hierarchy. The bishop of Alexandria was the ⲡⲁⲡⲁ,[45] the pope, the father of fathers, a title bearing the gravest of pastoral responsibility. My argument does not maintain that no corruption was found in Christian hierarchy; that would be altogether inaccurate and indefensible. Instead, part of the picture often neglected is a real, transformative, spiritual experience that might be lost on the modern mind, to its detriment. Before taking on the language of imperial honorifics—such as Eminence, Excellency, Reverence, among others—those who shepherded the flock of Christ understood themselves as reflecting the fatherhood of God Himself.[46] The model instituted by Christ is one in which "whoever wishes to be great . . . must be . . . servant [διάκονος], and whoever wishes to be first . . . must be . . . slave [δοῦλος]; just as the Son of Man came not to be served but to serve [διακονῆσαι],"[48] and where "many who are first will be last, and the last will be first."[48] Thus, Christ presents a hierarchy of servitude, which is paradoxical only externally to the tradition. When allowed its position within the submissive, humble, ascetical tradition of the developing early Church, the forceful repudiation of structured ecclesial leadership weakens. This leadership was premised instead on the very same spiritual ethics I attempt to recover in this book. Andrea Sterk, in demonstrating the early monastic ideals that became characteristic of the episcopate, does well to summarize the qualities emphasized in early Christian episcopal authority: "The ascetic bishop had seen God; he was a *bogovidac.* He had purged his passions, contemplated divine truths, and ultimately, like Moses, encountered the living Lord on Mt. Sinai. This vision, the fruit of the bishop's monastic vocation, was the true source of his authority in the church and the world."[49]

Again, this is not to say that positions of authority did not carry with them inherent temptations to corruption or that this corruption never came to fruition among leaders deemed spiritual. Yet this hierarchy of servitude ought not to be met with so avid a distrust and aversion so as to neglect any wisdom, especially one accessible in concrete spiritual practices, that this age might offer. Instead, it is within this ecclesial culture that one ought to envision a hierarchy in service of, and dare I say slavery to, the experience of truth, the service of the people of God, and the protection of the tradition, teaching, and faith "which the Lord gave, the Apostles preached, and the fathers preserved."[50]

Third, the spiritual context of the early Church Fathers, or more specifically their eschatological or anagogical contexts, are too often overlooked when critiques regarding the marginalization of women are placed on this era. I appeal here to Saint Gregory of Nyssa, the Cappadocian Father most central to this book. Consider, for example, how Gregory ascribed the majority of his spiritual progression, in fact his very salvation, to the angelic virtue overabounding from his blessed sister Macrina. In fact, the Scriptural passage in Philippians to which Gregory alludes in what comes to be coined as *epektasis* (ἐπεκτεινόμενος) is the same verse he uses to ascribe "the prize of" his sister's "upward calling" (τὸ βραβεῖον τῆς ἄνω κλήσεως).[51] She is angelic (ἀγγελικήν),[52] not by means of silencing her femininity but as participating in an eschatological reality as perfect (τελεία) in every kind of virtue (ἀρετὴν).[53] One cannot overstate the importance of the lens or context imposed *on* this example, because in the discussion that follows, whether his spiritual milieu is accepted or whether it is displaced by other interests dictates the conclusions, rendering Gregory a "patristic misogynist" par excellence or a champion of egalitarianism in an otherwise male-dominated era. For this reason, the feminist scholarship on Nyssen is not entirely settled, and his position as the norm or the outlier depends largely on the presuppositions of the reader, which modern scholars do not evade.[54]

A good example is found in Morwenna Ludlow's work on Gregory, specifically in her discussion of the bishop of Nyssa's relationship to his sister Macrina. Ludlow makes a "striking" observation that "women tend to be studied for their 'spiritual' and personal, rather than their political or institutional influence," an observation that neglects Nyssen's prioritization of spiritual unity with God above all else.[55] Similarly, Virginia Burrus, who self-identifies as a "perversely loving daughter" of a patristic corpus that she has allowed to "overwhelm" and "engulf" her, places on these texts a cultural context that is vastly incongruous from that in which they operate.[56] For example, in analyzing the texts of Athanasius of Alexandria, Gregory of Nyssa, and Ambrose of Milan, her assumption is that the motivating factor for, or at least the principle outcome of, their theological expositions is a silencing of femininity and feminized theological descriptors for the purpose of solidifying the masculinity of the divine and thus of the masculine state of ecclesial authority.[57] In deliberately ignoring the secondary resources that offer conflicting interpretations, she ignores the complex ecclesial and spiritual culture that informed these ancient Christian thinkers, ascribing to them agendas appropriate to, and at odds with, more modern sentiments.

As another example, Burrus's reading of the Cappadocian's *Vita Sanctae Macrinae* is too readily influenced by the lens she overtly professes, eclipsing the author's own emphases.[58] What is being critiqued here is not Burrus's methodology, which is sound, creative, and thorough. Nor do I even intend in this short space to contradict her assumptions. I only wish to point out that the assumptions—what John J. O'Keefe and R. R. Reno refer to as the "economy"—dictate or anticipate the conclusions. Though only using Burrus's text as a parallel to allegorical patristic exegesis, O'Keefe and Reno's observations here are helpful: "Decisions about the truth or falsehood of her interpretation of patristics literature will depend, to a great extent, upon whether or not readers think Burrus's assumptions about a feminist economy of personal and social life are true. The issue is not simply one of expressing preferences for one economy over another. Our 'faiths' interact with our interpretations in a mutually reinforcing fashion, making it impossible to distinguish between the organizing assumptions and the material results of interpretation."[59] Needless to say, any reader, and the modern reader no less, brings certain presumptions to a text, which is certainly not to be decried. But O'Keefe and Reno help to move the point forward: be wary not to read over and against the very lens with which many Church Fathers wrote, which might not do justice to the full breadth of their oeuvre. The patristic economy, or lens, developed throughout *Sanctified Vision*, with which I engage more thoroughly in chapter 5, captures some of the "spiritual context" to which I appeal and through which I believe space can be made for the Fathers to affect modern ethics.

Hans Boersma, more forcibly uncovering similar spiritual underpinnings, notes that "Burrus sees Gregory's work—contrary to his own intentions—as transgressing the homosocial worlds of gender." He continues, "I believe that recent appraisals of Gregory's theology of embodiment do not do justice to his overall thought."[60] In the instance of Gregory's exposition of Macrina, he is not silencing the femininity of his sister but is instead using a lens—an anagogical, eschatological, and spiritual lens—ignored in Ludlow and Burrus's assumptions that allows them to render one of the finest elevations of women in early Christianity: an accusation of misogyny by the bishop. Ilaria L. E. Ramelli, similar to Boersma, maintains that the only way to understand Nyssen's more sociological conclusions—for example, his denunciation of slavery and love toward the poor—is by first understanding his eschatology.[61]

In the same way, Macrina's *eschatological* transformation here and now—part of Gregory's spiritual or anagogical lens—was not a denial of her femininity but a celebration of her overcoming the fallenness in human nature and participating in the risen Christ. There is, in Gregory's worldview, no greater accomplishment nor noble *telos*; any silence on her femininity is an emphasis on her transformation in God—the goal of the Christian life for Gregory and the very impetus of his authorship.

Although insufficient to challenge the breadth of scholarship in opposition to the patristic corpus, I hope at least to have carved some space to allow the insights of ancient Christian spirituality to speak to contemporary ethical concerns. My concern here is not so much to defend a fabricated *consensus patrum* against cogent critiques but to temper the vociferousness through which many may come to distrust atavistic studies generally and early Christian studies specifically. If any clemency is to be granted, it might be in the same spirit assumed by Antony, Basil of Caesarea, and Gregory of Nazianzus, to name a few, to take that which is edifying from all we encounter despite the unpleasantries with which they might be associated.[62] In this book, then, that which is edifying is the spiritual praxis attested to by many early Christians as a spring of transformed life, confirmed by centuries of Christians thereafter, and preserved through embodiment (and thus verified in some ways and to some degree) by those Orthodox Christians, among others, who contemporarily assume similar spiritual *ethea*.

OVERVIEW OF THE BOOK'S CHAPTERS

In order to accomplish the objectives mentioned in this introductory chapter, the chapters that follow are laid out methodically. Put tersely, I hope to *situate, construct,* and *apply*. In chapter 1, I continue to *situate* this book in relation to virtue ethics—a task already begun in this introduction—first by describing in more detail what an Orthodox Christian ethics of virtue might entail and second by delineating points of comparison between Orthodoxy and the Aristotelian-Thomistic tradition. This latter concern, in a conventional fashion, allows me to address certain complexities within virtue ethics generally and Christian virtue ethics specifically, demonstrating how reenvisioning ethics, as suggested in this book, helps mitigate some contemporary virtue ethical issues. This sets the stage for the topics of chapters 2 and 3, spiritual struggle and the perpetual pursuit of God.

Moving on to the *constructive,* unconventional portion of this book, chapter 2 begins with a development of the concept of spiritual struggle. It is astounding that a concept of such paramountcy in antiquity and in the early Church would be entirely absent in modern moral philosophy, potentially due to the anthropological dissonance between these eras, as suggested above. In locating categorically the three origins of spiritual struggle, the concept emerges as one that allows a person to work in synergy with God's grace, confronts oppression communally, and culminates in purgative, virtuous struggle with God. An ethos of spiritual struggle becomes central to the pursuit of virtue; the former is an indispensable enabler of the latter.[63] The emphasis here on human responsibility in pursuing this change begins to push against accounts of virtue ethics that may diminish the import of human agency and that prefer instead to focus only on divine grace.

Chapter 3 moves to a concept more narrowly Christian than that of spiritual struggle. This chapter deploys two dimensions of Gregory of Nyssa's spirituality—*epektasis* and anagogy—to chart the relationship between three key topics: spiritual struggle, virtue, and God. These three concepts are otherwise fragmented, and thus are not presented in a comprehensive theory, and this is problematic; no Christian account before the Enlightenment would have imagined this dissociation. Three stages of the *epektatic* and anagogic ascent to God are uncovered, and these (spectral) stages, when coupled with spiritual struggle, serve as the Orthodox ethical framework of this book.

The first stage is the proper ordering of bodily passions to attain ἀπάθεια (passionlessness). In the second stage, the soul becomes like God and begins to acquire knowledge of God. Finally, in the third stage, a person experiences one of an infinite number of possible levels of unity with God, sometimes expressed as knowledge of God "in the darkness." While placing spiritual struggle within a framework of Godward spiritual struggle begins to address the tensions of self-centeredness and self-effacement prevalent in contemporary accounts of virtue ethics, more importantly, it provides the conceptual framework by which to understand a rather pragmatic ethic, one that is embodied in various Orthodox spiritual practices but that is not fragmented from its broader anthropological and theological assumptions. In this way, this book hopes to offer a model of ethics that stays true to virtue ethics' forebears, tending to their criticisms of modern moral philosophy.

Chapters 4 and 5 serve as the *application* of this ethics, turning to two of a plethora of its possible manifestations—asceticism and sacred reading, respectively. This model, which in some ways is developed retroactively from the practices themselves and back into the theoretical landscape of this book, can be applied to most components of human experience; and in chapter 4, it is applied to the body. Asceticism has had a long history both inside and outside Christian contexts. Yet contemporarily, it is hardly considered within virtue ethics as requisite to the aretaic life. This chapter, by applying this ethics to the body as a corollary, provides reasons why at least some form of contemporary asceticism ought to be recovered, especially as a practice attested to at least since antiquity. In analyzing early Christian ascetical experiences, three themes that parallel the stages of Godward spiritual struggle emerge: asceticism in relation to sexual continence; asceticism as angelification and restoration; and the body as the dwelling place of God. This analysis functions as one example of the overall theory of this project: that the application of Godward spiritual struggle to any form of Christian living (in this case, to a Christian's care for the body through asceticism) functions as a transformative portal to detachment from pleasures, the strengthening of the soul, and unity with God.

I continue in chapter 5 with the second example of Godward spiritual struggle, this time in relation to the practice of reading Scripture, *id est* to what might be rendered a Patristic *lectio divina*. I have chosen the body and reading as two points of application to demonstrate the versatility and latitude that this ethics grants in its application, while still maintaining enough specificity to avoid vacuous obscurity. At the same time, I hope to demonstrate in these two examples the move beyond deontological assumptions that actions in themselves are the only important considerations, but instead that the actions, though often meritorious on their own, are further transformed when placed within this ethical framework.

As an example of sacred reading, Scripture is sometimes considered to be an *informer* of virtue—a prescriber for particular actions that, when carried out, prove helpful in acquiring virtue—but not a *securer* of virtue. In other words, Scripture has often been viewed only as a source for rules, regulations, and suggestions for living a virtuous life. Yet what requires greater attention are ways in which to read Scripture as a transformative practice. There has been much debate among Christian ethicists and virtue ethicists as to the proper place of Scripture in the moral life. It is my suggestion that the practice of sacred reading, as implemented in the first few centuries of Christianity, is itself a transformative practice enabling the pursuit of virtue. That is, sacred reading, when practiced in certain ways embodied by the early Church, offers one degree of separation between reading and acquiring virtue—not two, which would imply one degree for its very reading and a second for the application of what seems appropriate for a particular context. Instead, there exists a spiritual struggle in the practice itself, one that encapsulates a way of life, a worldview, and a spirit that enable the acquisition of virtue.

In chapter 5, the first stage consists of a vulnerable, humble, Christocentric, and communal reading of Scripture. The second stage includes the embodiment of prayerful, virtuous reading. The final stage is one of full immersion and transformation into a new creation. Through a lens of God-ward spiritual struggle, the sacred reading of Scripture cannot be reduced only to an exercise of the intellect or a battle between an assortment of historical reconstructions. Though these certainly have their place in the discussion, sacred reading extends far beyond their reach. Similar to chapter 4, the application of this model consistently leads to the perpetual and transformative journey to virtue, beyond virtue, and ultimately to unity with God.

Chapter 6, by way of concluding, offers an honest appraisal—as far as I am able to look from the outside onto my own work—of this book; namely, it addresses the tensions that arise when providing the concrete examples of asceticism and sacred reading detailed in chapters 4 and 5. I address the particularism of this ethics, the tensions of the dignity of the body versus what may appear as a devaluation of the body, the risk of these concrete examples devolving into empty gestures, the difficulties of assessing an embodied or applied ethics, and certain methodological issues that I have in some ways been forced to implement. Thus, chapter 6 briefly assesses the contributions and shortcomings of the book as a contemporary Orthodox Christian ethics of virtue, grounded in a retrieval of Patristic and ancient Christian thought.

NOTES

Epigraph: Parfit, *Reasons and Persons*, 454.

1. Nietzsche, *Die fröhliche Wissenschaft*, III 108.
2. One paradigmatic thinker in this movement is John Caputo, who has made a career over the last half century out of the postmodern deconstruction of God, what he calls weak theology. See, e.g., Caputo, *Weakness of God*; and Caputo, *Insistence of God*.
3. Nietzsche, *Die fröhliche Wissenschaft*, V 343. All translations in this book are my own, unless otherwise noted, which I have been careful to document.
4. This shift is not being attributed entirely to Nietzsche; that would be historically inaccurate. Nietzsche, here, through only one articulated example, is being used as a representative of this shift that was in fact constituted by several other important shifts, captured more holistically and linearly as a process brought about by Scholasticism, the Enlightenment, modernity, and postmodernity, all leading to rationalism, scientism, and deconstructionism, among numerous other philosophical movements. Demetrios Harper makes a convincing argument for the interpretation of Kantian thought as a microcosm of the broader shift in modernity that separates ontology from metaphysics. Effectively, this shift is one of the elevation of morality over theology (or ontology), where "we are led to religious faith through a proper application of moral principles." See Harper, *Analogy of Love*, 24–39. Here, I am alluding to a complementary facet of this shift—one subsequent fulfillment or correlative of the "Kantian" shift.
5. Sanford, *Before Virtue*, 23.

6. Sanford, 61.
7. Edmund Pincoffs uses "quandary ethics" as a sort of denunciatory epithet that characterizes modern moral philosophy as a whole. Whether he participates in the unsuccessful shift to virtue ethics that Sanford presents is not entirely clear, though I would argue that Pincoffs falls into the category of "unconventional" virtue ethicists (see below) that include G. E. M. Anscombe and Alasdair MacIntyre. See Pincoffs, *Quandaries and Virtues.*
8. Sanford, *Before Virtue,* 69–80.
9. Anscombe, "Modern Moral Philosophy," 26.
10. Sanford, *Before Virtue,* 62.
11. Sandis, "Modern Moral Philosophy Before and After Anscombe."
12. MacIntyre, *After Virtue,* 52–55.
13. Harper, *Analogy of Love,* 58.
14. Harper, 75.
15. Williams, *Ethics,* 4.
16. Williams, 5.
17. Teleological frameworks have received their criticisms, including, but not limited to, the controversial requirement for a Creator who ascribes a teleological purpose to humans; the anthropocentricity assumed in teleological frameworks; the plurality of potential teloi that cannot be reduced to a singular telos; and the view that nature is primarily observational—it simply *is,* without being oriented at an end. While Nafsika Athanassoulis defends an Aristotelian account against these accusations, I do not pretend to hide my biases and starting points in this present work, because the "ethic" presented in what follows requires not only an acceptance of these presuppositions but also an involved dedication to them if the ethic is to be implemented with some degree of honesty. At the same time, I echo her sentiment that naturalistic teleology is hard-pressed to offer a normative ethical account. See Athanassoulis, *Virtue Ethics,* 81–96.
18. Saint Paul describes this same experience in Rom. 7:15–20.
19. Trimble, "First Philosophy," 27.
20. No Christians to my knowledge claim a state, or the ability to reach a state, of perfection. Yet I am intentionally conflating here an overconfidence in rationalism with the theological-anthropological assumption that humans are in a perfected state. What I mean to say is that this overreliance on reason, even if it is not meant to function as such, is in practice a neglect of the fallen reality of human nature.
21. The conflation between image and likeness is frequented more in modern times than during the early Church era. In this book, I do not emphasize this distinction, though in the backdrop is the understanding that though humans are created in God's *image,* it is through participation in God's grace through the Holy Spirit that a person grows in God's *likeness.* A helpful book on this discussion is by Lossky, *In the Image.*
22. See Boersma, *Embodiment,* for the development and application of this word as it relates to Gregory of Nyssa. "Anagogy" is referenced in parallel with *epektasis* as words that imply ascent and progress, respectively, in the same Godward spiritual journey.
23. Alfeyev, *Orthodox Witness Today,* 161.
24. Haldane, "Whither Moral Philosophy?" 93.
25. Roberts, "Varieties," 12.
26. One convincing purpose for choosing this era in particular is due to its ubiquitous impact on all Christendom; it was a time when the Church was *catholic,* despite the variety of opinions that fell within that unity. In carefully delineating how we ought to understand a

concensus partum, Bishop Hilarion Alfeyev makes a case for the framework within which to understand the Patristic corpus as a unified and orthodox, though pluriform, project: "Anyone working in the field of patristic studies should be well aware of this common context of the one faith for the entire patristic tradition. Any attempt to view the fathers outside their global context leads to a dead end. This is why secular scholars, self-avowed atheists, or agnostics intrinsically alien to the Christian tradition have great difficulties in trying to interpret patristic theology. It is impossible to comprehend the theology of the fathers and at the same time consciously distance oneself from the essence of their faith and spiritual experience. Therefore, even if the contextual method of reading the fathers does not necessarily require the scholar's adherence to the Christian faith, it does require at least a very high degree of trust in the experience of the fathers and the church of Christ within which patristic theology developed. Someone knowingly alienating himself from the patristic context, or aloof from the 'patristic faith,' cannot be a patristic scholar." It is also relevant to mention that this quotation is taken from a section where Alfeyev argues for a contextual reading of Patristics—that is, with an eye to the cultural, historical, linguistic, ecclesial, and theological peculiarities of each author's context. Still, this book appeals to the "global context" of the "patristic faith" and considers itself to be functioning from within that faith as a promising (and hopefully effective) effort in recovering patristic scholarship from within its own context, that is, from a contemporary context that relies formatively on the peculiarities of this ancient context. See Alfeyev, *Orthodox Witness Today*, 161.

27. Sanford, *Before Virtue*, 111.
28. The very field of ethics only developed in the post–Enlightenment West with assumptions poignantly opposed to early Christian sentiments, and in MacIntyre's words, to the theological, the legal, and the aesthetic. MacIntyre dates the transition of the word "moral" from general to about 1630–1850: MacIntyre, *After Virtue*, 38–39.
29. Nearly all defenses of the Fathers are on the biblical-exegetical front in relation to historical criticism, mainly from Orthodox scholars, in German. See Dragutinovic, "Interpretation of Scripture"; Nikolakopoulos, "Orthodox Critique"; Stylianopoulos, *New Testament*; and Stylianopoulos, "Perspectives." That so much interest, however, is invested in recovering a patristic exegesis signals, in part, the merits of exploring their spirituality; the two realities—Scripture and spirituality—can hardly be separated, even contemporarily.
30. One such critique is given by Kellner, "Introduction." A helpful response to this critique is given by Tholfsen, "Postmodern Theory."
31. One such critique, and where "kyriarchy" is coined, is made by Schüssler Fiorenza, "Introduction." See also Clark, "Women."
32. See King, *What Is Gnosticism?*; and Burrus, *Making of a Heretic*.
33. Ludlow, *Gregory of Nyssa*, 164.
34. Pui Him Ip suggests this much of *ressourcement* theologians in contrast to critical historians; see Ip, "'Back to the Fathers,'" 5.
35. See this important work that includes many perspectives across traditions on the topic of *ressourcement* theology; see Flynn and Murray, *Ressourcement*.
36. One accusation against a "return to the Fathers" as "ahistorical" "patristic fundamentalism" is made by Kalaitzidis, "From the 'Return to the Fathers.'"
37. I acknowledge the rejection of a narrative of persecution by historians. See, e.g., Moss, *Myth of Persecution*. This rejection is mainly concerned with dispelling a romanticized notion of uninterrupted persecution and especially with what this narrative might imply

for modern Christianity. However, my concern here is different; I only mean to point out that power and conviction of certain truths are delinked in the instance of martyrdom, which was prevalent in the early Church, even if not perpetual. This is evidenced further in the Coptic Church's resetting of the calendric year in AD 284 to the year of the martyrs (AM) under Diocletian persecution. See Papaconstantinou, "Historiography."

38. The allusion here is to Tertullian's famous "Plures efficimur, quitiens metimur a vobis: semen est sanguis Christianorum," in his *Apologeticus*, L.13.
39. One example is Beeley, *Unity of Christ*; he decenters Athanasius from his traditional role in Christological development, ascribing to him instead problematic dualisms.
40. For a more holistic picture of Athanasius that does justice to his broader context, see Gwynn, *Athanasius*, 105–58, including his more ascetical, spiritual context as well as his pastoral context.
41. Gwynn, 49, 152.
42. These stories exist in hagiographical accounts whose historicity might sometimes be challenged. For examples of monks fleeing, sometimes violently, from the call to the episcopate, see Sterk, *Renouncing the World*, 2–3; and Brakke, *Athanasius*, 113–20.
43. Coptic Orthodox Christianity—i.e., the See of Alexandria—was all at once the center of theological discourse in the early Church; an important source of the Christian monasticism and asceticism at the heart of the concepts developed in this book; the source of some of the most influential figures and doctors of the Golden Era of Patristics; and a Church that experienced persecution and oppression all throughout its existence. The combination of these elements gives it a unique position, which is especially relevant to the juxtaposition of premodern and postmodern sentiments. At the very least, it complicates the Western colonial narrative of the Christian institution as inherently oppressive, tyrannical, etc.
44. Virginia Burrus, *Begotten, Not Made: Conceiving Manhood in Late Antiquity* (Stanford, CA: Stanford University Press, 2000), 1.
45. The title "pope" was used some fifty years for the bishop of Alexandria before its appearance in Rome. See Gwynn, *Athanasius*, 22.
46. Bouteneff, *Sweeter Than Honey*, 171–72.
47. Mt. 20:26–28 (New Revised Standard Version). See also Mk. 10:43–45.
48. Mt. 20:16.
49. Sterk, *Renouncing the World*, 244.
50. Athanasius, *Letter to Serapion*, I.28.
51. Gregory of Nyssa, "Vie De Sainte Macrine," ed. Maraval, in *Sources Chrétiennes* 95, ed. de Lubac, Daniélou, and Mondésert (hereafter *SC* 178), 204.
52. *SC* 178, 192.
53. *SC* 178, 170.
54. Ludlow, *Gregory of Nyssa*, 164.
55. Ludlow, 204.
56. Burrus, *Begotten, Not Made*, 1.
57. Burrus. A similar thesis is put forth by Constantinou, "Male Constructions."
58. Careful, nuanced, and erudite as she is, Burrus does the same, with Gerard Loughlin, in "Queer Father: Gregory of Nyssa and the Subversion of Identity," where she, for example, makes asceticism virtually synonymous with queerness, defining both as "practices that center on *resistance* to normative discourses of sex and sexuality." See Loughlin and Burrus, "Queer Father," 147. Without responding as diligently as her works deserve, it is

not for the purpose of resistance to normative discourse that serves as the impetus for Gregory's writing on asceticism. Asceticism finds its import not as a result of its opposition to a normative position but as resistance against what becomes of human nature if its erotic desires are welcomed. It is not because it is resistant to normativity that it is good; its resistance to normativity is instead a corollary of Gregory's anthropology and eschatology. My point is only that much of the critical theory placed on Gregory does not do justice to his own tradition as one that positions spirituality, eschatology, and anagogy as highly as it does. My argument here is also that the best reading of Gregory would come from within a tradition that makes these same assumptions.

59. O'Keefe and Reno, *Sanctified Vision*, 111.
60. Boersma, *Embodiment*, 11.
61. Ramelli, *Social Justice*, chaps. 5 and 6.
62. Athanasius (writing on Antony) and Basil make reference to the prudent bees that take good honey from different flowers. Nazianzen's analogy references plucking roses amid thorns. Athanasius, "Salutate Priscillam," in *Patrologia Graeca Tomus LI*; hereafter *PG* 36.508–9; *SC* 400, 136; Basil, *PG* 31, 569; Gregory Nazianzen, *PG* 37, 1062. The apothegm "avoid the thorns; pluck the roses" (Τρυγῶν ἀκάνθας, οὐκ ἀπανθίζων ῥόδα)—mentioned here in Gregory Nazianzen's text—is also mentioned in *PG* 37, 1581. The latter (αἱ τὰς ἀκάνθας φεῦγε, καὶ ῥόδον δρέπου), however, has been attributed to Gregory's cousin, Amphilochius of Iconium, by Oberg, who edited "Amphilochii Iconiensis Iambi ad Seleucum," in *Patristische Texte und Studien*, and was noted by Hofer, *Christ in the Life and Teaching of Gregory of Nazianzus*, 26.
63. This is not to say that spiritual struggle is the only way to acquire virtue, but it is to say that spiritual struggle, when carried out in the way that is delineated in this book, will *always* result in the acquisition of virtue.

1

Which Virtue Ethics? Which Problems?

An . . . Orthodox ethic is a virtue ethic, but not a rationalistic one. The virtuous man is not Aristotle's *spodaios* in whom right reason alone reigns supreme. He is, rather, the new Adam, the man-god in whom divine love is incarnated and the creature is reunited with his Creator. . . . The moral life in all its conscientious attention to and striving for the good is finally taken up into the spiritual life. For the good is not simply the norm of life; it is the Divine Life Itself.

—Vigen Guroian

AN ORTHODOX CHRISTIAN POLITEIA?

I have already identified this book as one that is *conventional* in its mitigation and defense against mainstream virtue ethical accusations and *unconventional* in the suggestion that for ethics to be sufficiently grounded philosophically and embodied transformationally, it ought to be envisioned as a *subset* of spiritual formation. This chapter constitutes the conventional component of this book, highlighting the issues within contemporary virtue ethics that the ethical framework developed in this book addresses. Before addressing these issues directly and more than simply delineating between conventional and unconventional virtue ethics, this chapter first briefly positions Orthodox Christian "ethics" as one deeply engaged with ἀρετή (virtue) but whose concerns ultimately lie beyond virtue ethics.[1]

I cannot in such limited space develop an exhaustive Orthodox Christian ethics (assuming this endeavor were possible to begin with, which is doubtful), while also detailing the complexities it potentially addresses. Instead, this chapter's aim is only to further situate an Orthodox Christian ethics by pointing to its indispensable and ubiquitous components, and subsequently reflecting on the ethics' implications in a few relevant discussions of contemporary virtue ethics.

In Orthodox Christianity, the study of ethics as a distinct theological area is a recent development taking on a distinctive pattern.[2] Addressing ethical quandaries is seen as the responsibility of theologians, believers, clergy, and the laity—in a word, the saints, collectively known as the Body of Christ, conciliarly guided by the Holy Spirit.[3] At the same time, the good life is one of increasing unity with God, not one focused on conundrums and appropriate systems by which they are to be addressed. Western and Eastern approaches to theology have had their pros and cons: systematization in the former has led to deep analyses of complex topics, but it has often fragmented otherwise composite topics that require interdependence for the most accurate assessment. Conversely, nonfragmentation has preserved the holistic reality that characterizes the complexity of truths, but it has not allowed for the same depth of analysis as that engaged in Western systematic theology. Perhaps because Orthodox Christianity is less fragmented into theological subdisciplines, it has never itself subscribed to any particular ethics.[4]

With this understanding, the reliance of ethics on theology (or the reintegration of ethics and theology proper) is not an incidental or ancillary feature of this study; it is the necessary structure of any Orthodox Christian "ethics"—a term that deserves great caution when deployed, because it can only be used acquiescently as a tool of interlocution, not as an accurate identifier of Orthodox Christianity, past or present.[5] In its stead, as I have suggested elsewhere, the term *politeia* might more accurately describe the Orthodox ethos of this book.[6] Yet, due to potential political anachronisms with which the term might come to be associated (not to mention its variant usage in antiquity), it remains simpler to use the term "ethics" to describe this worldview. After all, the disciplinary isolation with which I have caricaturized modern ethics was never a consequence intended by ethicists; that modern ethicists have begun to realize its disintegration is a promising sign for the recovery of holistic ethical schemata.[7]

The broad and relatively underdeveloped field of Orthodox Christian ethics is characterized most notably by two overarching assertions.[8] The *first* is that Orthodox Christians conceive of ethics as resulting from the principal task of *uniting with God*.[9] God is the central orienting principle by which determinations of good and evil, right and wrong, and virtue and vice are made. More than this, it is the active, dynamic, and unpredictable pursuit of God that dictates, and often convolutes, Orthodox Christian ethics. Because of the centrality of this pursuit in Orthodox ethics, I will in the following chapter develop the concept of spiritual struggle. Spiritual struggle requires persistence despite the difficulties that may arise. It requires sincerity in its attempt to pursue God as the Being able to be experienced and known, yet mysterious and unable to be fully grasped. It requires humility in its communal model of discipleship to spiritual elders, in its fundamental ecclesiology, and in its submission to God Himself as the principal Guide for the journey. This Orthodox model would not be complete without the concept of *epektasis,* which provides the basis for this orientation.

Saint Gregory of Nyssa's theory of perpetual progress is one Patristic model, among others, by which to convey the pursuit of God as an eternal journey that begins now and continues in the afterlife, and by which to make a case for the necessary integrity between ethics, theology proper, and spirituality.[10] Though it may be the case that each of the components of this project also exists in non-Orthodox scholarship, I maintain that the combination of these concepts is distinctively Orthodox not only in intellectual theory but also in popular practice among the Orthodox faithful. Note the trajectory, then, of the lived ethics being developed in this book: in the lives of Orthodox Christians, it begins with God, it is embodied by the faithful in pursuit of this God, and I attempt to capture and articulate it in this book as an ethical framework by locating the central components of this lived experience. This book is, in a sense, a conceptual transliteration of Orthodox praxis, not a compilation of theoretical ethical resources that collapses, as may other potential ethical models, at the accusation of inapplicability.

The centrality of the pursuit of God in this ethics leads to the *second* hallmark of Orthodox Christian ethics—its *inherently integrative nature.* From an Eastern perspective, the holism to which I am referring might be best expressed in an Orthodox *spirituality* that excludes no facet of the human experience. Richard Schmidt is correct to note the understanding of spirituality that "prevailed in the West until the twelfth century" and "prevails even today in the Orthodox East" as including "Christian perfection, discipleship, faithfulness, devotion, obedience, piety, holiness."[11] He goes on to express a surprising contrast between premodern and modern notions of Christianity: The former understood theology and spirituality as synonymous, neither of which were separated from experience. Ethics cannot be separated from any other part of life but must be considered as part of the single fabric of life.[12] Most important for this integrity is the unity between ethics or actions, on one hand, and faith or beliefs, on the other hand. For this reason, many Orthodox Christian ethicists will begin with or at least devote much attention to matters of theology proper, rooted in Patristic writings, when presenting ethical stances.[13] The integrative method of this project results from a desire to stay true to Orthodox methodology, because no such methodology is outlined and because the project of constructing systematized methodologies is of little interest to most Orthodox Christian spiritualities.

Instead, this book arises from a need to present an ethical model that is not divorced from a worldview that integrates theology, motives, dispositions, beliefs, traditions, actions, embodied practices, and worship, among other components of spiritual life. At least some aspects of this integration were the sentiments expressed by the call of virtue ethics' forebears, as noted in this book's introduction.

Spirituality consists of the elevation of the spirit in perfect harmony with the heart, mind, and body to the eternal progression of the knowledge of God, which is a personal and conscious experience.[14] That spirituality includes the body is important because this project never intends to devalue the body. Instead, the body is to be disciplined and controlled for proper orientation to God, a point that will continue to unfold throughout this book. To this, Vladimir Lossky writes, "Negative theology is not merely a theory of ecstasy. It is an expression of that fundamental attitude which transforms the whole of theology into a contemplation of the mysteries of revelation."[15] Spirituality and the expression of negative theology are focused on real experience, and while this often includes ascent beyond the material, it is not limited to this. In fact, the material is required and is never separated from any aspiration to spiritual cultivation. Contemplation or inner disposition is not and cannot be separated from action or practice.[16]

Aristotle Papanikolaou unpacks this spiritual experience, positioning human nature's inability to make sense of spiritual experiences in relation to the apophatic pursuit of unity with God:

> The concept of "knowledge as union with God beyond reason" is not a denigration of reason in favour of experience; . . . if knowledge of God is possible, then it is not like the kind of knowledge we have through the operation of the mind. God is not a "thing" that can be conceptualized, which taken to its extreme becomes idolatry—projecting what we wish God to be. If God is the uncreated Creator who makes contact between the uncreated and the created possible, then knowledge as union with the uncreated is simply not like knowledge the mind has of created things. Union with God is a paradoxical fulfilment of nature beyond nature.[17]

The difficulty of articulating the experience of God through rational faculties does not preclude the reality of that spiritual progression. In fact, there is much to be said of God cataphatically, which is a topic discussed below that crafts the spiritual journey. However, Orthodox anthropology, as inherently integrative, does not limit spirituality to the intellectual realm but remains open to all modes of experience, especially those that are embodied. As we will see in future chapters, it is as though the body might learn something of God before the mind is able to grasp it.

At the same time, Papanikolaou here gives us a good example of this integrative nature, not as one of methodological necessity but as one that requires the juxtaposition of various concepts in order to accurately capture otherwise elusive experiences. To understand human nature, one must first understand the relation of the human being to God, the One who fulfills human nature. And yet, to understand that process of fulfillment—that is, knowledge of God through union with Him—one must have a robust understanding of the role of reason as one important, though ultimately insufficient, mechanism in the tapestry of Orthodox spirituality. To come to know the human being, one must first know God in all the capacities available to human knowledge. To come to know God, one must understand the human being's complex modes of existence. This circular, "paradoxical" journey leaves nothing of human experienced unturned; it is integrative in the fullest sense of the word.

Because of the two hallmarks of Orthodox Christian ethics—its emphasis of God as *telos* and its theologically interdisciplinary integration—Orthodoxy experiences a unique relationship with virtue ethics. One might conclude that conventional virtue ethics seems to be a potential avenue through which Orthodoxy can join contemporary discussions of ethics.[18] After all, similar to the field of virtue ethics, Orthodoxy is concerned primarily with a holistic way of life that emphasizes the formation of agents and communities of character and virtue. The Patristic heritage that is so formative for Orthodox thought is very much concerned with the acquisition of virtue by means of habituation in goodness. In a two-way process, one is to become loving, pure, holy, generous, patient, and the like in order to make good decisions, form good character, and transform inner dispositions. Vice versa, one is to form good character and inner dispositions in order to perform the actions and acquire the habits necessary to grow in virtue. This is all true, and yet might there be a subtle conflation here between virtue ethics and any discussion of virtue, especially in light of the discussion of conventional and unconventional virtue ethics in the book's introduction?

To be sure, Orthodox virtue ethics is a species of virtue ethics analogous to many "ethical" accounts in antiquity and through the medieval period. Insofar as Aristotle or Thomas Aquinas—themselves, not through their intellectual heirs—are virtue ethicists, contemporary Orthodox Christians are virtue ethicists. Aristotle and Aquinas both elevated the place of virtue in the pursuit of the good life, but when placed within Sanford's categorizations, they might not be immediately understood as conventional virtue ethicists. So, too, might Orthodox Christians function within an ancient mode of virtue ethical thought, elevating the aretaic life while evading the conventional categorization as "ethicists seeking a normative ethical model." In some ways, then, an Orthodox Christian virtue ethics might offer a contemporary instantiation of the type of virtue ethics functional in the traditional resources into which contemporary ethicists have tapped. If this is the case, then Orthodox Christians are not joining a Western virtue ethical model but adding a corrective to this way of thinking about virtue that has not done justice to its ancestry. This point is not one of triumphalism; it is an observation that this contemporary Christian community is indeed very much confused by the notion of ethics apart from an integrated life in God, and this confusion might echo the sentiments of criticisms leveled at modern moral philosophy.

In utilizing virtue ethics as the most fitting portal into the contemporary discussion of ethics, there exists a simultaneous, necessary subversion of virtue. Certainly, the acquisition of virtue in an Orthodox model is considered an excellency, and it could even be considered one of the τέλη (*teloi*) within the journey to God. Most ascetical texts in the tradition emphasize the acquisition of virtue. However, as this project maintains, the acquisition of virtue is only an inherent excellence insofar as this acquisition is understood as participation in God and growth in union with Him. The principal task of an Orthodox Christian ethics is becoming like God by loving God and loving one's neighbor. In this process, the acquisition of virtue and the formation of good habits function as markers in the pursuit of God. In other words, a person can confirm that she is properly oriented to God if she is acquiring virtue on a path of positive moral transformation.

Although it is possible that focusing on habituation in goodness and in virtuous actions as ends in themselves can and does lead people and communities to this knowledge of God, the assertion of this project as a contribution of Orthodox Christian ethics to virtue ethics is that the value of the acquisition of virtue is minimized outside a grace-filled, salvific, temporarily struggle-laden, perpetual life with God. This life—eternal life—with God begins here and comes to fruition perpetually and eschatologically. It is a life that is disinterested with one's own righteousness, virtuosity, or goodness apart from God. It is a life that hesitates to overstate the value of virtue and therefore of a model of virtue ethics whose purview does not extend beyond the scope of virtue. This is of the most direct contributions that the Orthodox ethical model of this book makes. Virtue ethics provides a critical shift away from overemphasis on rules, principles, and obligations and toward the transformation of people of goodness, virtue, and character. Yet virtue is to be lauded and pursued through spiritual struggle primarily as a means to communion with God, at some times, and as a *result* of this union, at other times.

ARISTOTLE, AQUINAS, AND VIRTUE ETHICAL PROBLEMS

But how might an Orthodox Christian ethics relate to the contemporary field of virtue ethics, especially in relation to Aristotelian-Thomistic ethics? Which complexities might it address, and which shifts might it make in the field's trajectory? To these questions we now turn, with special attention to five fundamental points of comparison: the unity of the virtues, perfectionism and (un)attainability, moral luck and moral effort, self-centeredness and self-effacement, and grace and works. Aristotle is not Aquinas, regardless of how much the latter depended on the former. I will be clear, then, to treat each author and his intellectual heirs in his own respect when conflation is neither helpful nor accurate. More precisely, Aquinas will prominently factor into the final and somewhat lengthy discussion of grace—a topic deserving significant attention to properly situate this book's ethics; Aristotle will be more thoroughly engaged otherwise. This structure will allow for the delineation of specific points of departure amid otherwise similar ethical frameworks broadly imagined.

The Virtuous Agent and the Unity of the Virtues

Aristotle, whose influence on contemporary virtue ethics cannot be understated, presents, in his *Nicomachean* and *Eudemian* ethics, an anthropology that emphasizes the perfection of human powers or potentialities within a comprehensive teleology. The focus on perfecting human nature, brought to perfection through habit (τελειουμένοις δὲ διὰ τοῦ ἔθους), leads to an emphasis on given conditions and confidence in fixed *teloi* (τέλη), fixed ends.[19] Contrarily, an ethics of spiritual struggle and perpetual progress relies less on a settled account of fixed ends. It exhibits a dynamism in the acquisition of virtue, in relation to each person's set of circumstances, and in the perpetual nature of the *telos* (τέλος) that drives the ethics. In other words, the shape of the journey of this ethics differs from that of an Aristotelian ethics of virtue as a result of the dynamism of human nature itself and the differences in τέλη. The τέλος of any contemporary ethics of virtue is the acquisition of virtue. The dynamic and perpetual τέλος in this project is unity with

God, aided by the acquisition of virtue, on one hand, whose marker *is* the acquisition of virtue, on the other hand.

Additionally, the emphasis in Aristotelian-based virtue ethics on an agent who requires little deliberation before ethical action has had implications for those who have yet to attain such unimpeded deliberation. For example, in Julia Annas's account of an Aristotelian-based virtue ethics, she presents the concept of "flow," which is unmediated by deliberation, is active not passive, and the experience of which is enjoyable in and of itself, although it also may fulfill a greater end.[20] A virtuous agent practicing such flow finds no interruption in the exercise of thought before acting virtuously.[21] In this way, an agent still in the process of acquiring such a natural emanation of virtue will often be viewed as lesser than the agent who already has acquired flow. One potential problem with such an understanding is that all human beings presumably fall into the category of agents who are still in process. Aristotle's "good man" (ὁ ἀγαθὸς) is a reality achievable here and now, but is at the same time an expectation that cannot be realized.[22] One of two scenarios would be required to rid Aristotle's ethics of this paradox. Either the *expectation* for a person adhering to his ethics of acquiring perfect virtue would need to be dismissed or at least lowered, or the ideal of a perfect virtuous agent would need to exist regularly in society to demonstrate the attainability of this ideal. In this vein, the spectrum of virtue that Annas admits exists in most if not all societies is a more helpful and realistic depiction in which most people find themselves en route struggling toward virtue.

It remains the case, however, that in a strictly Aristotelian ethics, this process—that is, the struggle—is sometimes the hurdle standing in front of the real goal: unimpeded virtue in a perfectly virtuous agent.[23] That is, when virtue becomes a natural emanation of one's character, the struggle has diminished and the agent is considered morally superior to the one who must still toil against particular vices. Put another way, the struggler is always subordinate to the virtuous agent par excellence. Jean Porter's comparison of those who struggle with those who have attained perfect virtue sheds some light on why this prioritization may be in place. Although there is value to those who struggle, the idea of elevating the position of those who have perfected virtue, and thus no longer need to struggle, safeguards against valuing the struggle as a good in and of itself—an inherent excellence. Porter maintains that today we highly value struggle, and that the reason for this may be that most people are struggling and have not yet perfected virtues.[24]

The pervasive reality of virtuous struggle complicates Aristotle's account of the virtues in which he admits a unity among the virtues that is both difficult to observe and to defend and that exacerbates a devaluation of the process of acquiring virtue.[25] For Aristotle, the acquisition of all the virtues is requisite for perfection.[26] To lack a single virtue is to not fully possess any virtue. In the same vein, to possess any single virtue in its perfect state, one must attain all others. As noted, it is difficult to pinpoint where in society a complete and perfect moral agent can be found, and Aristotle himself is aware of certain constraints in human nature.[27] In the same vein, most people can claim to exhibit partial virtue, but few will claim to possess complete, unified virtue. Even within this claim to partial virtue, there exists an observed reality that some of these partial virtues are more completely acquired than others. Could one conclude that partial virtue is no virtue at all? If so, again, then there exists no ideal agent; no matter the angle, the system is impractical and unattainable.

The Aristotelian unity of the virtues is partly Platonic in envisioning conflict as the result of a character flaw or a deficiency in virtue. Conflict, as a "flaw in character," presumably disrupts the unity that ought to exist in the "good life" and the "good" human being.[28] This means that all of a person's actions must be directed toward a particular end, and any actions that are incongruous with this focus are necessarily a result of vice.[29] The presence of vice points to a deficiency not just in the virtue with which that vice is associated but also to a number of other virtues. This is an all-or-none model in some ways, and in its need to denounce imperfection, it leaves struggle doubly subordinated—first because of the superiority of an agent who is unimpededly virtuous in comparison with an agent en route to virtue, and second because of the hyperexaltation of an all-virtuous moral agent.[30]

When juxtaposed with Christianity, however, the *flawed* saints of Scripture are nonetheless considered virtuous. Numerous characters that were exalted for one virtue or another are seen exhibiting moments of weakness and flaws in character. Among these is Moses the prophet, chosen by God as possessing the most humility of all His people in order to lead the Israelites out of slavery. This same Moses was also guilty of murder,[31] and of direct disobedience to God when he struck a rock twice instead of speaking to the rock as instructed.[32] The same partial possession of virtue is seen with Jonah the prophet, whom God chose to preach to the people of Nineveh but who was at the same time cowardly in his mission and petty in his complaints to God.[33] Similarly, Paul calls out Peter, the great apostle of Christ, for his hypocrisy, along with the blessed Barnabas, in their dealings with Jews and Gentiles.[34] The list goes on, and it is clear that throughout history (from Cyril of Alexandria's purportedly excessive austerity to Augustine's lasciviousness to Teresa of Calcutta's moments of doubt in God's presence), even "God's chosen" are imperfect and thus only possessing partial virtue, not a singular Aristotelian unity of the virtues.

The fullness of all the virtues in Orthodox Christianity is found only in the Paragon of Virtues Himself—God. God, the τέλος of this model, is the One in whom the unity of the virtues resides; the more one grows in unity with God, the more one's virtues *seem* complete. Only in this sense can one potentially argue that the unity of the virtues is, albeit in different ways, the ultimate goal for Aristotle and the Orthodox Christian. However, to understand spiritual struggle and perpetual progress as a pursuit of the unity of the virtues would be to miss the essence of the model as one whose τέλη require foci beyond virtue, to God, always perfect and always beyond human conceptions of perfection. It is a model that is at first sight paradoxical—calling for perfectionism, and yet exhibiting intrinsic unattainability.

Perfectionism and (Un)attainability

Alasdair MacIntyre appropriates an Aristotelian unity of the virtues in a way that complicates what otherwise might appear to be an inaccessible ideal. He writes, "It is in the course of the quest and only through encountering and coping with the various particular harms, dangers, temptations and distractions which provide any quest with its episodes and incidents that the goal of the quest is to be finally understood."[35] Virtue can be understood in light of a larger narrative, quest, or journey, and it is only through the difficulties confronted that the goal becomes especially clear. This is what determines success in the pursuit of virtue, and the singularity of this quest provides a unifying factor in what may otherwise appear as disparate virtues. For this reason, MacIntyre describes a virtuous agent as one who possesses "unity of a narrative quest."[36] The unity of this quest is made clear by answering what is good for humanity and what is good for me as a moral agent. This provides a more focused goal, with which one will be able to align one's actions, decisions, behavior, and so on.[37]

MacIntyre's framework is then one of uncertainties and complications; it is a journey in its most spontaneous understanding. The quest is not clear-cut; nor is it entirely definable or reproducible universally, given the infinite possibilities and circumstances of any person's life. Instead, it is a progression, a development in an ever-unfolding story of virtue, and each situation has its own particularities. Cultivating virtue in a series of progressions requires at least some level of exertion, and though some virtue may be present already to varying degrees in different people, there is always a possibility for development and further growth and cultivation.[38] This book, by developing the category of spiritual struggle, suggests a shift from virtue's *acquisition* to virtue's *pursuit*.[39] Understanding the pursuit of virtue in terms of a broader narrative of struggle renders the conversation more practical, relatable, and, in some ways, attainable.

What is more, understanding the pursuit of virtue as a progressive struggle more fully explains how a life of virtue can at the same time be both universal and particular. It is universal in that each person is somewhere along their own journey and somewhere along the spectrum of virtue. Each person is called to the aretaic life,[40] and no one can claim exemption from being formed by one narrative quest or another.[41] It is at the same time particular, because each narrative quest is shaped differently and because a number of responses to varying circumstances are expected of different people. Each person is immersed in a unique combination of times, locations, personalities, and expectations. No single journey can be exactly like another's; yet common ground can be found in the exertive implementation of human agency in this continual quest.

MacIntyre's appropriation is helpful, but more needs to be unpacked with attention to points of similarity and difference between an Orthodox ethics and Aristotle's *Nicomachean* and *Eudemian* ethics, especially in light of the perfectionisms portrayed in each ethics. One affinity between this ethics and a virtue ethics steeped in Aristotelian-Thomistic ethics is the formation of one's appetites. The appetitive part of the irrational soul, in an Aristotelian-Thomistic framework, should be brought under the control of reason.[42] Similarly, in this project, one is expected to detach from or overcome the base or fleshly desires of pleasure—that is, the appetite—in order to progress through spiritual struggle toward the strengthening of the soul. Another less exact affinity is the emphasis on virtue as a settled condition of character. For Aristotle, virtues are states that arise out of like activities.[43] Virtues are not emotions (πάθη) or capacities (δυνάμεις), which are given by nature.[44] Virtues are states that make a person good and allow the person to perform a task well.[45]

In the ethics of this book, virtue is also considered a state of character instead of an emotion or capacity. The emphasis on the journey to God is one in which a person makes progress only insofar as that person's state of character or virtuousness transforms in a succession of better states. A nuance here, however, is that progression and formation of character are construed in a more dynamic way, in which each consecutive state is concomitantly and paradoxically both complete yet incomplete. The agent is satiated in closer proximity to God yet encouraged in the pursuit of higher levels of assimilation in God's infinitude, a process that receives due attention in chapter 3.

Although Aristotle's ethics exhibits a similar dynamism, especially in a person's growth through habituation, Aristotle's τέλη are fixed. For Aristotle, ethics is modeled on his understanding of natural processes of change, and yet human nature itself is given and fixed. The virtues as a fulfillment of human nature—and thus the natural ends (τέλος φύσει) of his ethics—are fixed, though the process to those ends is dynamic.[46] For Orthodox Christians, human nature exists in tension between the fallen and the risen, the latter of which is the realization of human nature's potential. That is, human nature is fulfilled the more one progresses on the journey toward God. At the same time, the end is dynamic, which in turn shapes the journey itself. The paradox between simultaneously and perpetually being complete and incomplete is the essence of Gregory's theory of *epektasis*. This paradox also captures how, on one hand, this book agrees with the Aristotelian-Thomistic framework in which virtue is a settled state of character, and, on the other hand, it disagrees with this framework, asserting a constant grace-filled dynamism inherent to the journey toward God.

The Christian concept of divine grace pushes against Aristotle's ideal of perfectionism. For Aristotle, perfection in virtue is a τέλος that can be realized through human faculties and potentialities. It is within the power of a human being, insofar as the proper circumstances are in place, to acquire the virtues through hard work and processes of habituation, potentially to an idealized or perfected state.[47] As noted above, Aristotle's ideal of perfection is one that can be realized on this Earth, here and now. What it means in this book for a Christian to be "perfect" (τέλειος) is discussed below; but preliminarily, perfection requires divine grace, which both initiates and sustains the acquisition of virtue and the process of moving toward perfection. Without divine grace, the pursuit of perfection is impossible. Further, the Orthodox Christian model presented here utilizes a high Christian eschatology in which the road to perfection begins here and now and continues indefinitely, even and especially after death.[48] This is precisely a consequence of the model of Godward spiritual struggle. Perfection as full virtuousness is never entirely attained; nor does it need to be attained. Instead, in this Orthodox model, perfection is understood as a dynamic ascent, not as a completed summit. But would this not imply two levels of unattainability? In addition to the impossibility of attaining the unity of the virtues in this life, the model I am suggesting, by locating perfection in God, increases the chasm between agent and τέλος.

The two "unattainabilities," that of Aristotle and that of Orthodox Christianity, are quite different, and the difference rests in their contrasting expectations and perhaps a semantic redefinition of perfection. The expectation for Aristotle is for the actualization of a state of perfection that I am claiming is necessarily outside the capabilities of a human being. Again, human faculties and potentialities are incapable of ever reaching a state of perfection in virtue; yet this expectation remains critical to Aristotle.[49] Conversely, the unattainability of virtue in this project's model is intentional and must be realized by any person embarking on the journey. Though perfection is pursued, it is with an understanding that simply growing toward God *is* perfection. It requires, in a sense, redefining what perfection implies in relation to humans; perfection proper is a state that only belongs to God.

In a 1953 sermon by Bishop John Maximovich—a canonized Russian Orthodox saint—that still captures the experience of Orthodox Christians, he depicts the very essence of this mode of perfection as that of a struggler, as opposed to a victor:

> God's grace always assists a struggler, but this does not mean that a struggler is always in the position of a victor; sometimes the beasts did not touch the righteous ones, but by no means did they not touch them always. What is important is not victory or the position of a victor, but rather the labor of striving towards God and devotion to Him. Great is the Apostle Paul. . . . The Lord wants from the apostle the striving which cleanses his soul. . . . The power of God is effective when a person asks for the help of God, acknowledging the weakness and sinfulness of his nature. This is why humility and the striving towards God are the fundamental virtues of a Christian.[50]

The sustained effort of spiritual struggle is the measure of success, not the posture of victory or reaching a supposed state of perfection. A person in this ethical model should never expect to reach a final state. It is a journey that is inherently unattainable, on one hand, but that is always being attained, on the other hand. The differences regarding expectation lead to the differences in accessibility between these two ethics. Notice also the elevation of striving or struggling—central to Gregory of Nyssa's theory of *epektasis*—to the status of "virtue," a correlation that will not be made directly in the ethics proposed. Instead, struggle will at least be an enabler of virtue, if not an excellence in itself. More important, "perfection" is found in striving toward God; upward ascent to God, along any part of the journey, is by definition a transformative process that constitutes the ideal of Orthodox Christian perfection. Redefining perfection in this way has immediate consequences for the discussion of moral luck and effort, to which we now turn briefly.

Moral Luck and Moral Effort

The primary question at hand is whether a person can be blamed for a lack of virtue if certain circumstances prohibited the acquisition of virtue for that person. Nafsika Athanassoulis notes that "morality presupposes control, whereas luck is about lack of control and cases of moral luck are problematic because they bring the two together."[51] She continues: "There is unfairness in the way luck affects our lives, but a moral theory that can accommodate this offers a much more plausible picture of the kinds of lives beings like us live, than one which seeks to deny the influence of luck and tries to make us immune to all sorts of empirical factors that go towards making us who we are. The problem of moral luck is no longer a problem, but a correct account of what life is like for creatures like us."[52]

What Aristotelianism offers, in Athanassoulis's assessment, is an account of virtue that does not neglect the reality of luck as part of the human experience but that is at the same time not contingent entirely on one's context. She does admit, however, that for Aristotle, "while being prevented from acting once or twice has no effect on one's virtue, being entirely deprived of all the means for virtuous action does affect one's ability to be virtuous."[53]

Robert Merrihew Adams offers an account of virtue that is dependent on context and circumstances. When an agent who is otherwise able to resist temptations lapses and acts contrary to a given virtue due to certain circumstances, this agent is said to be dependent on conditions that enable the acquisition of virtue. Adams admits that this is rare but that this does not negate one's possessing that virtue for which there exist temporary lapses in its exhibition.[54] To have real virtue does not mean that one remains virtuous in all circumstances. As a consequence of moral luck, each person's optimal virtuosity is conditioned for certain contexts. The cultivation of virtue is facilitated by external conditions over which people have limited control, but perceptions of virtue (or vice) reflect social locations—class, culture, race, region, and the like. This means that virtue is dependent and conditioned, but it does not mean that virtue is not real.[55]

The dependency of virtue is also demonstrated in how one ought to see oneself in relation to the acquisition of virtue. Virtue should not be thought of as an individual achievement but as a gift—from nature, grace, and others.[56] This grace is expressed as originating from what Adams refers to as the transcendent goodness,[57] whose reality, he asserts, is far more important than "the reality of our virtue," a conclusion resulting from his emphasis on moral luck.[58] For example, the ability to live long enough to be able to change in a relevant way toward virtue is a matter of moral luck. Moral luck is the source of fortunate circumstances that are out of one's control. Adams accords moral luck more weight against those, such as Philippa Foot, who say that virtue is within reach of anyone who wants it.[59] He rejects this, maintaining a low view of moral effort. What is more important for Adams is for one to have a particular virtue, not the effort that goes into that process.[60]

It seems, however, that moral luck and moral effort do not need to be pinned in opposition to each other. Consider the effect that a shift of focus from virtue's *acquisition* to virtue's *pursuit*, only hinted at above, would have on this discussion. Aristotle focuses on averages or means between two extremes to approximate what may be considered a virtue.[61] In this way, his ethics are able to capture the vast and complex spectrum of differences that may exist among different people. Yet it may be assumed that this *spectrum* is fixed while *people* vary. This is true of any ethics of virtue that attributes a stagnant beginning and end to the acquisition of any given virtue. The emphasis on spiritual struggle in an Orthodox ethics challenges this notion. Instead, scales that shift relative to circumstances seem to encompass a wider breadth of circumstances and seem to capture more robustly the complexities of the journey toward virtue. One is expected, in relation to one's set of circumstances, to exhibit a certain exertion of effort, the sincerity of which becomes an important diagnostic tool and barometer for assessing the pursuit of virtue. Prioritizing effort over circumstance, however, does not imply that virtue becomes entirely a matter of relativity. What this shift *does* imply is that an action must not only be deemed good, nor only must moral motivation be present,[62] but also that sustained effort must be present in an ethos of spiritual struggle in order to more accurately assess virtuousness.[63]

The psychologist Angela Duckworth's work on grit, passion, and perseverance attests to the importance of these traits over skill or luck. Success is not achieved, according to Duckworth, through talent or genius but through resilience of the will and a focus on long-term goals—traits that can be learned and acquired.[64] Duckworth's concept of grit is similar to the exertion of effort in the concept of spiritual struggle, except that the former tends toward secular discussions of success while the latter, as developed here, is concerned more with "spiritual success," measured by intimacy with God and growth in a relationship with and a semblance of Him. Still, serious criticisms of the concept of grit might also apply to spiritual struggle.

One criticism is that encouraging perseverance can ignore or reinforce existing inequalities.[65] Although the response to this criticism is detailed in chapter 2, on spiritual struggle, and at the risk of stating the obvious, it is important to note here that this book does not justify or promote any sort of inequality, injustice, or oppression. To promote spiritual struggle is not to encourage a person or members of a group of people who are oppressed to remain as they are. Spiritual struggle is to be distinguished from suffering. The former is premised solely on freedom—freedom *from* vice, and freedom *to* choose the good. The latter is premised on external force and coercion. All forms of spiritual struggle must be free and uncoerced in order to distinguish struggle from suffering.[66] The emphasis of spiritual struggle on exertion and effort is encouragement to freely choose and focus on God in all circumstances, but it is not at the same time advocacy for inequality by any stretch. In fact, in the discussion of the journey to God in chapter 3, it will become clear that all strugglers, regardless of which level of spirituality they have attained, are on the same one path to God.[67] Additionally, it will become clear in the discussion on asceticism in chapter 4 that spiritual struggle is never a means by which one is to devalue the body. The denigration of the human body is opposed to the Godward ascent in this work. That is, the denigration of the body through any injustice, oppression, or inequality results in spiritual descent, not ascent.

Another, more problematic, criticism relevant to spiritual struggle is that because of preexisting circumstances, a person may not be able to exhibit the sort of resilience or perseverance required by such an ethics. An example of this is the case of children who grew up in poor socioeconomic circumstances. Paul Tough writes, "If you don't have the mental tendencies that a stable, responsive early childhood tends to produce, the transition to kindergarten is likely to be significantly more fraught, and the challenge of learning the many things we ask kindergarten students to master can be overwhelming."[68] He links this to grit when describing a conversation he had with Jack Shonkoff, the director of Harvard's Center on the Developing Child, who said:

> If you haven't in your early years been growing up in an environment of responsive relationships that has buffered you from excessive stress activation, then if, in tenth-grade math class, you're not showing grit and motivation, it may not be a matter of you just not sucking it up enough. . . . A lot of it has to do with problems of focusing attention, working memory, and cognitive flexibility. And you may not have developed those capacities because of what happened to you early in life.[69]

What this implies, then, is that demanding sustained effort from those who may not have those capacities would be unethical, unjust, and cruel. This is an important criticism. But, in the example of underprivileged students, it is not effort that is asked of them. What they are called to is the attainment of a measurable marker of success—that is, passing grades. The measure of success in educational institutions does not change in relation to circumstances; a student who receives a failing grade does not receive the credit needed to continue, despite any circumstances that may have preceded.

The analogy between educational grit and virtuous struggle does not hold on all fronts; but it seems that at the very least, the same *static* scale is used to measure success on either plane of these parallels, despite circumstantial variants. Consider how virtue ethical assessments of success are premised on the successful performance of an action that would be characteristic of a virtuous person: "The continent agent wins this struggle and does the right thing, so externally his behaviour is indistinguishable from that of the virtuous agent; however, whereas the virtuous agent's character flows smoothly and effortlessly into action because his desires are in line with his reason, the continent agent has to struggle to do what he knows is right. The incontinent agent loses this struggle and does the wrong thing, as his desires overwhelm his reason."[70] The vicious and the incontinent are deemed unsuccessful because the goal is the acquisition of virtue. The continent is successful only insofar as he or she has not succumbed to the whims of πᾰθος. The virtuous agent is the true *victor ludorum*. That the vicious and incontinent may have struggled is often inconsequential.

Instead, I maintain that (Godward) struggle *is* the goal, the measure. Circumstances do factor into the discussion of spiritual struggle, and the scale ought not to remain static. The measure by which a person's success is assessed is relative to that person's struggle against unfortunate circumstances, just as much as it might be measured according to a person's struggle against any vicious tendency. This shift is not far from the picture of God depicted in Matthew 25:14–30 or Romans 2, where the relationship between actions and circumstances is intrinsic to God's just judgment. The very model of spiritual struggle is premised on an egalitarian shift away from an absolute scale of *acquiring* virtue—to a relative, dynamic scale of *pursuing* virtue.

The egalitarian shift suggested here emphasizes the moral and religious value of sincere efforts to love God, but it is also a perfectionistic model in stressing the need to strive endlessly. The ethics is both an effort to recognize the moral value of flawed persons striving to love God better *and* one that distinguishes and elevates those who struggle in contrast to those with more muddled and mediocre hearts. Disparate circumstances do not jeopardize one's ability to struggle over another's; all are called to persevere. Those who do not struggle are encouraged to embark on the journey of spiritual struggle to God; and at the same time, those who struggle are indeed elevated above those who do not, not on the basis of a fixed, absolute scale, but in relation to each person's circumstances. In this sense, circumstances are no longer primary hurdles in the face of any person's acquisition of virtue.[71]

By asking how much one is *pursuing* virtue instead of how much virtue one has *attained*, the issue of moral luck becomes less prominent. Shifting from a focus on luck to effort implies that circumstances are no longer the sole determining or limiting factors in one's ability to become virtuous. However, moral luck is not replaced in its importance by moral effort. In fact, the question of moral effort undergoes a critical shift as well. Instead of asserting that virtue is within the reach of anyone who wants it, it is the *pursuit* of virtue that is within each person's capabilities, despite circumstances or context. It will become clear in the next chapter on spiritual struggle just how this is so and also why I am suggesting that spiritual struggle is so helpful to Christian considerations of the aretaic life. The natural continuation of this discussion requires an analysis of contemporary accounts of grace; but before this, it is worth noting briefly one more corollary of an Orthodox Christian ethics—that placing spiritual struggle within a framework of perpetual progress in God begins to assuage the complexities of self-centeredness and self-effacement in virtue ethics.

Self-Centeredness and Self-Effacement

Aristotle's conception of virtue is centered on one's own goodness.[72] Virtue is acquired for the self and for its own sake as an innate excellence. With an emphasis on the self's own goodness in an Aristotelian ethics, it is not difficult for the ethics to risk devolving into self-centeredness. Similarly, pursuing virtue for its own sake, without God as the ultimate purpose for or Paragon of that virtue, risks the self-effacement of virtue. In other words, vices such as selfishness, hubris, and complacency, among others, might often work contrary to virtue when pursued for its own sake, countered by unexpected vices. This book's ethics decenters the object of the pursuit of the good life. No longer is the self's own goodness the object of living a good life. Instead, in concert with Irfan Khawaja's observation that we ought to provide "an adequate account of the relation between well-being and virtue," within an adequate anthropology and psychology, the good life in this book is envisioned as the eternal and struggle-laden pursuit of Godlikeness through love of God and love of neighbor.[73] Virtue, in this model, becomes secondary to life with God.

Gregory of Nyssa's theory of perpetual progress and ascent enables the formation and placement of grace-enabled human agency on a path simultaneously toward virtue and toward a semblance of God. Briefly stated, the acquisition of virtue is a marker toward the infinitude of God. This could be an important reason why the early Church placed such weight on dogma and doctrine. To know God and His characteristics—in whatever capacity self-revelation allows—is crucial to the proper formation of a virtuous agent. This infinitude by definition can never be entirely reached but can always be pursued to attain higher, albeit partial, summits. *Epektasis* and anagogy enable a reorientation in the pursuit of virtue, enlivened by Christ's summation of the law and prophets into the two great commandments: (1) "Love the Lord your God with all your heart, and with all your soul, and with all your mind," and (2) "Love your neighbor as yourself."[74] In other words, one potential means by which to reframe the pursuit of virtue is as the pursuit of love of God and neighbor.[75] Placing virtue only as a marker that evidences one's embarkation on this spiritual journey means that similitude to God, unity with Him, and love of neighbor are the distinct τέλη—τέλη that capture the heart of the Judeo-Christian tradition.

This reorientation has an impact on discussions among virtue ethicists regarding the egoism or self-centeredness that an agent might risk in focusing on her own virtuousness and regarding the issue of the self-effacement of virtue ethics,[76] since the goal of acquiring virtue could potentially detract from the proper motivations that render certain actions virtuous.[77] These risks can never be entirely avoided but remain regular parts of the struggle throughout this journey. For example, Aristotle maintains that in order for virtue to be nobly good, it must be for its own sake, while virtue that is merely good is for the sake of other natural goods.[78] Yet placing God and others as the targets of virtuous actions safeguards against some of these risks and alleviates some of the preoccupation with the self and with virtue for the sake of virtue. Virtuousness itself, if it is no longer the chief concern, is also no longer the goal of virtuous *actions*; nor is it as encumbered with the temptation of hubris. Virtue for the sake of virtue—as is central to most accounts of virtue ethics—would no longer be the most salient of concerns for those who orient the pursuit of virtue onto God and others.

Take, for example, the suggestion that virtuous action should not be for the sake of happiness but for its own sake.[79] Virtues are virtues because they have intrinsic value as excellences in and of themselves.[80] To demonstrate this point, Adams cites the virtue of altruism. He describes it as an intrinsic, not an instrumental, good.[81] Altruism can include loving a person for her own sake and for the sake of wanting others to benefit from your service.[82] Yet the account Augustine gives us might help us make sense of how these apparent self-preoccupations and preoccupations with virtue can be held in healthy tension with the reorientation at hand. He claims that one can love the virtues and others for their own sakes as long as this love is ordered toward God. Only in this way can anything be loved truly and properly.[83] The difficulty of making selflessness a reality is addressed in part by the nature of the journey. The journey of spiritual struggle presupposes weaknesses, failings, and shortsightedness; but an orientation toward a semblance of God keeps the agent's focus away from these discouraging realities. Though the implications of Gregory's theory are discussed further in chapter 3, it is important to note here that one's orientation toward God not only prevents fixation on otherwise discouraging realities but also embodies the commandments to love God and one's neighbor. This reorientation, then, is a transformative, grace-enabled means to true selflessness.

Grace and Works

It has been difficult to hold off on the discussion of grace because it requires some recognition within most discussions in Orthodox Christian ethics, including those given above. Something might be lost when teasing out the issue of grace and works apart from the cohesive ethical theory, but this discussion aims to accomplish a few simple goals within the larger scope of situating this ethics. The first is that grace, whose understanding in Orthodox Christianity is relatively fluid, pervades every fathomable moment of the journey to God, and that this is a necessary component of any Christian ethics, distinguishing them from non-Christian accounts. Next, a response to grace is the bedrock of a Christian's relationship with God. This response—that is, works—are also indispensable for any account of Christian ethics, even in those who are keen to denounce works righteousness. In this respect, there is a consensus among all Christians, albeit with different emphases, within an arena whose bounds are Pelagianism and antinomianism. The emphasis in Orthodox Christianity (and in this book) is on the form that this response to grace takes, as the primary *voluntary* component of the journey, but without the classical Thomistic distinction between acquired/infused virtues.

Habituation through practicing the good is central to both Aristotelian-Thomistic virtue ethics and Orthodox Christian ethics. Character grows through habit; the virtues are perfected through habit.[84] The persistence inherent in the concept of spiritual struggle is premised on this notion of habituation. The more one practices the good with consistency and determination, the more one becomes good. For Aristotle, it is within human capacity to align oneself with the good. Because the good life is natural to humans, in that it fulfills given human nature, through reason a person can come through her own power to a realization of this latent potentiality. A person is limited only by knowledge, choices, circumstances, and habituation.[85] On the contrary, the anthropology presented in the introduction above assumes that a human being experiences significant limitations, including an inability to align oneself fully with the good. On one hand, humans can and must struggle to become good; on the other hand, virtue will never be completely secured without divine grace. It is easy to become dejected when a person does not reach certain levels of virtuousness; but the realization that the process of moving toward virtue is a grace-enabled, progressive, and transformative struggle lifts some of the responsibility off the shoulders of any given agent. Aristotle's nontheistic account carries with it a heavy burden (briefly discussed above) on the human agent in the process of acquiring virtue.

As is demonstrated below, the process of habituation in an Orthodox model is infused with a pervasive grace, so that the very desire, ability, and energy to do the good and persist in doing it are enabled by divine grace. Moreover, the types of actions at which spiritual struggle aims are specific in their orientation toward God. That is, in order to determine the proper actions for habituation, one must orient oneself toward God; and in this ethics, this orientation takes the form of a practice that is familiar to Christian living—for example, disciplining the body (asceticism), reading Scripture (sacred reading), and praying, among other practices. This process, though extending beyond Aristotle's nontheistic account, encompasses all of Aristotle's conditions for acts to become virtues: the agent must have knowledge, must *choose* the acts, must choose the acts *for* their own sakes, must perform the actions in the way that those who possess that virtue perform the actions, and must undertake the actions and not just philosophize about them.[86]

Grace and Virtue

Christian disagreement over the relationship between works and faith through grace stretches back to early Christianity. Most positions exist within a spectrum at whose ends are Pelagianism and antinomianism. The former denies the need for divine participation as requisite for salvation while maintaining human agency's ability to secure this salvation. The latter maintains that grace eliminates the need for any moral observance. In between these two extremes lies a broad consensus in which the indispensability of both divine and human agencies is acknowledged, each to one degree or another. This flexible model of divine–human co-agency is the realm within which spiritual struggle should be exercised.

It would be difficult to find a virtue ethicist upholding the merits of Pelagianism successfully, especially because it has been repudiated time and again since at least Augustine's time. This is not to say that there may not exist those whose Christianity maintains a strong Pelagian bent. In fact, Jennifer Moberly maintains that virtue ethics can often focus too much on human agency and not enough on divine grace.[87] But this extreme of the spectrum is difficult, in fact virtually impossible, to assert without ignoring the power of God the Trinity gracing humanity with salvation and eternal life. In this case, the qualification of this ethics of virtue as "Christian" would be suspect. Yet it remains that with the attention that is given in this book to the implementation of human agency in light of the discussion of spiritual struggle, the book might risk a similar accusation that is at least as "semi-Pelagian"—an accusation I anticipate and hope to dispel in multiple ways.

Grace is an indispensable component of any Christian account of virtue ethics.[88] There is no part of the journey toward virtue and a semblance of God that is not aided by unmerited grace. To begin, it is through the grace of salvation—that is, the economy of the Son of God incarnating, dying, and resurrecting—that the reconciliation between humanity and God is accomplished.[89] Grace is responsible for the enablement of the journey toward virtue. Yet, when discussing grace and works, this conception is not usually the focus, a likely result of its wide acceptance among Christians. Instead, the discussion of grace often centers on the role of divine agency in aiding humanity here and now, and how this agency affects any given person's journey. Hans Boersma's answer to this is found in Gregory of Nyssa's conception of grace in this journey toward virtue. Grace enables virtuous actions, which further enlarge the capacity for grace, which further enables virtuous actions, and so the cycle continues.[90] Orthodox Christians—in typically unsystematized fashion—do not go far beyond this loose, fluid, and even somewhat mysterious account of grace, in which grace is present from start to finish within every thought, action, decision, and so on.[91] Grace as unmerited, is a given, and so it is the synergistic *response* to grace, which is always free and voluntary, that occupies most Orthodox accounts. Though the terminology typically denoted in the Western discussion of grace is absent in the Christian East, the practical conclusions drawn therefrom help elucidate the mechanisms or parameters of grace that are functional in this book.

Augustine claims that pagans cannot be virtuous because their apparently virtuous acts are directed toward themselves and not toward what should be their ultimate end—God; and this is also true for the hypocritical Christian.[92] Union with God and imitation of God can only be achieved through one's active involvement with His grace. What pagans acquire is only a semblance of virtue, given that it is subsumed in and contingent upon self-sufficiency, which at the same time is filled with hubris. All things must be loved, according to Augustine, in relation to God. That which one loves, even people and virtues, must be ordered toward God. How, then, can a pagan possess true virtue? For Augustine, the answer is simple—they cannot. However, this does not by any means imply that Christians have been perfected in virtue. There exists a spectrum, and each person is at a different point along it. The spectrum is a gradual process of development in virtue by putting on Christ—the goal of virtue. Augustine does talk much of habituation, similarly to Aristotle, but Augustine maintains that bringing the appetite into submission does move one along this spectrum. Still, everything is graced. Despite his efforts, Augustine is aware of his own shortcomings and weaknesses, and these lead him to conclude that his putting on Christ, and even his will to do so, is a grace that is necessary for the acquisition of virtue.[93]

Aquinas is more gracious in granting the qualification of true virtue to pagans. Even if a pagan does not order all things in relation to God, the virtue they exhibit is still real, although it eventually must be directed toward God if virtue's fullest potential is to be realized.[94] Pagans are capable of good self-love as well as the good love of the commonwealth.[95] This virtue is real, incomplete, and not salvific, and on these points Jennifer Herdt agrees with Aquinas. Herdt's turn to the Thomistic theory on infused and acquired moral virtues sheds some light on Aquinas's understanding of grace. Aquinas's account of the acquired virtues is very similar to Aristotle's account of habituated virtues.[96] Acquired virtues are concerned with the natural end of human beings, while infused with the supernatural.[97] It is obvious that the theological virtues are infused, but Herdt asks what the function of infused moral virtues is, in comparison with acquired moral virtues.

Aquinas answers that actions that "may appear irrational from the perspective of acquired virtue may be fully appropriate from the perspective of infused virtue," because acquired virtues use human reason, while infused virtues rely on a divine lens.[98] In this way, infused virtues, which are graced or gifted to humanity, provide perspectives that aid in the further progress of acquiring virtue. Additionally, infused virtues do not render the recipient automatically virtuous; they only make one continent, and thus able to struggle, perform good acts, and refrain from evil ones. That is, *grace enables struggle*. To fully possess virtue, both acquired and infused virtues are needed, in conjunction with human agency.[99] This need for both acquired and infused virtues reflects one of Herdt's broader concerns—a holistic ethical model in which the bifurcation often characteristic of the moral life between acquired and infused, or in this book between the ethical and the spiritual, is broken down.[100]

Jean Porter's Thomistic account adds another dimension to this acquired/infused distinction. Aquinas' *infused* cardinal virtues can and do exist in those who do not possess the *acquired* virtues and in those who are still immature with respect to virtue. In these cases, living virtuously may be painful because the person has infused virtue but has been habituated in a life of vice to some extent.[101] More specifically, regarding the virtue of prudence, which is Aquinas's correlate to Aristotle's virtue of practical wisdom, just because one is infused with the cardinal virtue of prudence does not mean that the person is able to act prudently regarding earthly judgments. Prudence, for Aquinas, is primarily concerned with matters of salvation.[102] In this way, one who is infused with the cardinal virtues can err according to matters of seemingly obvious worldly logic. That person will still be on the road to virtue through virtue that has been graced or gifted. "The gifts are nothing other than the dispositions by which the justified individual is rendered amenable to God's inspiration." They are "habitual dispositions of the soul."[103] The person infused with virtue "consistently discerns and chooses the course of activity that is consonant with God's will."[104] In Thomistic virtue ethics, the one who is infused with virtues is seen as having fulfilled a native potentiality that has always been there. However, Aquinas does not offer a theory on the relation of acquired virtues to infused virtues, other than denying the continuity between the two. Understanding this relation, however, might provide a clearer understanding of the relationship between grace and works.

Michael Sherwin poses a question that might add a further nuance to this Thomistic account of acquired and infused virtues. Paraphrased, he asks, "What do we make of the adult who converts to a life with Christ but still has inclinations from his old life?"[105] In Thomistic terminology, what do we make of the person who has received the infused cardinal virtues (through the grace of the conversion) but lacks the acquired cardinal virtues (as a result of unfortunate old habits and the suddenness of the conversion)? This question yields another: Does one need to *acquire* some of the cardinal virtues before being *infused* with the more desirable cardinal virtues? Sherwin explains that just as the acquisition of cardinal virtues before one's conversion would come only through an agent's effort, so too would this exercise of agency be required even after one's conversion. Although the convert may not completely desire the good because of the residual effects of former vices, the adult convert should struggle to undertake good actions that are contrary to his or her disordered inclinations. This will build good dispositions—that is, acquired virtues: "When the acquired virtues are integrated into the life of grace, they begin the process of integrating our wounded nature into the activities that the infused virtues make possible. The acquired virtues, therefore, are not, as some recent commentators have affirmed, a prerequisite to living the infused virtues. On the contrary, for many adult converts, the infused virtues are what make developing the acquired virtues possible at all."[106]

In this way, one can embark on the life of grace and thus receive infused cardinal virtues before struggling to attain acquired cardinal virtues. Note here, also, that Sherwin is describing a tension within human nature that is not far from the Orthodox anthropological narrative mentioned briefly in the introduction. This tension in effect amounts to a very practical consequence: humans may have feelings, emotions, or dispositions, contrary to their own *eudaimonia,* and divine grace enables a fundamental reorientation of these disordered inclinations. For this reason, I maintain that it is one's anthropological narrative that dictates the nuances of one's theological, ethical, and spiritual conclusions.

Though an Orthodox account of grace might not be as detailed as the Thomistic account that has been used here, its conclusions might not be so divergent. The very impetus to embark on this journey, the ability to strive through its difficulties, and the progress to greater stages in the journey are all aided by divine grace. Grace is the *initiator, sustainer,* and *consummator*. Grace of the economy of salvation infiltrates and pervades all aspects of one's life and the journey toward virtue and a semblance of God. Much of this grace can be unseen and unnoticed and can come at times when a person seems otherwise unprepared. Thus, on one hand, grace is not summoned and is required in the acquisition of virtue, even in those who deny this schema. On the other hand, it requires a *response* in order to be brought to its fullest potential. Grace enables the acquisition of virtue; but the response required serves a critical function—ultimately, ordering virtue toward God.

Works and Antinomianism

Similar to Pelagianism, few would argue for a strict antinomianism, maintaining that grace eliminates the need for any human moral effort. However, antinomianism may attract more pale imitations than the Pelagian end of the spectrum. Evangelicals have historically erred more on the antinomian side due to Martin Luther's theology, but they have been cautious in doing so. In a number of Luther's works, he emphasizes the importance of grace over and against works. Among these texts are "On Two Kinds of Righteousness," "The Freedom of a Christian," "Lectures on Galatians (1935)," and "Answer to Latomus."[107] Luther asserts a clear distinction between faith through grace, on one hand, and all other works and actions, on the other hand. The former is concerned only with the "inner man," the soul, which Luther forcefully separates from the external, outer man.[108] This soul can be made clean, righteous, and justified only through Jesus Christ and Scripture, and not through any external acts.[109] Luther writes, "It does not help the soul if the body is . . . occupied with sacred duties or prays, fasts, abstains from certain kinds of food, or does any work that can be done by the body and in the body."[110] For Luther, it is not through external works that a person attains righteousness, but it is through Christ that a person acquires Christian righteousness, which in turn leads to good actions.[111] Christian righteousness is inherently "passive," not active; it is graced, not merited.[112]

However, Luther does not use this theology as an excuse for a life without discipline or good works. Instead, he warns that bad conduct reflects a person who has not been transformed through graced faith.[113] Although these external works do not justify a person, they are important. He writes: "Here the works begin. . . . He must indeed take care to discipline his body by fastings, watching, labors, and other reasonable discipline and to subject it to the Spirit so that it will obey and conform to the inner man and faith and not revolt against faith and hinder the inner man, as it is the nature of the body to do if it is not held in check." He continues, "These works reduce the body to subjection and purify it of its lusts, and our whole purpose is to be directed only toward the driving out of lusts."[114] Thus, at least to some extent, Luther recognizes the importance of purity of body, self-motivation, and struggle against one's debased tendencies—a concept that factors prominently in this work. He even exhorts his readers to study, read, meditate, and pray.[115] Yet it is Luther's anthropological insistence that actions have no bearing on a person's soul—that is, that the external cannot affect the internal, and that the body does not possess the ability to affect the soul—that ultimately sets him apart from the authors to whom I refer in presenting the concept of perpetual progress through spiritual struggle.[116] It seems difficult to once more evade the reality that narratives based on anthropological assumptions, despite their claims to a shared Christianity, will render disparate ethical conclusions. Luther argues for a strict bifurcation between "morality and faith, works and grace, secular society and religion."[117] His strong pushback against works righteousness left him at risk of a serious antinomian bent.

Joel Biermann, in *A Case for Character: Towards a Lutheran Virtue Ethics*, analyzes four Lutheran authors and admits that while the Gospel remains central to all four, their strict anti-Pelagianism sometimes leads to antinomianism.[118] He poses the Lutheran challenge as one in which the absolute and unconditional forgiveness of the Gospel can easily overshadow any place for ethics.[119] Biermann continues by pointing to a number of solutions to this problem, a problem that likely affects not only Lutherans but also many Christians. Antinomianism presents at least two important problems that render it unviable. First, its premise is inherently contradictory. It is difficult to envision a life in which no works are accomplished, in which human agency is inconsequential, and in which one's choices have no bearing on one's formation. Take, for example, Luther's forceful objection to any form of works righteousness that is thought to be acquired by the self. Luther is concerned with our entire beings, not isolated actions or even virtuous habits acquired piece by piece.[120] For Luther, the examined life—that is, the life of external works—is necessary, but it is not what makes us integral selves able to be in relationship with God. Hence, it is not worth living, and it deceives us into thinking we can rely on the virtues we have developed or acquired.[121] Further, and more aggressively, our own progress toward virtue is still sinful if it is our own. It can only be God's initiative that makes us virtuous, not our own efforts.[122]

Gilbert Meilaender claims that Luther does in fact care for the examined life of moral struggle by holding the examined and unexamined lives—Luther's language for lives of work and grace, respectively—in tension. This tension includes that between self-mastery of moral virtue and a self perfectly passive before God; between a virtue that one claims she possesses and on which she relies and a virtue that must be constantly reestablished by divine grace, and between a partial self and a whole self before God.[123] Meilaender admits that such tension cannot be fully resolved in the German thinker, though his argument that Luther cared for moral struggle is not entirely persuasive. Luther does acknowledge this moral struggle, for example, when he says, "Day by day the substance is removed so it may be utterly destroyed," but it may be for other reasons that Luther is not a strict antinomian, even if his disavowal of struggle as deceptive and sinful says otherwise.[124]

It is clear at this point that if there ever were an antinomian proponent, it would flow from the objections of Luther highlighted here. Yet my contention is that even Luther was not strictly antinomian and that the only way a Christian can fully lay hold to such a claim is either to have a view that compromises human freedom or, a different side of the same coin, to accept absolute predestination. Consider, further, some of Luther's contentions: virtues can only be fostered by not trying to foster them; true virtue is in realizing that we cannot build our own virtue; character does not depend on self-mastery but on becoming entirely passive to God;[125] true virtue requires faith first, not self-mastery; the self is whole and entire when completely submitted to God;[126] we are not righteous because of an intrinsic value but because of God's grace and remission of sins, which we receive when we acknowledge our sins;[127] salvation is complete dependence on God; we must cling to God in faith;[128] only when one realizes that there is nothing that can be done toward salvation, only then will that person have reason to turn to God; you will be delivered when you fully trust in Christ, which allows you to live righteously extrinsically;[129] and faith is a response of trusting extrinsically in another (i.e., God) in response to a promise.[130] These are just a few examples, but the contradiction is clear in each one. In order of their presentation, each of these claims carries some kind of action that has falsely been considered passive: *submitting* to and accepting the reality of our inability to foster virtue; *realizing* that virtue's acquisition is not in our control; *becoming* entirely passive to God; *putting* faith first; *submitting* the self entirely to God; *acknowledging* our sins; *depending* on God completely; *clinging* to God in faith; *realizing* that we are powerless to secure salvation without God; and *trusting* in God.

It is clear that these are all active, not passive, states of being. They are processes of *becoming*. Even when considering an action such as trusting that appears to be a passive state of being and that has been divinely graced, how is it that one achieves such a state? Is there no response to grace that is required in order for trust in God to be developed? Daphne Hampson pushes back against this question when she asserts that faith is not a work or an infused virtue but a response of trusting extrinsically in another (i.e., God) in response to a promise.[131] But to support this claim, a convincing qualification must be put forth distinguishing a work from a response. It would seem that this qualification exists only nominally. The question, then, is not whether some action, response, or work is necessary in order to acquire virtue or accept the gift. The point of contention is of an entirely other sort. Those who take Luther's suggestions strictly are ultimately concerned not to attribute an inherent and "interior quality of righteousness" to oneself apart from God; this would ultimately lead to pride and self-preoccupation.[132] The question is whether one thinks one is able to stand before God with any sort of righteousness.

There is no standing self apart from God's grace, and there is no righteousness apart from God's grace. This is precisely what spurred Luther's writings—the potential of viewing intrinsic righteousness as distinct from God's righteousness.[133] Instead of thinking that one, through much struggle, has reached an accomplished state of virtuousness, one ought to realize that "progress is nothing other than constantly beginning," and that life is for constantly praising and thanking God.[134] This constantly beginning, this way of life summarized by Luther, is a life of active repentance—a life of effort and struggle achieved in complete submission and realization of one's weakness.

But this turn away from self-righteousness is much different than claiming that there are not works, actions, or responses to God's grace that are necessary for salvation. As Herdt and others have argued, if virtue consists in the transformation and perfection of my agential capacities, if it is therefore something that is "mine," then we need an account of grace that makes sense of the operation of human agency in relation to grace.

Another problem with antinomianism relates to the matter of divine justice. To insist that works are unimportant in the acquisition of virtue would require a robust yet seemingly impossible answer as to why one person might be saved and not another, if all that mattered was God's grace. If works have no import in the discussions of salvation and the acquisition of virtue, one would be left with two options. Either moral progress has no bearing on one's relationship with God, and thus on salvation, or one's moral development occurs apart from the exercise of one's own agency. Regarding the former, each human being would be saved without differentiation, distinction, or consideration. Regarding the latter, one would have to accept a sort of double predestination in which works, actions, decisions, and the like have no bearing on the afterlife.[135] This would mean that regardless of one's works, some would be preselected for eternal damnation, a glaring contradiction of God's love and mercy, while others would be preselected for eternal salvation based on grounds unknown to humanity.

These two options, then, disregard any need for moral cultivation. First, morality would be rendered unjust favoritism by a God whose justice would contradict His impartiality. Second, morality would collapse into an absolute relativism in which no moral bounds could be affirmed because works would have no import regarding moral progress. If either of these were a reality, it would be a disastrous blow to Christianity. If morality was rendered entirely relativistic due to the misplacement of works within a Christian framework, moral chaos would (at least theoretically) ensue, assuming the application of such a conception. Moreover, could one defend a Christianity with a God whose conception of divine justice with regard to salvation necessarily and consistently contradicts any notion of justice one can envision?

Granted, in Romans 9:22–23, Saint Paul writes, "What if God, wanting to show His wrath and to make His power known, endured with much longsuffering the vessels (σκεύη) of wrath prepared for destruction, and that He might make known the riches of His glory on the vessels (σκεύη) of mercy, which He had prepared beforehand for glory."[136] As chapter 5 argues, individual Scriptural pericopes should be considered in relation to the entirety of the Scriptural corpus. Paul mentions these same "σκεύη" elsewhere, in his Second Letter to Timothy, the neglect of which would be a sure sign of proof-texting. He writes, "But in a great house there are not only vessels (σκεύη) of gold and silver, but also of wood and clay, some for honor and some for dishonor. *Therefore if anyone cleanses himself from the latter,* he will be a vessel (σκεύη) for honor, sanctified and useful for the Master, prepared for every good work" (emphasis added).[137] Notice the apostle's qualification in this letter. What one does—better yet, who one *becomes*—can aid in the transition between honor and dishonor, mercy and destruction. Active participation, never without God's grace, as noted in the previous section, is required for sanctification.

Between Pelagianism and antinomianism lies a broad consensus in which fits the discussion of Godward spiritual struggle. As long as one does not uphold the tenets of Pelagianism or antinomianism, then one accepts that, to some degree, both works and grace are necessary. Within this consensus a variety of opinions exist, with different emphases on (and different accounts of) grace and works. This spectrum is explored in subsequent chapters. It should become evident that the accounts of spiritual struggle and perpetual progress that are developed in chapters 2 and 3, respectively, strike an important and appropriate balance between divine and human agency within this loose but essential consensus.

A Contemporary Consensus between Grace and Works

Jennifer Herdt dedicates a chapter in her work, *Putting on Virtue: The Legacy of the Splendid Vices,* to discussing Saint Augustine's view toward pagans' abilities, or lack thereof, to acquire virtue. The main problem with "pagan virtue," according to Augustine, is self-sufficiency—pagans' belief that virtue can be acquired without external aid; and even more, that external aid would be considered a sign of weakness, not virtue.[138] In response, Augustine asserts that virtue is the perfection of the love of God, which is union with God. Virtuous activity is an expression of one's love of God and is constitutive of one's happiness and final end.[139] The same author in another work identifies Christian liturgy as the locus of a person's holistic ascent toward God and virtue and as a means of decentering the pursuit of virtue:[140] "By situating the growth of virtue in the context of worship we correct the insidious tendency to take pride in virtue as our own acquisition."[141] Herdt points to Augustine's stance on true virtue as being directed toward God, in love for Him, others, and creation.[142] A human's ultimate goal is imitation of God and union with Him, realized only through grace, because humans are not equipped with the independent ability to secure perfect union with God. Grace is essential, and one's active involvement with grace is what leads one to imitation of God and union with Him, in contrast to pagan virtue, which renders this union an affront to freedom, and thereby only a mere semblance of virtue.[143]

Yet even in his anti-Pelagian arguments, Augustine does not deny the need for works in addition to grace: "He will come with his angels in his majesty, so that before him all the nations shall be gathered, and he will divide them and place some on his right, whom, after recounting their good works, he will take into eternal life, others on his left, and, charging them with barrenness of good works, he will condemn them to eternal fire."[144]

In this same work against Pelagius, Augustine explains that good works are from faith, and faith is from grace. He is aware that works are necessary, but he is also aware that virtuous works cannot be carried through without divine grace.[145] Augustine strikes an effective balance, relating human struggle to divine grace. The former is realized by the latter, yet both are necessary for salvation. This struggle against sinful inclinations must be daily and constant.[146]

Again, Augustine, in his second treatise against Pelagius, *De natura et gratia,* captures the synergistic consensus of this section. If he had placed too much an emphasis on grace, he could have posited that merely becoming a Christian through baptism would be sufficient and that living a virtuous life would require no further works or actions. Instead, he seamlessly interweaves the dynamic between grace and works when discussing Christians who have neglected lives of holiness:

> We must not forget to urge them [those who are already Christians but neglect to lead holy lives] to godly prayers as well as to virtuous actions, and furthermore to instruct them in such wholesome doctrine that they be induced thereby to return thanks for being able to accomplish any step in that holy life which they have entered upon, without difficulty, and whenever they do experience such difficulty, that they then wrestle with God in most faithful and persistent prayer and ready works of mercy to obtain from Him facility. . . . I solemnly assert, that wheresoever and whenever they become perfect, it cannot be but by the grace of God through our Lord Jesus Christ.[147]

It seems at first that living this godly life requires a great deal of self-sufficiency and independent effort. It requires wrestling with God in prayer, virtuous actions, instruction in doctrine, gratitude and thanksgiving, and works of mercy. Yet after convincing his reader that rejoining the path of righteousness requires great personal effort, he reminds his reader that none of this can be accomplished without the grace of God.[148]

Thomas Aquinas, in his *Summa Theologica*, similar to Augustine, observes that a life of virtue consists not in following a prescription of actions or abstaining from other actions but in a certain way of life.[149] Recalling previous discussions of Aristotelian ethics, virtues cannot be emulated by mere mimicry, but certain motives and circumstances must accompany these actions until living virtuously no longer requires deliberation, flowing instead from a stable disposition of moral transformation.[150] To reach this stable state, one must struggle against inclinations and passions that are contrary to virtue. In expounding this point, Porter maintains that although struggle is praiseworthy for those who have yet to acquire perfect virtue, this struggle ought not to be praised as a good *in itself*, a reasonable conclusion that nonetheless requires clarification.[151]

Spiritual struggle, as a means to unity with God and virtue, must be considered good, because perfect virtue is not "rare," as Porter puts it—it is in fact impossible and necessarily unattainable. This becomes especially clear when Gregory's framework of perpetual progress is considered. Given that God, in an Orthodox ethical model, is the τέλος of spiritual struggle, and emulation of God as the Paragon of virtue is an unattainable feat, struggle on this side of the eschaton must necessarily be good. What this means is that Porter's qualification that one should be cautious in attributing inherent goodness to struggle is more of a technicality than an experienced reality. It is a qualification that might apply to the hereafter, where struggle will have no relevance. The struggle for sanctification, which is detailed in chapter 2, can never be considered counterproductive; it is a consistent source of good. Porter observes that it is only because there are more strugglers than there are nonstrugglers that the former are praised above the latter—"those who act readily and easily."[152] Though this may in fact be true, it is also the case that struggle itself embodies the way of life or ethos supposed within an ethics of virtue. To struggle is to make progress in virtue, which is as far as a person can proceed in "securing" virtue, because virtue's summit can never be reached.

Aquinas argues that God, in the outreach of grace, is the initial Mover. God's grace comes well before any good works, and it is only through grace that good works become feasible.[153] Further, it is not just good works that require grace; abstinence from sin is likewise dependent on grace. However, it is here—in the effort to abstain from sin—where Aquinas positions the necessity of human agency. In order to successfully abstain from sin and do good, human will is concomitantly necessary yet insufficient. Human agents must make some sort of effort. In fact, through grace, humans cooperate with

God for the purposes of their very salvation—eternal life: "God ordained human nature to attain the end of eternal life, not by its own strength, but by the help of grace; and in this way its act can be meritorious of eternal life."[154] In the same vein, he states that if "we speak of a meritorious work, inasmuch as it proceeds from the grace of the Holy Ghost moving us to life everlasting, it is meritorious of life everlasting condignly."[155] Thus, for Aquinas—similar to the conclusions drawn above—grace initiates, sustains, and accomplishes good works, virtue, and ultimately salvation for the human agent. At the same time, amid the journey, human agency plays a critical role in responding to, accepting, and cooperating with divine grace. This consensus is found all throughout Christian virtue ethical accounts.

Joseph J. Kotva, in *The Christian Case for Virtue Ethics,* mentions spiritual struggle in a section on sanctification, ultimately giving precedence to God's grace, rendering it an indispensable component of Christian virtue ethics and a distinct contribution to the field by Christianity. For Kotva, likeness to God is the goal of sanctification.[156] Sanctification is a process that begins here, continues now, and is perfected in the eschaton, requiring divine–human cooperation.[157] Drawing on three theologians—Kendrikus Berkhof, Milliard J. Erickson, and John Macquarrie—in his discussion of sanctification and eschatology, he demonstrates that although grace is responsible for freeing humans from sin toward the aretaic life, active responses and a genuine struggle are required of humans.[158] Kotva gives a glimpse of Gregory of Nyssa's framework, expounded on in chapter 3 below.

There is a tendency in Christian virtue ethics to conceptualize development in virtue as a journey of progressive struggle without necessarily naming it, but Gregory's theory does just that. Daniel Harrington and James Keenan, in *Jesus and Virtue Ethics,* deploy an understanding of Christian virtue similar to Gregory's: virtue is a journey of growth, progress, and striving. It should not come as a surprise, then, that their understandings of virtue ethics and of grace and works are also similar. Virtue ethics is "the appropriate response to God's initiatives and gifts."[159] In the same vein, Hans Boersma's *Embodiment and Virtue in Gregory of Nyssa: An Anagogical Approach* is one of the most helpful presentations of the relationship between divine and human agency. It is not entirely a coincidence that the most helpful of these presentations is found in a study of Gregory of Nyssa. Gregory's understanding of virtue necessitates a balanced interplay between both types of agencies. As mentioned above, grace enables virtuous actions, which enlarges the capacity for grace, which enables further virtuous actions, and so on.[160] Boersma expounds Gregory's conception of virtue, effectively describing this progress as growth away from a "measured body" and toward a virtuous body.[161] Gregory holds that human freedom is given within a participatory framework—that is, with God in Christ—who constitutes the journey and makes the very journey possible through grace. Gregory strongly affirms freedom of choice, which is maintained by God, whose grace sustains the continued efforts of the person in progress toward virtue.[162]

In this section, it has been my goal to demonstrate that works are needed and that a number of virtue ethicists—exemplary of the majority of virtue ethicists—appear to have reached a broad consensus that grace and works are both necessary to some degree in the acquisition of virtue. In all this, it should be clear that my elaboration on works in the form of a spiritual struggle should not be mistaken as a Pelagian sentiment regarding the importance of works *instead of* or *above* grace. I spend my time focusing on spiritual struggle in chapter 2 with a magnifying lens, in a sense. This lens certainly seems to inflate the importance of works, but the emphasis that should be placed on works versus that on grace, though certainly the goal of other projects, is not the goal of this one. In other words, portioning the emphases one should place on divine and human agency—beyond the conclusion that works are necessary—is not an endeavor I am taking up here. It is my hope that this magnifying lens be understood as such and not as an instrument to aggrandize the place of works beyond their facility. At the same time, the reason for an increased emphasis on human agency in the pursuit of virtue is because—put rather tritely—human agency is the only type of agency over which humans exercise autonomy. It could very well be the case that works are far less significant relative to the working of grace in securing virtue. Yet it remains that this arguably miniscule component of virtue's pursuit is all that a human agent has the freedom to exercise, informing a person's actions, behavior, logic, and character development. In this sense, works deserve their due attention, without forgetting that the discussion of the relative proportions and importance of grace to works is still open for debate.

CONCLUSION

By now, in the introduction and in this chapter, I hope to have situated to some degree the Orthodox Christian ethics of this book within the broader context of, or at least in some approximation to, Western moral philosophy, generally, and virtue ethics, specifically. Orthodox Christianity poses criticisms of Western moral philosophy not far from those of unconventional virtue ethicists. This ethics is at the same time an atavistic *ressourcement* of Patristic resources for modern application—for which I have hoped to create space; a transliteration of the lived experience of contemporary Orthodox spirituality into modern Western ethical language; and an ethical framework that utilizes as a starting point an Orthodox anthropological narrative, with all its ontological assumptions. The consequences of disparate anthropological assumptions are evident most clearly, though still subtly, in the discussion of Luther's view on grace as one that understood an inherent discord between the interior life and exterior life.

As a marginal virtue ethical work that accords in many ways with Aristotelian-Thomistic virtue ethical frameworks, it seemed necessary to approximate the potential points of departure between the models. In the process of situating this work, I have taken the liberty of suggesting the potential avenues of mitigation this ethics might lend some of the classical complexities within virtue ethics. It is not my contention that this ethics deals with these complexities entirely, but that they are ways to envision the ethical life that would not be uncommon to most Christians in approximately the first fifteen centuries of Christendom. Whether understood as the beatific vision of God, or union with God, the overwhelming experience of God to which these Christians (and even to those in antiquity) point is one of spiritual struggle—the first of two concepts in the constructive portion of this ethical framework. To these accounts, we now turn.

NOTES

Epigraph: Guroian, "Notes," 228, 231.

1. It would be more accurate, though unappealing, to use quotation marks for the rest of the book when deploying the term "ethics" as specifically Orthodox Christian because, as I hope becomes clear, ethics is not a functional category in the lives of Orthodox Christians as it is in Western philosophical systems.
2. Even the earliest Orthodox "ethicists" some sixty years ago, including Stanley Harakas and Vigen Guroian, foresaw that Orthodox Christian ethics would maintain a distinct approach among its Catholic and Protestant interlocutors. See, e.g., Guroian, "Eastern Orthodox Ethic," 228–44.
3. The early Church from its outset believed that when it gathered conciliarly it was to invoke the Holy Spirit in guidance of the Church on any particular decision, especially matters of belief or practice. See Acts 15.
4. This point needs no defense, but a good (and early) articulation of it is given by Guroian, "Eastern Orthodox Ethic," 240: "The most significant observation to be made about Orthodox theology is that it has never been rigorously systematic, not having such systematicians as Calvin or Aquinas. Indeed, Orthodoxy has consistently resisted such systematics."
5. Another dimension of this reparation is the reintegration of ethics and ontology. See Harper, *Analogy of Love.*

6. Meawad, "Liturgy as Ethicizer."
7. Jennifer Herdt, among others, sees this holism—the collapse of bifurcation in the moral life—as a critical task of Christian virtue ethics. See Herdt, *Putting on Virtue*, 96–97.
8. The difficulty of the project of differentiating between Orthodox ethicists and theologians —a task that would be unfruitful and that I do not take up—is another example of the integrated nature of the two disciplines. At the risk of excluding figures who have been important in the development of Orthodox Christian ethics, I must at least note a special edition of the *Journal of Studies in Christian Ethics* dedicated to the relationship between Orthodoxy and virtue ethics; see Hamalis and Papanikolaou, eds., "Modes of Godly Being."
9. On the topic of perpetual ascent to God, it is worth noting a mild disagreement between Orthodox theologians. Orthodox Christian theology or Orthodox Christian ethics are often made synonymous with that of Eastern Orthodoxy. Despite the majority of Orthodox writings in the West coming from Eastern Orthodox authors, there has been a recent increase in and influence from Oriental Orthodox authors in the academy. I mention this here as a reflection of my choice of language in describing the third stage of the spiritual journey. The language of *theosis* or deification, which I have attempted to avoid, tends to be problematic for Oriental Orthodoxy (and I suspect as much for Catholics and Protestants), or at the very least requires thorough elaboration. Some polemics between Eastern and Oriental Orthodoxy have arisen from the use of this term, and though it be semantic, where else might words be more important than in matters of theo*logia*?

   More specifically, one must clarify that when discussing deification, it is not implied that a person becomes God in His very nature or essence. Many Eastern Orthodox theologians agree with this clarification. E.g., see Maspero, "Deification"; Guroian, *Incarnate Love*, 14; Papanikolaou, "Theosis," 577; and Ware, *Orthodox Way*, 22, 74, 109, 125. Discussing the nature of God in relation to humans seems to be more an *apophatic*, rather than *cataphatic*, discussion. This is what Kallistos Ware, an eminent Eastern Orthodox theologian and bishop, asserts in the distinction between God's unknowable essence and His knowable energies: "Because God is a mystery beyond our understanding, we shall never know his essence or inner being, either in this life or in the Age to come. If we knew the divine essence, it would follow that we knew God in the same way as he knows himself; and this we cannot ever do, since he is Creator and we are created. But, while God's inner essence is for ever beyond our comprehension, his energies, grace, life and power fill the whole universe, and are directly accessible to us. . . . When a man knows or participates in the divine energies, he truly knows or participates in God himself, so far as this is possible for a created being. But God is God, and we are human; and so, while he possesses us, we cannot in the same way possess him," Ware, *Orthodox Way*, 22. God as totally Other, cannot be known in His nature and essence, though humans can participate in Him, grow in knowledge of Him, acquire virtue in emulation of Him, and unite with Him. I have also tended toward the language of "union" because it carries with it the centrality of the *epektatic* and anagogic process with a focus on God Himself and less of a focus on the individual himself or herself, which ultimately helps in guarding against a tendency toward self-centeredness in the acquisition of virtue. Instead, humans acquire a semblance of certain characteristics of God by fulfilling an inner, latent potentiality referred to as *likeness* to God. This semblance of and likeness to God is synonymous with participation in Him and union with Him. It is a union that is always incomplete, always dynamic, and always the *telos* of an Orthodox ethic, both Eastern and Oriental.

10. It could be that the Orthodox Christian model I am presenting in this book is similar to most Patristic and medieval Christian models, at least if we extend the language of unity with God to the "beatific vision of God," an extension I do not consider dubious in the slightest. For a brief analysis of Gregory of Nyssa's telic understanding of the beatific vision and unity with God, see Boersma, "Gregory of Nyssa."
11. Schmidt, *God Seekers*, xii–xiii.
12. See Harakas, *Wholeness*.
13. Wogaman, *Christian Ethics*, 270–81.
14. Lossky, *Mystical Theology*, 202.
15. Lossky, 42.
16. Lossky.
17. Papanikolaou, *Theosis*, 577.
18. See Woodill, *Fellowship of Life*, in which he suggests the complementarity of virtue ethics and Orthodox Christianity. In the two decades since this suggestion, a few scholars have taken up this task, especially in light of Maximus the Confessor's oeuvre.
19. Aristotle, *Nicomachean Ethics*, 1103a26.
20. Annas, *Intelligent Virtue*, 71–72.
21. Annas, 77. See also Porter, *Recovery of Virtue*, 103.
22. Aristotle, *Nicomachean Ethics*, 1124a25.
23. Annas, *Intelligent Virtue*, 28.
24. Porter, *Recovery of Virtue*, 115.
25. Aristotle, *Nicomachean Ethics*, 1145a1–2.
26. Aristotle, 1144b30–1145a5. See Aristotle's discussion of φρόνησϊς and an agent's possession of all moral virtue (ἠθικῆς ἀρετῆς) in contrast to natural virtue (φυσικὰς ἀρετὰς).
27. This is more fully discussed by Athanassoulis, *Virtue Ethics*.
28. MacIntyre, *After Virtue*, 157.
29. This is more fully discussed by MacIntyre, 219; but it is also accounted for throughout Porter's Thomistic account: "We can only attain our specific good . . . by sustaining a lifelong course of activity that is determine by our rational grasp of that in which the true human good consists"; Porter *Recovery of Virtue*, 166–67.
30. Though it would be difficult to support this Aristotelian model contemporarily without modifications, my pushback here is specifically against Aristotle (and Plato and the Stoics). Contemporary virtue ethics by and large seems to me unconvinced by the suggestion of the unity of the virtues as understood among the ancients. Nonetheless, virtue ethics always runs the risk of promoting conceptions of virtue in which ideal and complete forms exist and ought to be acquired; this book develops concepts aimed to dispel these potential misconceptions by elevating the place of struggle in the ethical life.
31. Exod. 2:11–15.
32. Num. 20:7–13.
33. Jon. 1–4.
34. Gal. 2:11–13.
35. MacIntyre, *After Virtue*, 219.
36. MacIntyre.
37. MacIntyre, 218.
38. Annas presents a case in which virtues are already present in a person naturally yet require further development. Complete virtue is an unattainable ideal, but there exists

a spectrum to virtue: it is not that one is either entirely virtuous or entirely not; Annas, *Intelligent Virtue*, 10–11, 64, 85.

39. Some discussions have called into question whether a person is able to claim possession of virtue or of particular character traits. See Athanassoulis, "Response to Harman"; and Athanassoulis, *Virtue Ethics*, 104–11. I assume that this acquisition is possible, but not without a fuller picture in place, including conceptions of grace, struggle, Godward (re)orientation among others, and a realization that the virtues one may claim to possess are never complete or exhausted but exist on a spectrum toward God, the Paragon of Virtue.
40. Issues surrounding unjust and oppressive circumstances and how they relate to the concept of spiritual struggle are addressed in chapter 2.
41. For a good discussion in addition to MacIntyre's, see Hauerwas, *Community of Character*, for another perspective on the function of narrative in a specifically Christian communal context.
42. Aristotle, *Nicomachean Ethics*, 1102b15–1103a3.
43. Aristotle, 1103b6–b22.
44. Aristotle, 1106a4–12.
45. Aristotle, 1106a14–18.
46. Aristotle, 1114b14–17.
47. Aristotle, 1103a14–b25.
48. Elaborating on this point might take me too far away from the topic, but I sense that divergent eschatological emphases are causes for different denominational approaches to Christianity. Though the hereafter receives little (comprehensible) description in Scripture, that what is fulfilled in the eschaton (perpetual transformation in God) begins here and now is clear. See, among others, John 17:3; Rom. 5:1–2, 12:1–2; 2 Cor. 3:18, 5:17; Gal. 2:20, 3:27; Eph. 4:22–24; Phil. 1:6; Col. 3:10; and 1 John 3:2–3. It is also worth noting that two elements often accompany references to earthly transformation: human struggle / suffering / death and the working of God.
49. Aristotle, *Nicomachean Ethics*, 1103a26.
50. Maximovitch, *Humility and Struggle*.
51. Athanassoulis, *Virtue Ethics*, 91.
52. Athanassoulis, 93.
53. Athanassoulis, 92.
54. Adams, *Theory of Virtue*, 158.
55. Adams, 161.
56. Adams, 165.
57. Adams, *Finite and Infinite Goods*, 28–81, 150–70. In this work, Adams uses the language of transcendent goodness, grace, and love to describe God, which he sometimes calls the "divine nature." Although this latter label may be problematic dogmatically, his points remain: grace is an attribute of God that characterizes all His love; divine love *is* grace; and God does not love only that which is perfect or the best but also that which is good or excellent. According to Adams, humans are good or excellent insofar as they resemble God, thus giving Him a reason to love.
58. Adams, *Theory of Virtue*, 170. It should be noted that in *Finite and Infinite Goods*, 81, it is clear that Adams maintains the classical tenet of apophatic theology when he maintains that the reality of this virtue is imperfect and fragmentary. For Adams, this means that there should be no hesitance in questioning human views of God.

59. Adams, *Theory of Virtue*, 163. Adams clarifies that while Foot does not make this claim explicitly, it can be deduced from her work: Foot, *Virtues and Vices*.
60. Adams, *Theory of Virtue*, 161–65.
61. Aristotle, *Athenian Constitution: Eudemian Ethics*, 1220b1–1222b13; Aristotle, *Nicomachean Ethics*, 1108b11–1109b26.
62. For a good exploration of moral motivation in virtue ethics and the criteria necessary to render actions virtuous, see Hursthouse, *On Virtue Ethics*, 121–60. Hursthouse's additional criterion and her main argument is that an action must be from a settled state of good character in order to be considered morally motivated. This is in addition to the obvious tenets that right thoughts, right reason, and good intent must accompany a virtuous action; but these are ultimately insufficient without a settled state of good character. Similar thought is found for Aquinas by Porter, "Subversion of Virtue," which is discussed below.
63. When discussing the need to safeguard against considering struggle as a good in itself, Porter admits struggle is necessary for the majority of people who have not yet perfected the virtues; Porter, *Recovery of Virtue*, 115. It seems reasonable and necessary to assume that no one is excluded from this categorization because none have perfected the virtues, a discussion receiving further attention in chapter 3.
64. Duckworth, *Grit*.
65. This criticism is detailed by Stokas, "Genealogy," where she tracks the development of the concept of grit in response to the resurgence in its interest due to Duckworth's research.
66. The distinction between suffering and struggling is picked up in chapter 2 in conversation with Weil, *Waiting for God*.
67. See Greer and Smith, *One Path for All*.
68. Tough, *Helping Children Succeed*, 50.
69. Quoted by Tough, 51.
70. Athanassoulis, *Virtue Ethics*, 115.
71. The point here is that in Aristotle's ethic there is perhaps too much at stake regarding circumstances. In contrast, spiritual struggle is relative to one's own circumstances; there are no circumstances in which the pursuit of virtue and thus of perfection are outside of reach. A potential limitation of this project is that there can be no way of determining the complex relationship between circumstance, spiritual struggle, and proximity to God, but the value (and self-effacing nature) of such a determination should be called into question.
72. Aristotle, *Athenian Constitution: Eudemian Ethics*, 1141b30; One good example can be found in Aristotle's discussion of the magnificent (ὁ μεγαλοπρεπής) and the great-souled (ὁ μεγαλόψυχος), Aristotle, *Nicomachean Ethics*, 1123a26–1125a27.
73. Khawaja, "David Solomon," 146.
74. Matt. 22:36–40.
75. Maximus the Confessor is one thinker central to most contemporary Orthodox virtue ethical accounts who helps envision the natural end of humanity as the fulfillment of love. The most recent and comprehensive of these accounts, noted above, is by Harper, *Analogy of Love*.
76. For fuller discussions of self-centeredness and virtue, see Annas, "Virtue Ethics"; and Huang, "Self-Centeredness Objection."
77. On the issue of self-effacement in virtue ethics, see Pettigrove, "Is Virtue Ethics Self-Effacing?"; Keller, "Virtue Ethics"; Martinez, "Is Virtue Ethics Self-Effacing?"; and Annas,

"Virtue Ethics." Ultimately, Annas makes the most compelling case against virtue ethics' self-effacement.

78. Aristotle, *Athenian Constitution: Eudemian Ethics*, 1248b37–1249a3. This observation is noted by Herdt, *Putting on Virtue*, 34.
79. Herdt, *Putting on Virtue*, 35.
80. Adams, *Theory of Virtue*, 24–25.
81. Adams, 65.
82. Adams, 68.
83. Herdt, *Putting on Virtue*, 54.
84. Aristotle, *Nicomachean Ethics*, 1103a14–b25.
85. Aristotle, *Athenian Constitution: Eudemian Ethics*, 1220a5–1228a15.
86. Aristotle, *Nicomachean Ethics*, 1105a25–b18.
87. Moberly, *Virtue of Bonhoeffer's Ethics*, 226–29.
88. Kotva, *Christian Case for Virtue Ethics*, 74.
89. I suspect that the Orthodox understanding of the economy of salvation as one of reconciliation—without as much a legalistic, technical payment of debt—is a primary reason that Orthodox Christians are not hesitant to speak of works. Works are not arbitrary rules to be followed but tools inscribed in human nature in order to align oneself with the embodied and spiritual process of reconciliation with God.
90. Boersma, *Embodiment*, 220.
91. See Barnes, "Orthodox View of Grace," 4–12, though his concern is more on how the Eastern Orthodox understanding of grace can make sense of the workings of grace on non-Orthodox Christians. Another helpful, but far earlier, account of grace in the Eastern Orthodox perspective that captures its vastness is summarized by Childs, "Eastern Orthodox Doctrine, 37–38: "1. The theology of grace is an inseparable corollary of Trinitarian theology. 2. Grace is all-pervasive in the sense that since the time of creation God's actions have been manifestations of grace. 3. The divine uncreated energies can be equated with grace and their operations a manifestation of grace. 4. The salvation of man is his divinization which involves the restoration of the grace lost in creation. 5. Divinization, described as the indwelling of the Trinity which is the inverse counterpart of the Incarnation, is according to the energies not the essence of God and is solely a function of grace. 6. Man's part in soteriology consists in the decision of his free will to co-operate with grace. 7. The divinization of Christians makes the active presence of God and his grace a dynamic ongoing reality in the Church."
92. Herdt, *Putting on Virtue*, 46.
93. Herdt, 47–48.
94. Herdt, 74.
95. Herdt, 76.
96. Herdt, 82.
97. Herdt, 84.
98. Herdt, 86.
99. Herdt, 90.
100. Herdt, 96–97.
101. Porter, *Recovery of Virtue*, 32.
102. Porter, 34.
103. Porter, 36.
104. Porter.

105. Sherwin, "Infused Virtue."
106. Sherwin, 47–51.
107. Luther, the works cited here, in *Martin Luther's Basic Theological Writings*, ed. Lull.
108. Luther, "Freedom of a Christian," in *Martin Luther's Basic Theological Writings*, ed. Lull, 393.
109. Luther, 393–94.
110. Luther, 393.
111. Luther, "Two Kinds of Righteousness"; Luther, "Freedom of a Christian," 135, 402–3.
112. Luther, "Lectures on Galatians (1535)," 19.
113. Luther, "Two Kinds of Righteousness," 136.
114. Luther, "Freedom of a Christian," 401.
115. Luther, "Lectures on Galatians," 23.
116. Luther, "Freedom of a Christian," 393–94. I wonder if Luther's bifurcation between the corporeal and the spiritual is an unintended disavowal of the incarnation—taking on real, material flesh consisting of intimately connected soul and body—of the Lord Jesus Christ. Is not the Christ the example par excellence that what is done in the body is essential and that without the body nothing "interiorly" nor "exteriorly" can be accomplished? In emphasizing the ontological transformation made possible only through the economy of salvation, one need not deny the corporeal experience of participation in that transformation.
117. Luther, "Lectures on Galatians," 21.
118. Biermann, *Case for Character*, 40–50.
119. Biermann, 54.
120. Meilaender, *Theory and Practice of Virtue*, 113.
121. Meilaender, 120.
122. Meilaender, 114.
123. Meilaender, 122.
124. Meilaender, 109.
125. Meilaender, 113–14.
126. Meilaender, 117.
127. Hampson, *Christian Contradictions*, 13.
128. Hampson, 30–31.
129. Hampson, 42.
130. Hampson, 49.
131. Hampson.
132. Hampson, 47, 50–51.
133. Hampson, 45.
134. Hampson, 49–50.
135. Double predestination refers to the belief that God predestines some to salvation *and* others to condemnation. The "double" here refers to the latter—the condemnation of the reprobate—as opposed to predestination, which includes only predestination to salvation. Much literature is available on this topic. For a detailed and earlier work on predestination and Calvinism, see Boettner, *Reformed Doctrine of Predestination*. For a close analysis of the main text in the book of Romans, from which this belief takes root, see Piper, *Justification of God*. For a more philosophical approach that attempts to reconcile between varying views, see Feinberg et al., *Predestination and Free Will*.
136. Rom. 9:22–23 (New King James Version, NKJV). I used the NKJV translation here and in the following biblical citation because there is a consistency in the translation of σκεύη

as "vessels," accurately connecting the two passages in Romans and 2 Timothy. Other translations, such as the NRSV, do not maintain this consistency in translation between these two passages.

137. 2 Tim. 2:20–21 (NKJV).
138. Herdt, *Putting on Virtue*, 52–53.
139. Herdt, 55.
140. Herdt, "Augustine," 26–27.
141. Herdt, 23.
142. Herdt, 22, 28.
143. Herdt, *Putting on Virtue*, 47–48.
144. Augustine, *On the Proceedings of Pelagius*, 121.
145. Augustine, 84, 147, 164. These are just a few instances, but it should not come as a surprise that the need for divine grace in relation to any good work is found all throughout *On the Proceedings of Pelagius.*
146. Augustine, 56.
147. Augustine, "On Nature and Grace."
148. This is a minor point of contention with James Wetzel; see Wetzel, *Augustine*. He does not deny *that* Augustine believes that the initial conversion of a believer is in the divine will, but he does not entirely agree that this is always the case. Moreover, Wetzel expresses similar sentiments toward Augustine's consideration of perseverance as a graced gift.
149. Porter, "Subversion of Virtue," 100–102.
150. Porter, 103, 108–9.
151. Porter, 115.
152. Porter.
153. Aquinas, *Summa Theologica* (hereafter *ST*), I-II.114.5.
154. *ST* I-II.114.2; translation taken from *"Summa Theologica" of St. Thomas Aquinas.*
155. *ST* I-II.114.3; the same translator.
156. Kotva, *Christian Case*, 72–74.
157. Kotva, 76–78.
158. Kotva, 71–76, 90–91.
159. Harrington and Keenan, *Jesus and Virtue Ethics*, 71.
160. Boersma, *Embodiment*, 220.
161. Boersma, 211–50.
162. Boersma, 220.

PART II

Developing the Ethics

2

A Case for Spiritual Struggle

When spiritual trials disappear, Christianity disappears.

—Søren Kierkegaard

Setting the stage in the previous two chapters to begin the discussion of spiritual struggle highlights part of the problem—that this concept is, for the most part and depending on how one defines spiritual struggle, entirely absent in ethical (and other scholarly) literature.[1] The two most prominent literary fields in which the term appears are those of popular spirituality, especially that of Orthodox Christianity, and clinical psychology. Regarding the former, the same spiritual struggle (πνευματικὸς ἀγώνας) mentioned in works of spirituality are the topic of this chapter, to make the point that the spiritual, especially in its exertive form, cannot simply be separated from the ethical in Christian ethical accounts; the ethical emanates from the spiritual. In fact, there is reason to believe that even ancient non-Christian accounts, which are explored briefly below, would not envision the ethical life as free of struggle. Yet it remains that the absence of spiritual struggle from the ethical literature is not incidental but is likely reflective to some extent of a broader contemporary consensus on the topic.

If a concept were to be neglected within a society, culture, or religion, this would not typically or necessarily signal alarm; but in this case, spiritual struggle has been part of—if not the center of—all accounts of Christianity, at least before the Reformation.[2] This chapter does not trace an accurate history of how or why this may have occurred, though I hope I have already begun expressing its import within Christianity, philosophical ethics, and applied ethics. Instead, the singular focus of this chapter is to delineate what constitutes spiritual struggle, especially as embodied in Orthodox Christian ethics, yet without being limited to the experience of Orthodox Christians. Spiritual struggle is a phenomenon recorded throughout history in various schools, camps, and religious traditions, and sometimes under different guises. The authors who are portrayed in conversation below represent a broad range of thought, describing overlapping components of spiritual struggle. This breadth—both geographical and temporal—is intentional, with the hopes of bolstering the validity of this experience, to an extent, by locating commonalities found among otherwise disparate writers. Of course, struggle does take special forms in Christianity, considering the many presuppositions, especially anthropological ones, that would inform their instantiation. Yet it remains that both the East and West, and the ancient and medieval periods, all attest to this religious experience. So it is with this in mind that we tap into the primary sources available on this topic that might help elucidate this largely forgotten, and perhaps deliberately abandoned, way of life. In this respect, this book here reaffirms its countercultural or marginal approach, defining struggle as a good—requisite for both human flourishing and virtuous formation.

Regarding the latter—the use of struggle in the field of clinical psychology—the technical term "religious/spiritual struggles" is defined as "distress or conflict in the religious or spiritual realm,"[3] or "tension, strain, and conflicts about sacred matters."[4] Of these, there are six types of religious/spiritual struggles, as summarized in table 2.1.

On one hand, table 2.1 helps identify some of the origins of spiritual struggle that are discussed throughout the chapter, for which I suggest more succinct categorizations. On the other hand, as conveyed in this table, and as discussed throughout the expanding collection of psychological articles on this topic, there seems to be a disconnect, albeit one of subtlety and nuance, between religious/spiritual struggles understood as "conflicts" (or, as another study puts it, as "disruption"[5]) and spiritual struggle in the pursuit of God. In the psychological literature, spiritual struggles are conflicts *with* religion, difficulties brought about as a person appropriates certain concepts and beliefs into his or her life. They are struggles, at least in their descriptions, whose resolutions might suggest revisions, emendations, or modifications to the areas of religion that cause friction. In a word, they are struggles to be forgone, not embraced.

However, as this chapter unfolds, what will become clear is that spiritual struggle is more accurately struggle *within* religion—and, in this case,

Table 2.1. Types of Religious/Spiritual Struggles

Divine struggles	Anger or disappointment with God, and feeling punished, abandoned, or unloved by God.
	Sample item: Felt angry at God.
Demonic struggles	Worries that problems are caused by the devil or evil spirits, and feelings of being attacked or tormented by the devil.
	Sample item: Felt attacked by the devil or by evil spirits.
Doubt-related struggles	Feeling confused about religious/spiritual beliefs, and feeling troubled by doubts or questions about religious/spiritual questions.
	Sample item: Felt troubled by doubts or questions about religion/spirituality.
Moral struggles	Tensions and guilt about not living up to one's higher standards and wrestling with attempts to follow moral principles.
	Sample item: Felt guilt for not living up to my moral standards.
Struggles of ultimate meaning	Concerns that life may not really matter, and questions about whether one's own life has a deeper meaning.
	Sample item: Questioned whether my life will really make any difference in the world.
Interpersonal struggles	Conflicts with other people and institutions about sacred issues; anger at organized religion; and feeling hurt, mistreated, or offended by others in relation to religion/spirituality.
	Sample item: Felt as though others were looking down on me because of my religious/spiritual beliefs.

Source: Exline et al., "Religious and Spiritual Struggles Scale."

within Christianity. Recalling the functional definition of spiritual struggle in this book, it is the exertion of effort in all conceivable dimensions of human existence—including the physical, emotional, psychological, intellectual, and spiritual—with the intent to attain a semblance of, knowledge of, and intimacy with Jesus Christ in community, for God, and for others. Certainly, the struggles listed in table 2.1 are inherent in the concept of spiritual struggle, but not as a spectator looking at religious beliefs as only one component (and, in this case, one problematic component) of life. Instead, spiritual struggle makes up the experience of a person subsumed *within* a tradition, pursuing spirituality *despite* the conflicts that arise; it entails not only an analysis of conflict *with* sacred matters but also an active, persistent pursuit of the subjects of those matters.

Be that as it may, there might be a reason not to dispel any of these religious/spiritual struggles so quickly in our analysis of spiritual struggle. Just as virtue is not outside the reach of non-Christians, spiritual struggle is also possible—though ultimately (and, similar to Augustine and Aquinas), orientation to God is what grounds both concepts in this virtue ethical account.[6] This will at least be clear in Aristotle's and the Stoics' accounts of spiritual struggle discussed below. To demarcate certain struggles as irrelevant would work counter to the vast complexity welcomed under such a flexible, less systematized model as that of the Orthodox ethics proposed here. Moreover, the struggles that are topics in modern psychology should not be minimized, even if they seem external to a Christian "struggler," because the accounts of spiritual struggle to which we turn below delineate different types of spiritual struggle—those of lower and higher orders. In fact, the categorizations of religious/spiritual struggles given above, at least in their titular forms, can be situated in each of the three origins of spiritual struggle analyzed in this chapter.

WHY "SPIRITUAL STRUGGLE"?

The concept developed here is not ambiguous; as two sides of the same coin, the term simultaneously constitutes the praxical formation and ethical framework of Orthodox Christians and is established all throughout the Christian Scriptural canon. This dual reality should come as no surprise, because it is through the embodied experience of Christians attesting to the Gospel of the risen Christ that Scripture came to be codified.[7] The Greek New Testament term from which this concept originates is ἀγωνίζομαι, used to describe the act of striving, laboring, competing, or struggling.[8] The references are many, and they are by no means ancillary considerations; it is Jesus Christ's command in Luke's Gospel to strive (Ἀγωνίζεσθε) to enter the narrow gate,[9] it is the term used by Saint Paul in his first and second letters to Timothy to fight the good fight (ἀγωνίζου τὸν καλὸν ἀγῶνα), a strife (ἀγωνιζόμεθα) based in hope that he himself fought (τὸν καλὸν ἀγῶνα ἠγώνισμαι).[10] Saint Paul uses the same term to describe one's labor (ἀγωνιζόμενος) for an imperishable crown,[11] obtained through synergistic striving through God's work (ἀγωνιζόμενος κατὰ τὴν ἐνέργειαν αὐτοῦ).[12] It is a perpetual struggling (πάντοτε ἀγωνιζόμενος) embodied in spiritual practices, such as prayer, referenced by Saint Paul.[13]

At first it might seem that the struggle described here appears too close to asceticism for sizable distinctions to be made. However, just from the biblical references, it is obvious that spiritual struggle encompasses so much of the Christian life, and the fact that it can be embodied within and applied to different spiritual practices suggests that, categorically, this concept is more overarching than what might be signified in asceticism. One can argue that an Orthodox Christian ethics is fundamentally ascetical, and this would not be entirely inaccurate. Asceticism, the topic of chapter 4, is the disciplined training of the body to regain control over bodily desires in order to exact a more profound, inner transformation of being, character, or personhood. However, the framework I am suggesting here is one in which asceticism is only one instantiation of spiritual struggle—that is, spiritual struggle applied to the body. One's progress in God is not only challenged or impeded by bodily desires, though one can make the argument that these are the most prevalent deterrents from the fulfillment of human nature in God. Instead, spiritual struggle is required on all fronts of human experience, a delineation emphasized in the functional definition of spiritual struggle provided in this book.

Spiritual struggle, then, functions more as a worldview, lens, and even modus operandi for Christian life, and as such, it can be applied to different aspects within that life. Spiritual struggle can be applied to Christian prayer, which requires consistent effort and dedication of time, energy, and focus, communally in the Body of Christ. Similarly, it can be applied to meditation—struggling to center oneself in order to experience the presence of God—and to penance—a self-evaluative and self-emptying struggle that requires what is often a difficult look at one's true state of virtue, or lack thereof. Among many other practices, spiritual struggle can also be applied to works of charity, which are often premised on self-sacrifice, and to the observance of other Christian rituals and traditions that might require human effort at the mercy of, and in synergy with, divine grace.

The two components of this term, "spiritual" and "struggle," have direct implications. More secular terms, such as "moral effort" or "moral struggle," or simply speaking of an ethics of virtue or a virtuous struggle, would not entirely capture what is meant by spiritual struggle. Potentially carrying polemical or historical baggage, words such as "spirituality," "pietism," and "religiousness" underemphasize the persistence, perseverance, and work that are requisite to the spiritual struggle under consideration here. "Struggle" is meant to convey tenacity. "Effort" does not immediately invoke resolve but carries with it traces of intermittency. "Strife" is a close replacement, yet it can at times be mistaken to include feelings of bitterness or anger, much the same as "grief."

Søren Kierkegaard, who laments that spiritual "trial" has become a rarity among Christians and that it is not sought after any longer,[14] uses the word *Anfægtelse,* which avoids Luther's melancholic *Anfechtung* that only captures *Anfægtelse*'s dimension of despair.[15] Simon Podmore translates *Anfægtelse* as "spiritual trial," but Kierkegaard's association of this term with only the higher order of struggle would limit the wide range conveyed by "spiritual struggle" in this book.

Turning to the term "spiritual," the obvious implication is one of religious overtones that are specifically not secular. As attractive as a more universal term might be, spiritual struggle in this project does necessitate a belief in Jesus Christ, because He is ultimately the Paragon of Virtue whom Christians seek to imitate. This does not mean, however, that those who do not profess such a belief cannot acquire virtue through struggle. Consider Aristotle's ethics, for example. Certainly, the effort required in the lifelong process of habituation is filled with struggle. Struggle is requisite to the acquisition of virtue: "Both craftsmanship and virtue come about in what is more difficult, for, indeed, even the good is thereby better."[16] That is, the good is better when it is difficult. He continues by explaining that the target of virtue is easy to miss and hard to hit.[17] The road to virtue is difficult, and it is in fact often the road of *most* resistance, not least. Aristotle recognized the transformative nature of struggle, and in doing so he foreshadowed similar sentiments expressed centuries later in Jesus Christ's description of the narrow gate.[18]

Aristotle is clear that one can have the right end (τέλος) but the wrong actions, the right actions but the wrong end; or both can be wrong; or both can be right.[19] Virtue chooses the purpose or action by which to reach the end, and the correctness of the choice's end is the job of virtue.[20] Said more succinctly, virtue is what allows you to choose the right actions toward the right end. Thus, character is assessed by the purpose for which a person acts, not entirely from the act itself. If spiritual struggle is exertion oriented to God, the term "spiritual" is what denotes this orientation. God is the τέλος that can never be entirely reached, and the actions that one must take in order to pursue virtue require a persistent orientation and reorientation toward this infinite, though partially knowable, end.

The absence in Aristotle's theory of the defined Christian God that would develop in future centuries might, at the risk of being overly simplistic, render his endeavors merely "struggle." Similar to Aquinas's assessment of pagan virtue, "pagan struggle" is true and even transformative to some extent, but it is not salvific if it is not oriented to God. That this struggle might still be transformative only points to an inscription within human nature that is affected by our embodied practices, actions, decisions, dispositions, and relationships. Ultimately, however, this transformation falls short of the anthropological problem stated at the outset of this book—that humans are separated from God and can only be reconciled to Him through active acceptance of, or participation in, the salvific economy of Jesus Christ.

Chapters 4 and 5—which address spiritual struggle applied to the body in asceticism and spiritual struggle applied to Scripture in sacred reading—will demonstrate clearly that struggle for, in, and through Christ creates an entirely different form by which to embody a given physical practice. That is, beyond simply being a locus by which to decenter the self, Christ transforms all struggle. This ontological chasm—evidenced by the tensions between virtuous and vicious desires typical of human experience—cannot be overcome by mere effort, and one's struggle must eventually be redirected to God if one desires to tap into its fullest potential in fulfilling human nature's end. Aristotle's unattainable ideal, which was criticized in chapter 1, is nestled in this same problem—that without a robust theological account, the τέλος of human nature is neither clear in any agent nor attainable within human potentialities. Who is the σοφός (wise), or the σπουδαῖος (zealous), why are there not more of them, and on what basis would struggle guarantee this perfection?

Similar to Aristotle, the Stoics shared the view that through reason, the fulfillment of human nature in virtue can be realized.[21] Yet their multivocal account of struggle in the acquisition of virtue is riddled with paradox. The most obvious contradiction in the Stoics' discussion of moral struggle is the assessment of the effects of struggle in a person who has yet to reach perfection—the status of the σοφός (sage). The struggle of such a person is rendered worthless, as expressed clearly in Cicero's *De Finibus*:

> For just as a drowning man is no more able to breathe if he be not far from the surface of the water, so that he might at any moment emerge, than if he were actually at the bottom already, and just as a puppy on the point of opening its eyes is no less blind than one just born, similarly a man that has made some progress [*processit aliquantum*] towards the state of virtue is none the less in misery than he that has made no progress at all [*nihil processit*].[22]

Cicero denies the benefits of partial moral progress, defending his position despite the inherent paradoxes (*mirabilia*) that exist.[23] Though one is either good or bad, without an in between state, moral progress is still encouraged because it is possible to reach the level of the sage who uninhibitedly does good in perfect freedom and wisdom and without a need for deliberation.[24] The caveat remains that unless this level is reached, any and all moral progress made that falls short of this pinnacle is rendered useless. Gradual change (*προκοπή*) leads to radical change (μεταβολή), but the gradual without the radical is as good as no gradual at all.[25]

Plutarch, a Platonic anti-Stoic of the early first century AD, believed that moral progress is really found in this μεταβολή. A fundamental flaw arises in Stoics' thought, according to Plutarch, when they admit that there sometimes exist those they call σοφὸς διαλεληθώς—wise men who were not aware of their becoming wise.[26] He asks how this could be, because such a sudden change must be noticeable. He concludes that either their conception of μεταβολή is mistaken or that there can be no σοφὸς διαλεληθώς. Moreover, if even the greatest moral change (μεταβολή) can sometimes be unnoticed, how would smaller change be noticed? There could be gradual moral progress, unbeknownst to the Stoics. Plutarch pushes the Stoics into a corner, where they must admit that partial moral progress is valuable or that all those who have undergone μεταβολή, successfully rendering them sages, must be aware of their accomplishment. Because many of those whom the Stoics followed as moral guides were not considered sages, and because they chose to follow some and rejected following others, the Stoics did indeed differentiate between those struggling for moral progress and those who were morally depraved. They followed some leaders who were not sages but did not listen to others at all because of a judgment they had placed on them. Degrees between vice and virtue did exist.[27] One way or another, the Stoic philosophy on moral progress could not stand without modification.

Epictetus gets the closest to providing a solution.[28] He admits that virtue leads to happiness (εὐδαιμονίαν) and detachment (ἀπάθειαν), and progress (προκοπὴ), and that any progress toward virtue is progress toward its effects.[29] It would seem, then, that Epictetus would admit that there is value to a person who struggles. However, his divide between internal (disposition and attitude) and external (precepts and actions) left him unable to make this admission. The problem, as Geert Roskam points out, is that if moral progress is an internal endeavor that is evidenced by a person's moral consistency, then if a person falters, that person was never a sage and his or her struggle is not valuable; and if a person does not falter, there is no way to tell if that person is a sage because one cannot assess internal disposition.[30] The Stoics remained pragmatically aware of the need for moral progress but theoretically unable to attribute any value to the one who progresses.

What is most telling, however, is that the Stoics demonstrated an awareness that their common experience of moral struggle contradicted their doctrinal theories. Despite the apparent paradoxes, struggle was a widely attested religious experience even among the Stoics, whose theological assumptions were markedly different than those of the Christianity that would follow.[31] Pagan struggle, though at times offering intimations of a theism similar to that of Christianity, is ultimately insufficient. Without an account of human nature that considers God as its end and the Fall as an ontological chasm to that end, how could the Stoics, with their doctrinal assumptions, make sense of their visceral intuition that struggle is necessary? What is needed is an account of *spiritual* struggle that is dogmatically dependent on a robust account of the Christian God. Turning to the ethos functional in the lives of contemporary Orthodox Christians, explicating the three possible origins of spiritual struggle provides a fuller picture of what this concept might entail.

STRUGGLE AGAINST BASE DESIRES: THE SELF AS COOPERATOR WITH GOD'S GRACE

First, spiritual struggle may arise from one's own weaknesses or base desires. This origin might also include the category "moral struggles" mentioned in table 2.1. As one of the "lower" orders of struggle, it is an experience demanding exertion against passions that have made their abode deep in the recesses of fallen human nature.[32] Elder Paisios of Mount Athos, a twentieth-century Eastern Orthodox monk who was recently canonized as a saint, locates the fight against bodily passions as originating in one's thoughts. One must endeavor to get rid of any thoughts that pollute the soul and must struggle to cultivate good thoughts that purify the heart. In fact, "Progress [πρόοδος] in [the] spiritual life depends on thoughts [λογισμὸ]."[33] Only when this purity of thought (mind) and heart has been obtained does Paisios speak of a person's entitlement to divine succor.[34] According to the elder, purifying one's thoughts, an action aided and rewarded by God, makes room for Christ Himself to dwell within.[35] The war between evil dispositions and the indwelling of Christ begins with thoughts and extends to all aspects of life.

A surprising juxtaposition might be made here between elder Paisios's account of this lower level of struggle and that of Epictetus, who, as noted above, was an outlier in some ways to traditional Stoic thought. In a short passage from his *Discourses*, he describes the struggle against certain impulses, the purpose of which is to prevent bad habits from forming and to aid in the formation of good ones.[36] Reminiscent of Aristotle's model but with significantly less elaboration, habituation requires struggle because only by constant repetition of good actions can one purify oneself of what is undesirable—including anger, distress, and lust, among others. Habituation in the good through struggling against negative impulses ought to be gradual, with increasing increments of good actions and decreasing increments of bad ones. In this way, bad habits will be completely destroyed. Among these "actions" (ἔργων) on which Epictetus elaborates are impure thoughts. He advises to set one's mind on pure things and to sacrifice to God when impure impressions (φαντασίας) attack.[37] He says to struggle against the lingering of any thoughts. If a thought is identified as bad, get rid of it right away without entertaining it. The more one does this, the more one will be equipped to resist any impure thought.[38] Epictetus advises the struggler to call on God for aid in the struggle, so that by catching any bad action early on, it does not risk becoming a full-blown habit.[39] Similarly, Paisios finds that the more one is drenched in sin, the more one must engage sincerely in struggle against the passions to attain purity. "Good habit [Καλὴ συνήθεια], my child, is virtue; a bad habit, passions [πάθη]."[40] One must struggle to make all habits good, and though ultimately for Paisios the purpose of this lower level of struggle is to prepare a person in accepting Christ, both Epictetus and the elder agree that one critical locus of spiritual struggle is in the mind.

Notice Paisios's model of purification here: the struggle against evil desires, graced as they may be, make way for divine indwelling. The discussion of works and grace in chapter 1 becomes especially important here and helps us elucidate the concept of spiritual struggle. Consider the inverse model of purification put forth by Luther, who held that the struggle to crucify the flesh was only in order to align the body with an already-purified soul. He writes, "Since by faith the soul is cleansed and made to love God, it desires that all things, and especially its own body, shall be purified so that all things may join with it in loving and praising God."[41] It is because the soul has been purified by Christ that bodily passions ought to be crucified as well. Paisios, conversely, places a graced purification of the body before the soul's purification, which makes room for Christ's indwelling. Neglecting bodily cleansing, for Paisios, means piling rubbish onto rubbish, under which reality becomes obfuscated. For Paisios, without the intentional purgation of one's impurities through graced spiritual struggle, the likelihood of self-deception drastically increases. What is at stake is the indwelling of Christ: there would be no room for Christ's indwelling amid a self that desires that which is contrary to Christ. For this reason, the ascetical and monastic treatises of the early Church, of which Paisios is a spiritual heir, emphasize the lower level of struggle against one's passions. Strugglers are more virtuous than those who do not struggle.[42]

For example, in Saint Athanasius's *Vita Antonii*, the acquisition of virtue in Saint Antony's life required human struggle and effort. This effort is described as intensive and intimidating, but it is on this road that virtue is to be acquired.[43] Virtue is within human nature (κατὰ φύσιν)—a potential that is easily within the grasp of any who desire.[44] But the effort, which included discipleship under a spiritual elder, must be sustained, focused, and unrelenting.[45] Antony was the prudent bee (σοφὴ μέλισσα) who went from flower to flower taking any and all good pollen he could find.[46] In his efforts, he discovered firsthand a truth of Scripture—the inverse proportionality between the body and the soul. The weaker one is—within limits, he adds—the stronger the other is, again within limits.[47]

Yet an emphasis on austerity in struggle was never meant to overshadow divine grace. This road to virtue, which Athanasius describes as the reason for Antony's and all other monastics' asceticism, was not contingent entirely on those who embarked on this journey.[48] Antony continued striving (ἐπεκτεινόμενος) for things ahead,[49] but Athanasius ultimately attributes Antony's successes to God.[50] Antony's ἆθλον,[51] and God's work, function as appositives in Athanasius's writing.[52] Healing, exorcism, and all other feats come *through* Anthony's prayers and ascetic discipline, but *from* God.[53] This grace-enabled struggle, then, required the human being's efforts but were rendered naught without God's grace.[54] More than that, it was God's very grace that infused the desires, strength, and ability to embark on the journey in the first place. The κατόρθωμα belonged to God, the Σωτῆρος.[55]

Again, what appear as hints of Pelagianism are dispelled when considered further. Consider Paisios's account of the dynamics of grace and works. He claims that awareness of one's sinfulness is what moves God. Paradoxically, for Paisios, divine grace is unmerited; yet there are still things humans can do to receive grace.[56] The grace one receives is undeserved in comparison with what one does, but one can still act in a way that wins the favor and the grace of God. For the elder, the way of life that moves God's grace is awareness of one's sinfulness and need for God.[57] Progress is made in struggling for self-realization, penitently and with reliance on God: "As one progresses (προχωράει) spiritually, the more the eyes of his soul are purified and the more he sees the magnitude of his faults; so he is humbled, and the Grace of God comes."[58] In the opposite direction, God's grace can be resisted to an extent through a lack of spiritual struggle.[59] Importantly, Paisios, though starting with an understanding of grace that seems dangerously Pelagian, reaches a conclusion with which even Luther would have agreed. For the Athonite, Christian spiritual struggle is meant to lead to an embodied, realized, and unreserved submission, faith, and trust in God. God, in Psalm 81, expecting the Israelites to assume a posture of submission, asks them to do their part by opening their mouths wide, for only then can He fill them. This posture of submission is the means by which to accept God's undeserved and overabundant grace, which is always trying to find its way into all people.

Teresa of Avila, representative to some extent of the spiritual struggle embodied by medieval Western mystics, places austere Christian spiritual struggle at the service of complete submission to God. Teresa was keen to demonstrate that struggle in religious observance leads to virtue, believing that God took pleasure in her infirmities, by which she shared in the Lord's very pains.[60] She saw the narrow road of righteousness as a gradual one that leads to heaven.[61] In letting go of worldliness—that is, attachment to worldly pleasures—she struggled in prayer, which she believed to be the door to grace.[62] Yet she is clear that unless this struggle ultimately led to a state of complete submission to God, it was all in vain: "I used to pray to our Lord for help; but, as it now seems to me, I must have committed the fault of not putting my whole trust in His Majesty, and of not thoroughly distrusting myself. I sought for help, took great pains; but it must be that I did not understand how all is of little profit if we do not root out all confidence in ourselves, and place it wholly in God".[63]

While positing that nothing can be done outside of complete reliance on God, Teresa never let go of the belief that this complete dependence ought to be accompanied by sincere struggle. God at the same time gives grace to those who struggle and persevere but also gives grace to sinners while they are sinning, both of which were familiar experiences to her.[64] Teresa and Paisios—though geographically, historically, and denominationally disparate—come to the same conclusions regarding spiritual struggle against the passions: one must struggle with determination while exhibiting complete faith, trust, and reliance on God and His grace.

We cannot of course rummage through all accounts of spiritual struggle against the flesh, which would at the very least incorporate the entire ascetical, monastic, and mystical corpus; but one more medieval Western mystic's account is helpful here. Julian of Norwich, in her popular work *Revelations of Divine Love,* identifies the struggler as one who seeks, endures, prays, strives, and repents.[65] Struggling through this life's pain is directly proportional to the solace of the next life: "The harder our pains have been with Him in His Cross, the more shall our worship be with Him in His Kingdom."[66] One must feel the purgative process of sorrow in order to experience God's mercy and grace.[67] All this struggle is deemed necessary by Julian, but in the end only God's grace mends us. When we sin, we become unlike God, and He allows us to go through difficulties, after which His grace and mercy restore us.[68] In this way, the interplay between works and grace is beautifully painted, with one never nullifying or overstepping the bounds of the other. God's unmerited grace alone is able to restore the downcast struggler, but this person must be just that—a *struggler*.

Distinct from Aristotle and the Stoics, the aim of the spiritual struggler is a similitude with God that is dependent and that envisions the vicious life as a matter of separation from God. Julian's experience of this spiritual struggle, in concert with the other authors discussed in this section, leads her to conclude that one cannot see God while still living in sin because His will and sin are antithetical; sin makes one unlike God.[69] There is no evil worse than sin, and this is the primary reason for spiritual struggle—to cast out sin through sincere prayer and travail—in a word, purgation.[70] The more one realizes one's sinfulness, the more one is able to repent. And the more one repents, the more one is given grace.[71] The purpose of life for Julian is penance—a realization of one's weakness that leads one to experience and rely on God, not on the self.[72] The subtle paradox between spiritual struggle and grace that we are seeing over and again—that it is unmerited and at the same time increases with increasing contrition—leads us to an important conclusion: *Spiritual struggle enables submission to God in the self-realization of one's weakness and sinfulness, thereby actualizing one's reliance on and acceptance of God's grace.*

The word "intimacy," selected in defining spiritual struggle, was carefully chosen to describe the literal cooperation between divine and human agency therein. It is characteristic of God in Scripture to encourage the participation of human agency within His divine plans. There are many instances where it is clear that God could have accomplished certain tasks on His own but instead chose to involve humans. God tells Job that in order for his friends to be forgiven, Job must pray for them.[73] The blind man had to go (while still blind) to the lake to wash his eyes, although Christ was there and able to heal him immediately.[74] The disciples had to give out the food after Christ miraculously multiplied the loaves and fish, which could have also miraculously been distributed through Christ.[75] Paul had to go to Ananias to recover from his blindness, although the same God who initially appeared to Paul (Saul) could have very well healed him of his blindness.[76] God raised Lazarus from the grave but commanded humans to unwrap his grave clothes, though the former is immeasurably more difficult than the latter.[77] The examples that illustrate God's desire to include humanity in His divine economy are many, and Moses's life—upon which Saint Gregory of Nyssa's theory is formed, and to which we will turn in chapter 3—is a good example of this divine–human cooperation. At this point, it should be clear that part of God's plan is for humanity to participate with Him in His works—which, from humanity's perspective, is in effect His grace. The essence of this cooperation might be difficult to assess in its particularities, but at least on the surface, God in His love cooperates, calling for the participation of human agency in the economy of salvation. This participation results in submission to God, which in turn enlarges one's capacity for and receptivity of God's grace.

STRUGGLE AS COMMUNAL CONFRONTATION OF EXTERNAL OPPRESSION

The second origin of spiritual struggle, which is also considered of a lower order, are extrapersonal forces. The two most relevant branches within this category of struggle are those originating from demonic powers or evil forces in the world and those that spring as consequences of other people's poor or malicious thoughts, decisions, and actions—that is, actions that are antithetical to the fulfillment of human nature in God. As categorized in table 2.1, these could be labeled "demonic struggles" and "interpersonal struggles." The former are illustrated descriptively in the *Vita Antonii* and become a theme in desert spirituality and its literature. When the demons could no longer bear Antony's ἀσκήσεως, fearing that he would soon fill the desert with this blessed struggle, they tortured him so excessively that Athanasius describes Antony as nearly dead from the blows that could not have been inflicted by mere humans.[78] Interestingly enough, the type of struggle entailed here is nearly identical, if not exactly the same, as that entailed in the struggle against one's own passions. The role of the demons in relation to humanity—in Antony's example, and also as evident in the account of the Fall of humanity in Eden—is temptation, and the defense against these temptations is a grace-enabled spiritual struggle that brings the passions into subjection. External demonic temptations do not penetrate the "inner human" who is fortified and disimpassioned through spiritual struggle—a struggle that shuts out demonic temptations.[79]

The Epistle of Saint James is not ambiguous on this point: "But one is tempted by one's own desire (επιθυμιας), being lured and enticed by it; then, when that desire has conceived, it gives birth to sin, and that sin, when it is fully grown, gives birth to death."[80] That is, temptation effectively weakens a person only if one succumbs to temptation out of weakness; and a person will not succumb if the passions and dispositions to sin have been bridled through grace-enabled spiritual struggle. Barring the discussion of Jesus's (in)ability to sin, in the face of Satan's temptations, Christ is not brought to sin because there was no place in Him that desired those temptations. It is not coincidental that His sinless flesh was brought into subjection through sleepless nights, early mornings, and persistence and toil in prayer.[81] That His flesh was already sinless lends more credibility to the argument for spiritual struggle; though He did not need them, Christ still insisted on embodying this struggle as a sanctifying exemplar, paralleling His acquiescent theophanic baptism and paving the way of struggle for His followers.[82] Christ is clear that the fight against demons requires prayer and fasting, two methods of struggle common at least to Christians of the Patristic and medieval eras.[83] In this way, whether the struggle originates from demonic powers or from one's own base desires, the praxical response is the same—cooperate with God's grace to bring your passions under subjection, thereby extirpating temptations.

However, spiritual struggle originating from other people might often take on a different form. Spiritual struggle, despite its seemingly individualistic qualities, is communal through and through. Spiritual struggle necessitates the community of the Body of Christ—the Church. John Zizioulas's observation that the Church Fathers describe the persons of the Holy Trinity with πρόσωπον or ὑπόστασις and never with ἄτομον (individual) means that they understood personhood as inherently relational, not individualistic.[84] As beings made in the image of God, humans are persons, formed in and through relationships. We are amalgamations of different relationships and experiences. To overemphasize human individuality, as has happened more vociferously in modern times, is to risk miscalculating the end of humanity and the means to that end. Even the hermits who took on lives of complete isolation never understood themselves as pursuing individualistic lives but ones for the flourishing of their communities, to which they always belonged.[85]

The disruption of the peaceable communion of God's people is a cause for evil that must be struggled against. Disharmony in the collective unity of humanity brings about ills that can be opposed and eliminated through spiritual struggle. This is precisely what constitutes structural oppression, which is at the same time the imposition of oppression *and* the absence of the communal harmony intended by God for His creation. Again, one's anthropological presuppositions are important here. When any part of God's creation veers from its intended purpose, not as a matter of utility but regarding the fulfillment or τέλος of its nature, the detrimental consequences of this disruption ripple out into the rest of creation. The distinction between "person" and "individual" deserves much more attention than I am able to give it here, but this important discussion would end with a simple conclusion, which suffices for our purposes: humans, as persons, are communal, and one's τέλος cannot be reached in a hyperindividualized neglect of others.

Spiritual struggle is communal by nature. Technically, one cannot envision a scenario, barring extreme circumstances or exceptions, in which a person does not belong to a community in one sense or another. It is more a matter of identifying a number of communities to which one belongs than of assessing whether one lives in a community. Personhood exists as a result of communal interactions in any capacity, and it is especially meaningful when the group gathered is confessing and professing a common faith grounded in love of God and neighbor—that is, the Church. The picture painted here of spiritual struggle within a community is indeed idealistic, but the concept of spiritual struggle never forgoes a reality of shortcomings and temporary failures. To perpetually fall and subsequently rise is inherent to spiritual struggle. It is to always aspire and to be satisfied more in the process of transformation than in actually attaining a supposed summit in that aspiration. Spiritual struggle means to move into the future, strive; it is *epektatic* and anagogic.[86] It never means to be stagnant but always to delight in the life that is lived vibrantly in, for, and through God and others.

Inherent in the concept of spiritual struggle is the idea that the agent's exertion is always oriented outwardly—toward the promotion of God's word and kingdom, for the benefit of others through one's own transformation, and toward growth in a semblance of God for the sake of the good of the world and the flourishing of humanity. Stanley Hauerwas, who championed the centrality of community in virtue-ethical formation, makes clear that part and parcel of the successful formation of a community is a shift in perspective from one's own to that of the entire community.[87] The interest of the larger body of people must not contend with or be seen as distinct from a person's interests within that community. Moreover, we are often deceived into thinking that we are able to maintain individualistic worldviews while prioritizing the desires of others over our own. Hauerwas contends that this is nothing more than self-deception; we must see ourselves as part of a community if we sincerely desire to put others above ourselves.[88] Our individualistic worldviews must give room to a more communal one. Placing oneself above others may seem impossible to uphold indefinitely, but the concept of spiritual struggle helps make this prioritization possible.

Thus, at the heart of this ethics are the chief commandments of Christianity, which are understood as embodying all the law and prophets—the commandments to love God with all your being and to love your neighbor as yourself.[89] In a word, these commandments turn one's focus from the self to the other. Without selflessness in community, there can be no sincere love of neighbor, because love presupposes sacrifice, and sacrifice presupposes an ability to place another's desires and preferences above one's own. This reprioritization cannot happen outside a community, regardless of how loosely this community might be defined. If spiritual struggle is not understood within a community and without selflessness, it risks the self-preoccupation, self-centeredness, and self-reliance about which Luther was rightly worried and against which he argued so ardently.

If the passive, inadvertent disruption of the right relation between persons in community is a cause for spiritual struggle, then how much more might overtly malicious interactions between communities and persons within those communities bring about especially unfortunate forms of struggle? If humans are meant to exist in community in order to actualize "human-nature-as-it-could-be-if-it-realized-its-*telos*,"[90] then the disruption of this communion is amplified to one degree when there exists a lack of appropriate intimacy between people and communities and to a second degree when that disruption is overtly malevolent, such as in instances of oppression, violence, and injustice. One might rightly label these instances as causes for involuntary suffering that might still be combated through a spiritual struggle that demands (re)presencing the divine through proper orientation to God. Structural violence that originates from the injustices of other people, groups, and institutions falls into this second category of spiritual struggle, without implying that injustices or oppression of any sort should be sought after or tolerated.[91] What it means instead is that in the face of suffering, a response of spiritual struggle might create an opportunity for the acquisition of virtue through the pursuit of God where otherwise no virtue would exist.

Consider the example of slavery, as noted by the early twentieth-century philosopher Simone Weil. She refers to *malheur* as a category even more harmful than *souffrance,* though the distinction might not be immediately relevant for our purposes because the suffering we are discussing includes the anguish of the *malheur* described by Weil. *Malheur* is so devastating to Weil that she is astonished that "God has given *malheur* the power to seize the very souls of innocents and as sovereign master to grip them."[92] She seems to have expected that unjust circumstances, misfortunes, or afflictions would not have been so far reaching, crippling a person's soul, in the sight of a just God. Her observation is unsettling, an account also described in part by contemporary ethicists.

For instance, Lisa Tessman—in her examination of the effects of oppression on moral progress, or its lack thereof—coins the term "burdened virtues."[93] These virtues are "burdened" because of deleterious circumstances causing barriers to their bearer's flourishing. In a sense, virtue is delinked in these cases from Aristotle's conception of the good life or human flourishing. Instead, they "forfeit their bearer's well-being because they are self-sacrificial or corrosive or crowd out other valuable traits."[94] Tessman believes that conditions of oppression do not just damage the victim's morality through a sort of trauma that is experienced after the fact but they also cause moral limitations and burdens by creating circumstances in which there is no good way to live, in the traditional sense.[95]

In a similar vein, Lisa Cahill coins the term "adverse virtue" to describe the deliberations, actions, and choices that might be facilitated by unjust circumstances. It is worth noting her full definition here:

> Such choices are not virtuous in the sense of finding just the right mean or balance between extreme alternatives, nor are they virtuous in the sense of being reasonable or of being fulfillments of all that human beings are meant to be. Yet neither are they necessarily best understood as forays into "sinning bravely"—into doing what one "knows" is wrong, but trusts will be forgiven. Nor are they "exceptions" to moral rules that can be clearly defined and justified in light of specific excusing circumstances, fitting neatly into a predictable worldview where their scope and repeatability can be controlled. To deem such choices essentially sinful is to undervalue the difficulty, worth, and courageousness of human attempts to discern the best way through impossible situations. . . . Nevertheless, to regard acts of adverse virtue as "acceptable" social practices is to accept the causing circumstances, underwrite the practices that may have helped cause the adversity, and create social institutions and policies that facilitate their repetition in the future.[96]

Cahill delicately navigates the difficulty of deeming examples of laudable character in deleterious circumstances as virtuous at the risk of turning a blind eye to the societal forces that have facilitated, and continued to facilitate, these circumstances. On one hand, what is deemed unvirtuous cannot be rendered virtuous merely on account of adverse circumstantial limitations. On the other hand, there exists a lamentable suffering that must be accounted for when searching for virtue in adverse circumstances or instances of suffering.

One helpful navigation through these issues is Aristotle Papanikolaou's application of virtue ethics to the new category "moral injury." He notes one type of suffering—the devastating effects of moral injury, defined as "a state of being in which the combat veteran experiences a deep sense of having violated his own core moral beliefs."[97] In combining Maximian anthropology and modern psychoanalytical schemas, Papanikolaou optimistically uncovers a way in which struggle in God can rewire the detrimental effects of war on the brain, resulting in the ability to love. Elsewhere, he writes that "the virtue of love is something that must be learned; it requires humans to engage in ascetical practices that allow us to acquire the virtues, which then form the building blocks for acquiring the virtue of virtues, which is love."[98] To access these healing portals, one can implement an ethos of spiritual struggle embodied in respective practices. In this sense, "violence does not make love impossible."[99]

The point in all this is that in the face of extrapersonal suffering, spiritual struggle oriented to God might still be an occasion for acquiring virtue through proper orientation to God. It might be an opportunity to realize the presence of God in situations that might otherwise seem to be God-forsaken. In the discussion of moral luck in chapter 1, I noted that circumstances do not affect one's ability to struggle spiritually, because spiritual struggle is measured by exertion relative to any set of circumstances. For some, merely carrying the will to survive might be just as exertive as the ascetic who fasts and prays for days without interruption.

With regard to profound cognitive disabilities, an objection is raised to an ethics that prioritizes human agency in the free pursuit of likeness to God: if freedom is necessary to attain this dignity, might we unintentionally be marginalizing those with profound cognitive disabilities from attaining their very *telic* purposes?[100] The premise of this objection is that certain actions afford a person the dignity of "likeness" in the "imago-likeness binomial." I agree that "dignity should not be evaluated from the perspective of human agency or human capacities, but in relation to Christ's all-encompassing sacrificial act."[101] However, in this ethics, the ends, as far as human capacity is concerned, is the Godward struggle itself, which is not always contingent on particular actions. That different types of suffering are included in this struggle implies not a need for freedom of action but for making the divine present amid one's struggle—a reality that might not, in certain circumstances, require human volition at all. To be sure, there is a significant emphasis in this ethics on the grit, volition, and action requisite for the embodied pursuit of God. Yet the reality remains that though those who possess this supposed freedom must embody it as implied in other forms of struggle, those whose capacities take on different forms are already embarking on the grace-enabled pursuit of God laden with struggle, potentially attaining more advanced levels on this journey than those without similar physical disabilities. As noted in chapter 1, struggle is relative to circumstances, not to be evaluated on any absolute scale. Moreover, I have been intentional in not limiting experience or knowledge of God to any cognitive, intellectual, or physical capacity; in fact, an ethics of Orthodox spiritual struggle is necessarily opposed to such interpretations. The argument may be taken so far as to admit that those using their volition in embodied spiritual struggle are looking to imitate those who are in fact perpetually making God present in their struggle through disability.[102]

STRUGGLE AS PURGATIVE, VIRTUOUS ENCOUNTER WITH GOD

The third possible origin of spiritual struggle is God, which is rendered in the psychological literature as "Divine struggles." Reminiscent of this type of struggle is Jacob's wrestling with God in the book of Genesis. As it appears in works of Christian spirituality, this struggle is of a higher order or stage because it deals directly with God Himself. Søren Kierkegaard describes this experience most clearly, distinguishing spiritual trial (*Anfægtelse*) with God from temptation, which originates in oneself or from others, as detailed above. He writes, "While temptation points to a darkness within, spiritual trial orients the self, anxiously, towards an Other. Spiritual trial can thus be understood as encountering the numinous boundary, the limit, between the self and a Holy Other."[103] He continues: "Temptation attacks the individual in his weak moments; spiritual trial is a nemesis upon the intense moments in the absolute relation. Therefore, temptation has a connection with the individual's ethical constitution, whereas spiritual trial is without continuity and is the absolute's own resistance."[104] When one is still warring against the flesh and its base desires, this is temptation, and it is not the supreme form of religiousness to be sought after. It is necessary but must be surpassed.

Kierkegaard's model might be depicted as a three-rung ladder, where the lower rung is the temptation just mentioned. The second rung, which is always transitory, appears when confronted by anything to be struggled against, thereby opening a portal toward the higher rung, which includes things of the Spirit. It is on this higher rung where the bounds of the limitless are expanded to the human being who has engaged the pinnacle of Christian existence for Kierkegaard—*Anfægtelse*. When Christians look upon all aspects of life and relate it to God, when they are focused on the religious every day, spiritual trials will arise. But this intense focus is rare, and thus comes Kierkegaard's lament that Christians experiencing spiritual trials is a rarity. What is more, "when spiritual trials disappear, Christianity disappears—as it has disappeared in Christendom."[105] Only when one lives as an authentic Christian, according to Kierkegaard, will one experience spiritual trials, thus successfully making progress. Even feeling God-forsaken is a spiritual trial to be fought against, because we have the consolation of the God-forsaken Christ.[106]

Similarly, Julian of Norwich, in her autobiographical account, recounts the struggles she went through on her journey to God through illness and anguish. In movements of solidarity with the suffering Christ, she recalls His pain as encouragement to endure her own pains, which are often spoken about as originating outside herself—that is, externally.[107] The interplay between internal and external origins of suffering with and for Christ is explicit in her work.[108] She embraces a reality in which God allows turmoil in life as a means of purification.[109] God expects our patience in the difficulties that befall us, and many of these difficulties befall us outside our control. Although Julian indeed was responsible for some of her requested sufferings, she admits that struggles come and go as God pleases, and we are often not in control of what comes at us, only at how we react to it.[110] Yet in all this, the solace of the struggler is in the realization that God never leaves us alone but suffers with us.[111] She is hardly concerned with the acquisition of virtue, except in her discussion of the higher parts of the human that are geared toward virtue, in opposition to the lower parts geared toward bodily passion.[112] Struggle is what allows a human to switch from the lower to the higher, and focusing on God is ultimately what allows Julian to rest assured that "all shall be well"; the passions of Christ protect against her own inevitable struggles.[113]

At times, however, one cannot decipher as clearly as Kierkegaard or Julian do when their struggle is *with* God and when a struggle is *toward* God but against certain impediments, obstacles, or hurdles in that journey. Even if one could decipher the difference, a difference especially pronounced for Kierkegaard, it remains that isolating spiritual struggle with God from an otherwise holistic journey is not the experience of many and might not capture this journey's complexity. It could be that with regard to some base desires—for example, gluttony—a person could be weak, still fighting against temptations. That same person could also be well beyond base desires in the struggle to pray earnestly and wholeheartedly. Categorizations between temptations and trials, lower and higher desires, and external and internal, are often less organized and might be considered nonlinear, as detailed further in chapter 3. For now, two brief accounts of struggle with God might illuminate dimensions of this complexity.

Consider Teresa of Avila's spiritual struggle applied to the practice of prayer. The first stage of prayer is very labor intensive and is not always accompanied by sweetness or solace. It is an acceptance of suffering because Christ has suffered, but God often consoles and gives grace through these intense struggles. If any virtue can be acquired in this stage, it is through God.[114] The second stage is less labor intensive and leaves the struggler reaping more benefits. This stage includes the prayer of quiet—that is, the quieting of the mind and the will—but these are not entirely ridden. This is part of the struggle of this stage. It is also filled with more grace, and thus more virtue, and is attained by many.[115] However, few progress past this stage to the third stage, where the pleasures of the flesh and of the world become the most dreaded sufferings that the soul can imagine after having experienced such joys and detachment. There is no more labor in this stage, but there is a great deal of virtue acquisition in which the soul becomes united with God.[116] Finally, the fourth stage is complete death to the world. A struggler in this stage only experiences bliss and divine union. It is a mystical state in which the senses are suspended, so little can be said of this state. Attaining this stage, according to Teresa, is worth all the trials and struggles in the world just for a taste of the glory of the Lord.[117]

Another medieval Western mystical account to consider here is John of the Cross's "La Noche Oscura," or "Dark Night," which at first glance might appear to be an elaboration on what Teresa of Avila left unturned—the mystical fourth stage of prayer that is inarticulable. However, Teresa's fourth stage includes no suffering, at least not any suffering that one can be aware of while in this state. John's dark night is just that—dark. It is imbued with pain, warfare, strife, and labor. Though only Teresa's first stage of prayer is riddled with struggle, both John and Teresa are aware that this pain is produced by much the same causes. For Teresa, labor is required, and pain is experienced when ridding oneself of worldly attachments. Similarly, John's darkness is experienced when God flows into the soul and purges it from its imperfection and ignorance. The more impurities and weaknesses in one's soul, the more painful the soul's purgation. The Divine light is not full of pain or darkness, but its incompatibility with the darkness that already exists in the soul causes a fire within. The old human must die, and the new human emerges in a new, divine radiance.[118] The road of struggle is the only sure profitable road upon which one ought to tread. John captures the concomitant difficulties and benefits of pursuing this path of suffering: "Another reason the soul has been safe in this darkness is because it has been suffering; for the way of suffering is safer and even more profitable than that of enjoyment and activity (*hacer*). First, in suffering, the power (*fuerzas*) of God is added, while in enjoyment and activity, the soul exercises its weaknesses and imperfections. Next, in suffering, the soul is exercising and gaining virtues, becoming purer, wiser, and more cautious."[119]

John touches on the many facets of the struggle-filled journey to God. Suffering leads to virtue; and in this way, the soul becomes prepared for the indwelling of the Divine, of God. Spiritual struggle is requisite on the road to God, or is the very road. Virtue is a marker that a person is en route toward

God, and though it is in some ways an excellence in itself, it is ultimately at the service of unity with God.

CONCLUSION

It should not come as a surprise that our exploration of spiritual struggle has brought us to the topic of unity with God, or divine indwelling. Richard Schmidt's work summarizing the experiences of thirty-two Christian spiritual women and men over twenty centuries might be distilled in the title he gives spiritual strugglers: "*God Seekers*." All along in our discussion, the orienting principle has been God, intimations of which might even appear among Aristotle and the Stoics. Cyclical as it may seem, spiritual struggle is at once a lifestyle that begins with orientation to God and ends in unity with God.

In response to some accusations pinned against virtue ethics, an ethics of virtue centered on spiritual struggle is an accessible moral pathway, is pragmatic in nature, and is reflective of commonly attested experiences of virtue in Christian traditions.[120] Though I have tapped into a variety of primary resources, my hope has been to provide a definition that is representative of spiritual struggle as it functions among Orthodox Christians. That I have used such a variety of spiritual experiences within the Christian tradition lends credence to this ethics' relevance, applicability, and transformative potential.

Our exploration in ways might lead to an understanding of spiritual struggle as hypersensitivity to the divine responses to human exertion. In this way, the emphasis on human agency is not inherently selfish or self-centered but is preoccupied with a constant (re)orientation toward God, even in its focus on human mechanisms. Its outward orientation is also engaged within the unitive love found in community, the disruption of which has devastating effects on the telic realization of persons, communities, and societies. Spiritual struggle amid this suffering might make possible the presencing of the divine in otherwise evil circumstances.

As we have seen, spiritual struggle is a process that is grace enabled all throughout. God's grace enables the struggle, leading to a state of submission to God, which in turn opens a person up to actualizing the fullness of this grace. Spiritual struggle is a purgation that rids the self of any attachments or desires preventing fuller intimacy with God. By means of an elaboration on Gregory of Nyssa's theory of the spiritual journey as *epektatic* and anagogic, the focus of chapter 3 is the Godward dimension of spiritual struggle, expressed as perpetual progress and ascent. There, I examine how conceiving of the journey as one that is never-ending casts new light on what it might mean to struggle, to be virtuous, and to claim moral progress. The conceptual framework of this ethics, summarized as Godward spiritual struggle, will then have been laid out for specific implementation through concrete Orthodox Christian spiritual and devotional practices.

NOTES

Epigraph: Kierkegaard and Hong, *Søren Kierkegaard,* 548.

1. One of the few books that uses the term moral struggle as its central topic—David Clairmont, *Moral Struggle and Religious Ethics*—is a comparative study between Christianity and Buddhism and not an attempt to elaborate on the term. In *Struggling with God,* Simon Podmore also suggests this term to translate Kierkegaard's *Anfægtelse,* but he ultimately ends up sticking with "spiritual trial" so as not to add another word to the list of possibilities for *Anfægtelse* (pp. 47–70). In going through an in-depth analysis of the difficulties of pinning this concept to one English translation, his discussion of the various possibilities provides a good picture for its fuller meaning. *Anfægtelse* does capture some of what spiritual struggle means in this project, but ultimately "spiritual trial" for Kierkegaard is not the same as spiritual struggle here; the former is struggle only *with* God, whereas the latter is struggle *toward* God but with three distinct origins discussed throughout this chapter.
2. Boersma, "Gregory of Nyssa," 146.
3. Exline, "Religious and Spiritual Struggles," 460.
4. Pargament and Exline, "Religious and Spiritual Struggles."
5. Keith, "Process of Resolving Spiritual Struggle," 1.
6. See Herdt, *Putting on Virtue,* 46–61, 72–82, on pagan virtue in Augustine and Aquinas, respectively.
7. For an example of the pervasiveness of communal reading events in the early Christian era prior to any codification of New Testament books, see Wright, *Communal Reading.*
8. Similar to the Coptic word ⲡⲓⲁ̀ⲑⲗⲟⲫⲟⲣⲟⲥ, the Greek ἀγωνίζομαι is a term that is often used to describe those striving in an athletic competition, as Saint Paul also describes the journey to the kingdom of heaven. This points to the embodied, muscular dimension of spiritual struggle. For this reason ⲡⲓⲁ̀ⲑⲗⲟⲫⲟⲣⲟⲥ when translated from Coptic and attributed to the heavenly saints, is sometimes rendered "victorious," "struggle-bearer," or "struggle-mantled," as interchangeable synonyms. See Greer and Smith, *One Path for All,* where they describe the aim of martyrs, saints, and ascetics as a "lifelong contest" via Gregory of Nyssa's oeuvre.
9. Luke 13:24.
10. 1 Tim. 4:10, 6:12; 2 Tim. 4:7.
11. 1 Cor. 9:25.
12. Col. 1:29.
13. Col. 4:12.
14. Podmore, *Struggling with God,* 52–54.
15. Podmore, 54–70.
16. Aristotle, *Nicomachean Ethics,* 1105a8–10.
17. Aristotle, 1106b31–33.

18. Matt. 7:13–14; Luke 13:24.
19. Aristotle, *Athenian Constitution: Eudemian Ethics*, 1227b20–23.
20. Aristotle, 1228a1–2.
21. Cochran, *Protestant Virtue*, 49.
22. Cicero, *De Finibus Bonorum*, 267.
23. Cicero, 268.
24. Roskam, *On the Path to Virtue*, 9–15.
25. Roskam, 24–29.
26. Roskam, 229–36.
27. Roskam, 242–44.
28. Additionally, Cochran observes that "Epictetus suggests an understanding of God as more of a personal being than that held by other Stoics"; Cochran, *Protestant Virtue*, 14.
29. Epictetus, *Discourses*, I.4.3–4.
30. Roskam, 116–24.
31. Cochran, *On the Path to Virtue*, 13–18.
32. Among others, Gregory of Nyssa uses the lower/higher categorization to distinguish between different stages in the journey to God. This terminology will be helpful in the next chapter; the higher stage is deemed so as it is the τέλος of the spiritual journey.
33. Παϊσίου, *ΠΝΕΥΜΑΤΙΚΟΣ ΑΓΩΝΑΣ*, 33.
34. Παϊσίου, 35.
35. Παϊσίου, 66.
36. Epictetus, *Discourses*, II.18.
37. Epictetus.
38. Epictetus.
39. Epictetus, 157.
40. Παϊσίου, *ΠΝΕΥΜΑΤΙΚΟΣ ΑΓΩΝΑΣ*, 66.
41. Luther, "Freedom of a Christian," 401.
42. E.g., in the epilogue of Methodius's *Symposium on Virginity*, a character named Gregorian is arguing that those who experience no concupiscence are better than those who struggle against it, since the former are far from any lust and have the Holy Spirit always dwelling in them. Yet another character named Eubolion—the character with whom Methodius is ultimately in agreement—makes a number of analogies, e.g., the pilot who has steered many ships, the wrestler who has beat many opponents, the doctor who has healed many patients, and the wise man who built his house on the rocks. These people are compared to the one who has struggled, and for this reason Eubolion concludes that the soul that struggles against concupiscence is stronger than the soul that has no such passions in the first place—a conclusion slightly contradictory, however, to the notion of struggle as making room for Christ's indwelling. It remains that struggle is elevated here, and the force that makes virtue stronger is perseverance. See Methodius, *St. Methodius*, 159–62.
43. Athanasius, *Vie D'Antoine*, ed. Bartelink, in *Sources Chrétiennes* 400 (hereafter *SC* 400), 142–44, 164–66.
44. *SC* 400, 188–90.
45. *SC* 400, 152–56.
46. *SC* 400, 136.
47. *SC* 400, 152, 172–74.
48. *SC* 400, 256.
49. *SC* 400, 154.

50. *SC* 400, 374.
51. Struggle in this text is sometimes rendered ἄθλον, capturing the athletic dimension of ἀγώνας. The latter, however, is still used frequently throughout the text.
52. *SC* 400, 150, 240, 352.
53. *SC* 400, 174, 238, 358.
54. *SC* 400, 144–46.
55. *SC* 400, 150.
56. For a fuller discussion on the superabundance and unmeritedness of grace, see Cassien, "Conference XIII." Cassien makes it clear from the outset that nothing good can be done in this life without the grace of God. Furthermore, even the impetus toward or desire for good, the ability to do the good, and the opportunities that arise for the good, are from God. God is the one who provides the spark, enlarges the spark, and gives the opportunity for the spark to grow. Another dimension of the dynamic between grace and struggle is a comparison that Cassien makes between what is input and what is output. Humans put in efforts that are rather small and dainty, yet the grace that results is insurmountable. This is another dimension of the unmeritedness of grace. Not only does God give grace to those who do not deserve it, but He does so in an amount not proportional to those who may deserve at least some grace. Cassien continues to another factor in the immensity of grace—its superabundance; it comes even when humans are unaware of it or not seeking it, and it comes in an amount that almost cannot be resisted. Yet, the doctrine of irresistibility that would develop in future post-Enlightenment Christianity is countered by Cassien's explanation that turning to evil can in fact become a resistor to grace. God will still do all He can without overstepping the boundaries of free will, but constant opposition to grace is indeed able to create a resistance to grace as a result of free will. A number of these observations are typical of ascetics in early Christianity, play important roles in Orthodox Christian theology, and are at play in the backdrop of the asceticism presented in this chapter.
57. Παϊσίου, *ΠΝΕΥΜΑΤΙΚΟΣ ΑΓΩΝΑΣ*, 85–87.
58. Παϊσίου, 90–91.
59. Παϊσίου, 50–57.
60. Teresa de Avila, *La vida de la madre Teresa de Jesus*, VII. 9; VII 18, 24.
61. Teresa de Avila, VIII. 7.
62. Teresa de Avila, VIII. 13.
63. Teresa de Avila, VIII. 18.
64. Teresa de Avila, XI. 1–5.
65. Julian, revelation X.
66. Julian, revelations XXI, XLVIII, LXXVIII; translated from Middle English by Grace Warrack.
67. Julian, revelation XLVIII.
68. Julian, revelation LXI.
69. Julian, revelation LXXIII.
70. Julian, revelation LXXVI.
71. Julian, revelation LXXVIII.
72. Julian, revelations LXXVII–LXXVIII, LXXXI.
73. Job 42:7–8.
74. John 9:6–7.
75. Matt. 14:13–21, 15:32–39; Mark 6:30–44, 8:1–10; Luke 9:10–17; John 6:1–14.

76. Acts 9:3–19.
77. John 11:38–44.
78. *SC* 400, 156.
79. *SC* 400, 198.
80. James 1:14–15.
81. Matt. 4:1–11, 14:23; Mark 1:13, 35, 6:46; Luke 4:1–13, 5:16, 6:12.
82. Matt. 3:13–17; Mark 1:9–11; Luke 3:21–22; John 1:29–34.
83. I acknowledge that the authenticity of καὶ νηστείᾳ (and fasting) is a point of textual dispute; but at the very least, this addition would have been the result of an early Church practice of fasting, and as such, central to the ethics proposed here. For a somewhat poetic but nonetheless insightful elucidation of a biblical perspective on fasting, see this Lenten prayer from the Coptic Orthodox liturgy: Coptic Orthodox Diocese of the Southern United States, *Divine Liturgy*, 429–31.
84. Zizioulas, *Communion and Otherness*, 174–76.
85. Saint Paul the first hermit, for example, in conversing with Saint Antony after several decades of solitude, is chiefly concerned to know how humanity is faring. See Jerome, *Trois vies de moines*, 166.
86. This dimension of spiritual struggle is unpacked in chapter 3.
87. Hauerwas, *Community of Character*, 135.
88. Hauerwas, *Peaceable Kingdom*, 9, 28–29.
89. Matt. 22:37–40.
90. MacIntyre, *After Virtue*, 53–54.
91. One contemporary example of struggle amid suffering imposed externally can be found in the Coptic Orthodox Church, which has witnessed one positive and paradoxical result of oppression—the proliferation of the Gospel of Christ. Evidenced by their use of a calendar whose year was reset after the mass extinction of hundreds of thousands of Coptic Christians, this Church prides itself on the blood of the martyrs, whose line of blood has been shed almost consistently for nearly two millennia. See Papaconstantinou, "Historiography." Yet this still does not and should not translate (although at times it did) into a pursuit or welcoming of oppression. See Gruber, *Sacrifice*; Hassan, *Christians versus Muslims*; and Tadros, *Motherland Lost*.
92. Weil, *Attente De Dieu*, 78.
93. Tessman, *Burdened Virtues*, 4.
94. Tessman, 5.
95. Tessman, 6, 81–106.
96. Cahill, *Theological Bioethics*, 119–20.
97. Papanikolaou, "Trinity, Virtue, and Violence," 123.
98. Papanikolaou, 122.
99. Papanikolaou, 130.
100. Maican, "Holiness."
101. Maican, "Overcoming Exclusion," 509.
102. Sophie Cartwright reads Gregory of Nyssa, to whom I turn in depth in the following chapter, as locating autonomy and self-determination in vulnerability. See Cartwright, "Vulnerability."
103. Quoted by Cartwright, 178.
104. Cartwright, 179.
105. Cartwright, 202.

106. Cartwright, 184.
107. Julian, *Revelations*, revelations XXVIII, XXXI, XXXVII–XXXVIII.
108. Julian, revelation LXV.
109. Julian, revelation XXVII. On one hand, the origin of struggle here can be considered external because God allows it. On the other hand, the real reason God allows it is because humans are infested with sin that must be purged if they are to be with Him and like Him. "For that contrariness [which is in us] is cause of our tribulations and all our woe, and our Lord Jesus taketh them and sendeth them up to Heaven, and there are they made more sweet and delectable than heart may think or tongue may tell" (revelation XLIX). Similarly, "But for failing love on our part, therefore is all our travail" (revelation XXXVII). Translated from Middle English by Grace Warrack.
110. Julian, revelation XXXI.
111. Julian, revelation LXXX.
112. Julian, revelations LII, LV, LVII.
113. Julian, revelation LXIX.
114. Teresa de Avila, *La vida de la madre Teresa de Jesus*, 306–7, XI.11–25.
115. Teresa de Avila, XIV.1–XV.14.
116. Teresa de Avila, XVI.1–XVII.14.
117. Teresa de Avila, XVIII.1–XXXVII.3.
118. San Juan de la Cruz, *La Noche Oscura*, V–X.
119. San Juan de la Cruz, XVI.9.
120. For a full discussion of this accusation and its defenses, see Begley, "Practising Virtue." A direct example of this accusation is given by Truscott and Crook, *Ethics for the Practice of Psychology*, 8, of the impracticality of applying virtue ethics to the contemporary assessment of psychologists. Authors who have defended against such an accusation include Oakley, "Virtue Ethics," 197–99; Vardy and Vardy, *Ethics Matters*, 77–78; and Swanton, "Practical Virtue Ethics." Yu, "Practicality of Ancient Virtue Ethics," demonstrates that ancient Greek and Chinese virtue ethics help the modern reader remember that the issue of practicality is more than asking what does moral philosophy tell us to do. Finally, Baker, "Virtue Ethics," offers a fuller picture of how virtue ethics can be rendered most practical.

3

Onward and Upward

The Perpetual Godwardness of Spiritual Struggle

> . . . always being changed to what is better, and from glory to glory being transformed; in this way, let him turn . . .
>
> . . . πρὸς τὸ κρεῖττον διὰ παντὸς ἀλλοιούμενος καὶ ἀπὸ δόξης εἰς δόξανμεταμορφούμενος οὕτω τρεπέσθω . . .
>
> —Saint Gregory of Nyssa

The Orthodox Christian ethics of this book, as it is developing, is a lifelong journey, not a series of actions or systematized methods to be deployed. It is an ethics that requires a spiritual struggle that is a commonly attested religious experience and modus operandi that finds grounding in Scripture; that arises from a person's evil inclinations, actualizing a reliance on God, that is a grace-enabled communal endeavor that extirpates evil of all sorts; and that is a purgative process leading to unity with God. The focus of this chapter is to unpack the most important component of spiritual struggle—its Godward orientation—with the hope of detailing what Godward progress along this journey entails and implies; until this point, it has been given only cursory attention. An Orthodox Christian worldview is inherently eschatological, shaped at every corner by its anticipation of unity with God and its orientation toward God even in the mundane. One ancient Patristic author who articulates this worldview especially well is Saint Gregory of Nyssa, whose writings have helped shape Orthodox Christian thought throughout the centuries.

Hans Boersma, in concert with the ethics of this book, reminds Gregory's readers that the anthropological question of the human τέλος reshapes one's eudemonistic ethics: "St. Gregory makes us aware that human beings cannot find their true identity, and therefore cannot flourish, when they exclude serious reflection on the transcendent purpose of the human person."[1] The "transcendent purpose" to which Gregory points is a struggle for purification of soul in order to orient oneself properly to God. This reorientation is as practical as any ethics for Gregory, implying first a turn away from those things that deter a person from fulfilling their τέλος in God. Boersma puts into perspective what is at stake for the contemporary application of the ethics of this book in neglecting Godward spiritual struggle:

> The reductionism inherent in the modern abandonment of the beatific vision is, therefore, much more serious than may at first appear. It means a turning away from the infinite God who gives all good things in the vision of Christ in favor of a reorientation of the human gaze toward this-worldly goods. The loss of the beatific vision as the purpose of human existence leads to a "spirituality in which nothing any longer exceeds the ebb and flow of this-worldly human desires. Gregory knew human nature well enough to recognize that our desires are infinite. When such infinite desire is directed away from its proper telos of the vision of God in Christ, the objects of desire inevitably end up holding their immanent sway over human existence in frightening ways, holding us in a form of bondage that, ironically, we have willed into existence by our own misshapen desires. We are perhaps more than ever in need, therefore, of the witness of St. Gregory of Nyssa: only when with Gregory we redirect our gaze upon God in Christ can human persons find their true identity and aim.[2]

I hope, then, in this chapter to conclude the constructive portion of this book by explicating the "Godward progress" representative of an Orthodox Christian ethics. Organizing this chapter is intrinsically onerous, because it requires divorcing concepts that are so interwoven that even pulling at the seams will compromise their integrity. Nonetheless, one might envision this spiritual struggle of Godward progress through two overarching themes of the Cappadocian: progress to God as *epektatic* (a perpetual striving), and anagogic (a perpetual ascent). Within these two categories, one can begin to understand the theological, spiritual, and "ethical" implications of the Nyssen's vision of the spiritual journey in and to God. After expanding on his theory, I turn to the difficult task of systematizing his theory of the spiritual life into stages along a spectrum, better preparing us for the application of this ethical model.

GREGORY'S THEOLOGICAL INTEGRATION

Born in about AD 335, Gregory of Nyssa is one of the three heralded Cappadocian fathers that include his brother Basil the Great and Gregory of Nazianzus.[3] These three Cappadocian fathers affected much of the developing theology of the early Church and the centuries that followed. Their contributions include writings on the doctrine of the Trinity, the Person of the Holy Spirit, responses to Christological controversies, ascetical treatises, and what would be characterized in modern times as spiritual teachings. It is not coincidental that much of the dogmatic, Christological, and anthropological presumptions that constitute Gregory of Nyssa's eschatological theories are transferrable to contemporary Orthodox Christianity, as a Church that identifies closely with its Patristic heritage. The same conceptual integrity found within Orthodox Christianity discussed at the outset of this book is characteristic of the theories developed in Gregory's texts.

For example, in Mary Emily Keenan's description of Gregory's theology, she describes the spiritual life as a sort of organic whole, taking into consideration the intellectual, the physical, the psychological, and the spiritual.[4] In a rare occurrence, the scholarship since Keenan has been nearly unanimous on this point. There exists no realm of the human experience that does not affect all other realms. This is no less the case among Orthodox Christians. For this reason, Han Urs van Balthasar explains that for Gregory, dogmatic theology and mystical theology are one and the same—a notion not easily accepted in modern times.[5] Along similar lines, Sarah Coakley challenges Jean Daniélou's modernization of Gregory in which epistemology/philosophy and spirituality are separated.[6] Gregory did not conceive of a separation between the sensual and the spiritual but understood the human journey as a continuum between fallen sensuality and redeemed sensuality—"a human continuum of epistemic transformation."[7] The "spiritual senses" in Gregory are no less tied to sensual perception. Morwenna Ludlow cites the unitive realms in what she calls Gregory's "moral psychology": synergy of body and soul, whose archetype is the Incarnate Christ; and synergy of human and divine agency.[8]

What is most important in insisting that Gregory writes with a certain theological holism or integrity is understanding that his theory of Godward progress was never intended as a mere theory but as an applicable ethics engaging a person's integrated whole:[9] "One's life, in its pursuit of virtue, must at all times be a unified endeavor."[10] It seems that Gregory is at the very least just as interested in encouraging his readers to *act* on his theological excurses as he is in getting them to *understand* his theological premises. He is interested not just in imparting knowledge but also in getting his reader to embark on the journey he is presenting.[11] This might begin to explain his occasionally imprecise theological language, which sits uncomfortably alongside other instances of hypersystematization in certain theological treatises.[12] Gregory's precision is obfuscated at times by his desire to encourage a practical ethics of spiritual journeying.[13] It is a journey accessible to all, and it is this accessibility that makes the ethics proposed in this book especially suitable for the twenty-first-century Christian.[14] The sentient, the spiritual, and the intellectual are all enmeshed in this singular journey. The integrity of his theology translates directly into the accessibility of his ethics as one that does not distinguish between theological knowledge and spiritual formation. Growing in knowledge of God *is* the transformative journey itself, and this growth could never be separated from the composite integrity that is human nature.

Typical of many early Church Fathers, Gregory's theological integrity included a Christianization of philosophical currents of his day, especially in his theory of spiritual progress. Ludlow claims that it is in Gregory's later works that *epektasis* really becomes his own through a fusion of Platonic associations and biblical conceptions.[15] Coakley agrees, pointing out that Gregory seems to have changed his mind over time in his discussion of what spiritual sense might mean.[16] She points to different stages in his development, beginning with a Platonic sense, to realizing that the body can be transformed through the Holy Spirit and union with Christ,[17] that "cognition, ethics and ascetics" work as one in Gregory's thinking,[18] that the "eye of the soul" is the constant that can be dragged down by the body or undisturbed through purification from passions,[19] and that "progression of sensuality [proceeds] from baseness to Christlikeness."[20] Thus, the writings of Gregory that include his theory of *epektasis*—his most sophisticated expansion of the spiritual life—are often dated as the latest of his writings, coming after his *De anima et resurrection*.[21] These writings, which help unpack Gregory's theory, include his treatise titled *De perfectione*, his commentaries on the Beatitudes, the Psalms, the Song of Songs, and his "De vita moysis."

EPEKTASIS: IMMUTABLE AND INFINITE PERPETUITY OF GODWARD PROGRESS

To begin unweaving Gregory's spiritual tapestry, one component of the journey is the *perpetual* nature of progression in God. The Cappadocian uses the character of Moses to express progress in God through Pauline terminology—a life of *perpetually* striving or straining (ἐπεκτεινόμενος) toward those things still to come.[22] Jean Daniélou coined the term *epektasis*,[23] which is more properly referred to as a theory instead of a doctrine because it is a word that is contemporarily used to summarize Gregory of Nyssa's sense of the spiritual journey.[24] Though it is premised largely on theological arguments, it does not necessitate the creedal affirmations typical of doctrines proper. *Epektasis* describes a journey in which the human soul grows perpetually through an orientation toward God, in desire of God, and toward likeness of God. It is a journey in which the soul is always filled as it progresses but simultaneously always desires more because of God's infinitude—the basis of the eternality of the journey.

One might best understand the perpetual nature of *epektasis* in at least two dimensions: it is perpetual, in that it is immutably stable in the Good, that is, God Himself; and it is perpetual, in that it is infinite growth in an infinite God. Gregory's assertion regarding the former is a significant departure from the Platonic thought with which he otherwise exhibits significant overlap.[25] Anthony Meredith points out at least three basic theological and philosophical principles in Gregory that find their origin in Plato: (1) God as goodness, reality, and being; (2) God as beauty; and (3) the way upward as a demanding task and also a "return to origins."[26] He adds to these three claiming that Gregory shares with Platonism a belief in the "spirituality of the soul and the existence of a supreme, changeless spirit."[27] All these principles aid Gregory in piecing together a fuller theory of *epektasis*.

However, there is an important distinction that Gregory makes without which perpetual progress would have been philosophically inconsistent. Platonists hold that change is inherently bad, while stability is good. It is not hard to see how starkly opposed an essentially dynamic theory as *epektasis* would be to such a tenet. Though Gregory ultimately does deny this premise, he does not entirely forgo this claim. Instead, there is an element of stability in his theory of perpetual ascent: as the epicenter toward which perpetual progress is oriented, God is the stable Good in which humans ought themselves to remain stable.[28] In other words, progress in the Good is the only constant, a paradoxical aphorism ("change is the only constant") still used in the twenty-first century. For Gregory, mutability need not be condemned because humans can participate in a "mutable immutability,"[29] a state in which a person does not alternate between bad and good but is paradoxically at rest in the good and at movement along a spectral ascent.[30]

Further, it is the responsibility of a Christian not only to imitate Christ's virtues but also to participate in His immutability. For this reason, the ethics of this book as one beyond virtue ethics cannot be boiled down to an *imitatio*

Christi that extracts the virtues of Christ separating them from participation in Him. Christ, for Gregory, is a rock that is immutably in the good;[31] in fact, Christ is the Good Himself.[32] When a Christian puts on the virtues of Christ through detachment and imitation, that Christian becomes constant in the good, as much as human nature will allow.[33] Becoming Christ-like, having union with God, and residing in Him—dynamically through perpetual growth, but statically through constancy—are the inexhaustible "ends" of spiritual struggle for Gregory.[34]

The τέλος of the spiritual journey is both dynamic and static. It is dynamic, in that growth and progress never cease. It is static, in that a person remains consistently and stably in God—the good—by making progress toward similitude with Him. Gregory presents this Christian τέλος as the only means to attain perfection. Gregory concludes his *De perfectione* by explaining how mutable humans can participate in an immutable God, pointing to the anticipated trajectory of the *epektatic* journey:

> Now the most beautiful task of change (τροπῆς) is growth in the good, since the one who is changed to things more divine is always being created (ποιούσης) into that which is better. So then, that which seems fearful (I mean the changeability (τρεπτὴν) of our nature) can serve as a wing for flight to greater things, since it is to our detriment (ζημίαν) if we are unable to accept change for the better. Therefore, one who knows [this] ought not to be grieved for this purpose—that his nature is mutable (μεταβολὴν); rather, by always being changed to what is better, and from glory to glory being transformed; in this way, let him turn.[35]

In defending a notion of mutability that was in his time considered inherently problematic, the Cappadocian defines his conception of the virtuous life not as an Aristotelianism of final telic attainment but as *perpetual* progress toward that which is immutably but infinitely good. Virtue is the result of constant flight toward and pursuit of God-likeness, who is at the same time Goodness itself and is also God incarnate, able to be emulated.

The second dimension of the perpetuity of Godward spiritual struggle—its infinitude—is a natural progression from the discussion of im/mutability. Gregory's understanding of the journey to God was geared toward Origen, who, similar to the Platonists, took issue with the ascription of mutability to humans.[36] The scholarship comparing the two theologians is extensive;[37] but regarding our exploration of *epektasis*, Origen, similar to Plato, viewed "absence of limit and form as a defect."[38] What this meant for Plato, and would come to mean for Origen, is that God Himself is finite, because infinitude for Origen would have implied defectiveness.[39] Origen states: "For we must maintain that even the power of God is finite [πεπερασμένην], and we must not, under pretext of praising him, lose sight of his limitations [περιγραφήν]. For if the divine power were infinite [ἄπειρος], of necessity it could not even understand itself, since the infinite [τὸ ἄπειρον] is by its nature incomprehensible [ἀπερίληπτον]."[40] For Origen, ascribing infinitude to God's power would have meant that God would not even be able to comprehend Himself. Infinitude implied defect for Origen, and Gregory would come to disagree strongly with this view, because if there were an end to God, there would also necessarily be an end of the journey toward Him. Gregory maintained God's infinitude, which would render humanity's participation with this infinite God an infinite journey.[41]

Yet Origen's conception of God as finite created another problem, this time anthropologically. If God is finite, then humans can reach a point of perfect satiety in God. In other words, if God has a limit, this limit can be reached in which the desire for God and assimilation to Him are exhausted.[42] Humans would in this way have a limited capacity by which to participate in God.[43] Gregory, dissatisfied with this notion, makes a distinction between human participation in God here on Earth and thereafter in the eschaton. Origen does not distinguish between the two in terms of capacity. Gregory, however, asserts that humans possess an increased capacity for participation with God in the eschaton, where the original state of humanity is restored. This distinction in turn seems to appease Origen's anxieties regarding satiation.[44]

For Gregory, what appears to be a state of satiation as one progresses through virtue turns out to be the beginning of a newly discovered stage of virtue.[45] In the "De vita moysis," the human soul is one that experiences the beautiful, whose origin is God, and that is drawn toward a thirst and desire for more of that beauty and for what lies behind that beauty. This thirst—an image of the ascent toward the infinite God—is always filled and at the same time never satisfied when it realizes that there is more to be desired after reaching each subsequent level of the ascent.[46] Similarly, Moses never stopped ascending; nor did he set a limit on his ascent. There always remained in front of him a step higher than the one previously taken.[47] So, too, does the human soul constantly grow in its desire for God, only to realize that there is nothing binding this desire's satiation.

In homilies 4 and 5 of Gregory's commentary on the Beatitudes, Gregory maintains that inherent in each human being is an inclination toward the good, against which each person has a choice.[48] The more this desire for the good, righteousness, justice, or salvation—in a word, God's Divine Will—is fed, the more it grows in its desire for them:[49] "We need an unceasing desire for higher things, which is not content to acquiesce in past achievements; we ought to count it loss if we fail to progress further."[50] This forward or upward striving is perpetual; it is always satisfied in growing but at the same time enthralled with its infinite potential. This is a potential founded on Gregory's understanding that virtue is modeled on the Godhead. That is, participation in the virtues is at the same time participation in God and union with Him.[51]

Gregory echoes the same in Homily 8 on "In Canticum Canticorum," and this is where it is especially clear that the limit of virtue is unbounded. The soul journeys continually to loftier levels of glory in a progression toward God, who remains unchanged, infinite, and ineffable. He cites the example of Paul, who kept ascending toward God, never standing still, but always striving onward toward the unbounded. The person who tastes a little of the Lord by partaking of the good will continue to grow in this participation for eternity, as previous experience incites a desire for more of this experience. Each new arrival of the sojourner immediately becomes a new departure, a continuous crescendo in which human mutability works as an ally of the soul, established immovably in the good. Gregory writes:

> Consequently, the Word wills that we, mutable as we are according to nature, not decline toward evil through change, but rather to have change as a coworker in the upward path of higher states through the ever-unfolding growth toward the better, with the actual result that we are made to succeed in the unchangeability toward evil through the mutability of our nature; to this end, the Word has evoked the memory of beasts that were once dominant as a kind of teacher and guardian for the estrangement from evils, so we may succeed in both steadfastness and inerrancy in good states by turning away from the worse, neither coming to a halt in change for the better nor being altered toward evil.[52]

This process is possible only because human beings are made in God's image and likeness, thereby equipping them with the capacity to experience God in a way unlike the rest of creation. The potential to continue growing in God's likeness is necessarily unlimited because God Himself is unlimited; this growth can never reach an end. In effect, the chasm that exists between finite humans and the infinite God is always being bridged partially but never fully.[53] At stake for Gregory is eternal life itself. Gregory must defend God's infinitude in order to uphold the impossibility of human satiation by God, thereby affirming the perpetuity of the spiritual journey toward and in God. The bishop of Nyssa associates this earthly, struggle-laden journey of virtue with an eternal life that begins now and continues after death.

Though Gregory's theory hinges primarily on Philippians 3:13, it seems that at the same time he is providing an exegetical expansion of John 17:3: "And this is eternal life, that they may know you, the only true God, and Jesus Christ whom you have sent." In this way, eternal life, understood *epektatically*, begins now and continues eschatologically.[54] The endeavor at hand is one of knowing God and participating in Him. For this reason, in interpreting Gregory, Coakley recognizes that "it is . . . the doctrine of *Christ* that is at stake, whereas the spiritual senses are the epistemological means of progressively internalizing that doctrine."[55] Only by preserving the *epektatic* nature of life in God—that is, eternal life—could Gregory make sense of "ethics," which in his schema is the spiritual means by which to make progress on this perpetual journey.

God's infinitude, for Gregory, means that in His essence and nature He is unknowable.[56] Often termed "apophaticism," the unknowability of God that results from His being infinite is a reason Gregory and others use the concept of darkness. The image of darkness implies invisibility, incomprehensibility, and inexhaustibility.[57] Gregory points his readers to Psalm 17:12, where "God made darkness his secret place."[58] Yet God does not remain altogether unknowable, and this is critical to forming the desire that propels the *epektatic* journey. God is accessible through his loving activity toward humanity; and as such, He is knowable relatively through His attributes.[59] Often termed "cataphaticism," ascribing positive characteristics to God will always be limited because humanity is limited and because humanity's limited knowledge can never fully grasp the unlimited God. Gregory acknowledges the positive and negative attributes of God and is described by Joseph O' Leary as torn between two currents: apophaticism and metaphysical cataphatic reasoning.[60] The more God is approached, the more concepts and images fall short of His description.[61] This reality, however, is not a deterrent from embarking on this journey.

"Apophatic theology is not a theology of distancing or discouragement, but a song to the infinity of the Life and the Good."[62] It is precisely because God is infinite and humans are finite that growth in knowledge of and intimacy with God is eternal.[63] In the human soul's capacity for infinite growth, it experiences a "continual crescendo,"[64] resulting directly from God's concomitant incomprehensibility and accessibility.[65] The fixed chasm between the infinite Creator and finite creation, upon which Gregory insists,[66] is not a boundary to participation in God but serves as the very platform by which humans are drawn to God.[67] More specifically, it is not simply the presence of this permanent chasm in combination with humanity's curiosity that encourages participation in God. Instead, the cataphatic traits known by humanity through God's self-revelation serve as important attractors to the *epektatic* journey. Theology proper and ethics are harmonious contingents in the soul's progress to God, a progress that is not only *epektatic* but also anagogic.

ANAGOGY: GODWARD PROGRESS AS ASCENT IN GOODNESS, VIRTUE, AND PERFECTION

If Gregory's theory of the spiritual life were nothing else, it would be dynamic. Gregory understood the spiritual journey as one of ascent (anagogy) or descent, without the possibility of stagnancy.[68] There could be no neutral space where one's thoughts, actions, decisions, interactions, spiritual practices—and, in a word, spiritual struggle—had no effect on one's internal or spiritual disposition. Godward spiritual progress demanded the integrity characteristic of Gregory's worldview. For example, in the "De vita moysis," he considers arrogance and pride (ὑπερηφανίαν) as a downward descent away from God and virtue. Falling into arrogance is no different than falling (πτῶμα) in bodily passion (πάθος).[69] He envisions the life of virtue as one that is dynamic and that requires constant struggle. He maintains that "stopping on the road to virtue (ἀρετὴν) begins the road to evil (κακίαν)."[70] Moreover, "those who are lax on the upward and difficult course of virtue" (ἀναπαύονται δὲ οἱ τὴν ἀνωφερῆ καὶ δυσπόρευτον τῆς ἀρετῆς πορείαν) will find themselves descending further down into fleshly attachments, away from the soul's light, airy, and unhindered ascent.[71] Evil must be stopped in its tracks from the very first trace of its temptations.[72]

A similar picture is portrayed in his *Inscription of the Psalms,* where he imagines the progression of the Psalms as an exposition of the soul's ascent away from evil and toward God.[73] Instead of presenting rigid categories, Gregory presents a smoothly transitioning and overlapping spectrum of development in virtue through the pursuit of a God-likeness that is imprinted within human nature.[74] Again, the spectrum can be put in reverse when evil—that is, a life in opposition to the attributes of God as revealed in Scripture and in the person of Jesus Christ—is chosen. This ultimately moves one from an otherwise concomitant process of becoming human and like God to becoming bestial or dog-like (κυνῶδες).[75] The choice between progress and digression is a product of the free choice of any given human and is within the grasp of all people, despite potential maleficent circumstances.

In Homily 5 of "In Canticum Canticorum," he speaks of the bride's ascent: first, she hears his voice, after which she continually draws nearer to Him in a variety of obfuscated and changing images.[76] The bride's journey is any person's journey in this ascent. Similarly, he understands the command of Christ to the paralytic to take up his bed and walk as a command to move toward greater perfection.[77] A person must, according to Gregory, *voluntarily* begin the journey toward virtue and God by first getting rid of the little foxes in one's life—that is, of all vice in pursuit of the pure life.[78] After ridding oneself of vice, Gregory points to the positive component of this journey. "'It is not enough for you,' he [the bridegroom] says, 'to get back up from your lapse alone, but advance also through progress in good things, concluding the race in virtue.'"[79] As noted in his commentary on the Psalms, Gregory does indeed speak of an end to virtue, but ultimately it seems that Gregory is talking about some sort of relative end or feeling that one has acquired virtue at least partially, without compromising his assertion that the road to perfection is perpetual. It is the soul that is constantly transformed as it is progressively drawn into a higher beauty of the Divine nature that remains immutably in infinite good. The soul "is being led by the hand to the heights in an incremental ascent through the upward paths of virtue" (ἐν βαθμῶν ἀναβάσει χειραγωγουμένην διὰ τῶν τῆς ἀρετῆς ἀνόδων ἐπὶ τὰ ὕψη).[80] In this way, virtue is the means and the marker toward an end never fully attained. No matter how magnificent one may deem a certain glory, there is always a greater glory beyond it, which ever-inflames one's desire toward God.

Eventually, as described in the "De vita moysis," the soul's ascent reaches its climax when knowledge of God is seen as light, attracting a person's soul through its brilliance. Interpreting Egyptian wealth (ὁ καλῶς τὸν Αἰγύπτιον),[81] in the Exodus account as worldly knowledge, Gregory even carves a space for the pursuit of "outside education" (ἔξω παίδεθσιν) or philosophy, maintaining that it can be profitable but that it ultimately risks tainting the truth.[82] As one approaches closer to the Divine, one realizes that reason and the senses fall short of expressing these experiences. For this reason, Gregory also uses the language of darkness in his experience of God. It is in this luminous darkness (λαμπρῷ γνόφῳ)[83] that one is able to draw near to God through faith to learn about other images presented in Exodus.[84]

The first example Gregory gives is that of the heavenly tabernacle, which teaches those on the journey toward virtue that they ought to be comfortable with mystery, with not knowing.[85] That which is beyond comprehension is felt beyond all doubt to exist. Its ineffability does not contradict its existence; it only implies its inability to be articulated.[86] Next, he describes the earthly tabernacle as a teacher of the importance of self-control and "mortification of the sinful flesh" (νέκρωσις τῆς ἁμαρτητικῆς σαρκός) through asceticism.[87] This is signified through the skin that is dyed red, like blood, and the coverings made of hair, which resemble death in their callousness—their inability to feel.[88] The earthly tabernacle points to the notion that "the grace that is blooming through the Spirit does not come about in others unless they first make themselves dead to sin [ἁμαρτίᾳ νεκρώσειαν]."[89] God assists those who live a life of virtue.[90] Finally, Gregory describes the priestly garments whose names are "rational," "doctrine," and "truth" (δήλωσις λόγιον ἤ ἀλήθεια), pointing to the adornment of the soul by virtue.[91] The long garment reveals the continuous nature of virtue, which should not be cut short but should extend perpetually.[92] In his descriptions of both the lower struggles against the passions and the inarticulable experience of God in the darkness, Gregory is clear in these writings that the anagogical dimension of the spiritual journey, because it is Godward, is one of increasing virtue, goodness, and fulfillment (perfection).

Gregory depicts virtue as consisting of two parts: virtue that pertains to right conduct (ἤθους) and a good conscience (ἀγαθῆς συνειδήσεως), and virtue that pertains to the divine (τὸ θεῖον) and to matters of faith (πίστεως).[93] Both of these are necessary in order to begin ascending to God-likeness; but the former, for Gregory, is usually of a lower tier on the "ladder of divine ascent," while the latter is encountered higher up the ladder. Gregory uses the image of the mountain in Exodus to further describe the ascent to God. The further one is able to ascend, the "greater and higher doctrine (διδασκαλίαν) of the mysteries" one is able to comprehend.[94] Reminiscent of the Orthodox Christian anthropology presented at the outset of this book, in order to ascend, "the dead and earthly skins placed around (our) nature at the beginning when we were made naked by not listening to the will of God, ought to be removed from the feet of the soul."[95] Deadness, according to Gregory, is found in the pleasures and passions of the body, and this state is reached by those who do not acknowledge God.[96] Purity—that is, a clean soul attained through outward struggle and reliance on God—is necessary to ascend the mountain.[97] There exist lower and higher parts of the soul. Faith increases when the latter prevail.[98] Just as the body is weighed down by gravity, the soul's natural trajectory is upward when it is released from earthly pleasures and attachments.[99]

In his commentary on the Psalms, Gregory perceives of the aretaic life in spectral terms, that is, on a spectrum through which progress can be made and assessed. Virtue is a journey that has a beginning, a progression, and an end.[100] Similar to his commentary on the Beatitudes, he does discuss an *acquisition* of virtue (ἀρϵτῆς κτῆσις), albeit one that is relative to God and has a similitude to Him, and not absolute in the sense of perfect or complete acquisition.[101] "A life perfect through virtue," for Gregory, is nothing more than a perpetual progress in participation in God.[102] To demonstrate this point, Gregory writes, "The acquisition of virtue (ἀρϵτῆς κτῆσις) thus belongs to blessedness and, according to itself, looks towards the living, for this [virtue] is the beginning and end of everything considered good."[103] He continues this thought by adding that "the limit of human blessedness (ἀνθρωπίνης μακαριότητος) is likeness to the divine (τὸ θεῖον ὁμοίωσις)."[104] Gregory correlates virtue with goodness and blessedness. This participation in blessedness he explicitly defines as likeness to God. The process he provides is simple: humans begin by detaching from evil and then continue on to goodness through imitation of Christ through virtue directed toward God.[105] This orientation is contingent on participation in a perfection, a goodness, and a blessedness defined by and in God.[106] That is, the pursuit of virtue, as defined in God as paragon, is the ultimate end toward which one is oriented.

Gregory likens this process to God the sculptor chiseling humans into His divine likeness.[107] We are to participate in God, not for virtue's own sake, nor for some satisfaction that attaining virtue might bring about, but because life is a continual process of increasing in the likeness of God. In other words, it is not enough to love the good if that good is perceived outside God as its source; one must love God. God is the Archetype, and human understanding of virtue is predicated on Him. The purpose of life is to be called a servant of God as a result of a sublime and virtuous life.[108] Gregory explains that when Moses sees God's back, the reader is to understand that God is the one to be followed. Humans can only see His back because He is the guide of virtue; and in order to grow in this virtue, one must follow His commandments, way of life, words, example, and constant instruction.[109] He describes the armor of the soldier of virtue (ἀρετῆς ὁπλίτης) as God Himself, without forgoing the essential position of struggle.[110] Spiritual struggle is the means by which perpetual progress continues: "For only the activity (ἐνέργεια) towards virtue feeds its [the flight's] power by exertion (καμάτῳ), not slackening the intensity through work, but increasing it."[111]

Gregory, in his commentary on the Beatitudes and in the "De vita moysis," describes Christ Himself as absolute virtue (ἡ παντελὴς ἀρετή),[112] in which there is no limitation through time or satiation.[113] This is a good example of the inconsistency, or perhaps of the use of paradox, in Gregory's writings. Even in employing virtue (ἀρετήν) as a reward (γέρας) that can be acquired, he is not implying that virtue is an end in itself or is good for its own sake.[114] This would directly contradict his belief expressed in the same homily that growth in virtue is at the same time growth in God, which cannot be limited. "True virtue," according to Gregory, is God Himself, and yet he leaves room for the acquisition by humans of partial virtue. Growth in virtue, which he makes clear requires struggle and exertion, consists of perpetually increasing degrees of growth and transformation in God.[115] The perfection of each virtue and all virtues resides in an unlimited and perfect God. Yet people can claim possession of a virtue, albeit incomplete possession, to the degree that they participate in God through grace-enabled spiritual struggle.

After quoting Psalm 43:1, "'I shall be satisfied when Thy glory shall appear," Gregory writes that true virtue (ἀληθὴς ἀρετή) is goodness that is untainted by any evil.[116] For the Cappadocian, God is virtue and is untainted Goodness.[117] The Divine nature, whose very infinitude is one of Goodness,[118] remains immutable (ἄτρεπτος), unaltered (ἀναλλοίωτος), and unlimited (ἀόριστος) in the good, and stability in the good increases the intensity of the ascent to God.[119] The perfection of human life, as described by Gregory, is to grow in God's Goodness and become stable in the good by following an innate inclination (ἐπιρρεπῶς) toward the good.[120] Though Beauty is more than this, the attractive "pull" toward Goodness is sometimes termed Beauty. God's infinite Beauty, as such, is not redundant but always new and desirable. The more one discovers this Beauty, the more one is enticed to continue its discovery.[121] David Balás's reading of Gregory's *Contra Eunomium I* reveals Gregory's understanding that the principal means of participation in God is through His Goodness. God in His very essence and nature is absolute Goodness, and humans are able to participate in this Goodness through humanity's sensible and intellectual capacities.[122]

Thus, perpetual ascent can be summed up with this consideration of God's Goodness: "Spiritual life consists in an ever-growing participation of Divine Goodness—that is, in an infinite progress of our knowledge of and union with God—and this progress is to continue in all eternity."[123] But Balás is aware of the broader implications of referring to God as Goodness. Goodness "includes all perfections with a special emphasis on virtue."[124] That is, Goodness extends beyond a simple attribute, encompassing the essence of what it means to be virtuous. God is the paragon of virtue.[125] Gregory captures this well when he describes God's positive traits and characteristics as "incorruptibility, eternity, immorality, goodness, power, holiness, wisdom, and every majestic and sublime conception."[126] All five primary sources utilized in this chapter are inundated with "virtue" terminology, and in his "De vita moysis" and commentaries on the Beatitudes and the Psalms, Gregory is explicit in describing God as the paragon of virtue. God is virtue's very source; it is through God that humans come to know what virtue is. At the same time, growth in God is growth in virtue.[127] But can humans ever fulfill the commandment to be perfect as God is perfect?

Gregory claims that matter and senses have definite limits, while virtue's only limit is that it has no limit because virtue is based in God, who by nature is unlimited and infinite.[128] For this reason, it is impossible for those who pursue a life of virtue to ever reach perfection; perfection is a continual process of the soul.[129] Gregory, similar to Aristotle, envisions the road of virtue as a narrow mean between two neighboring extremes or evils, but Gregory's understanding of perfection—because it is defined in relation to the Christian God who is the paragon of virtue—will ultimately be at odds with some of the Greek philosophy that characterized his time, a philosophy that viewed change as an inherent imperfection.[130]

As discussed in some detail in chapter 2, in a perfectionist ethics like that of the Stoics, the value or merit of intermediate stages is relativized and qualified. All that matters is whether a person attains a final state of perfection—in this case, the status of the sage. Drowning 10 feet underwater is the same as drowning 100 feet underwater; one must break through the depths to the surface of the water for any of the effort to matter. By contrast, in a developmental account of moral and spiritual progress, intermediate stages of moral and spiritual growth would likely meet with approbation. Gregory is at odds with the Stoic perfectionist model; he goes so far as to relate progress to perfection.[131] In a sense, suggesting a sort of synonymy between progress and perfection appeases the Scriptural commandment to be perfect as God in heaven is perfect.[132] This, of course, begs the question as to what constitutes progress; but this task will be left to the discussion of the forms in which spiritual struggle can come to be embodied.

More than his departure from Stoic moral progress, Gregory's theory directly challenges the Aristotelian focus on one's own goodness as the object of the moral life. For Gregory, grace-enabled struggle allows a person to embark on the journey toward God—the τέλος of the ethics.[133] Gregory does not believe that a final state will ever be reached on the journey of virtue but that humanity by its nature is in constant flux and that perfection is found in this dynamism.[134] Aristotle similarly takes into account an inherent dynamism in the life of goodness; but the contribution of Gregory's thought is to redefine the goal of the life of virtue—and progress therein—as a perpetual process in which progress implies success and as a process necessarily decentered from the self. The Cappadocian writes, "The perfection of human nature is in always desiring that which is better (τῷ καλῷ),"[135] found in God who is Goodness. A sojourner on the road to perfection is "through daily growth always becoming better and always being perfected and never reaching the boundary of perfection. For this is truly perfection, to never stop increasing towards the better nor to limit perfection with any boundary."[136] In this way, he redefines perfection as progress towards one's τέλος, that is, the God who perfects (completes, fulfills) human nature.

Gregory goes on to liken this road toward perfection as friendship with God. It is a road that is predicated on freedom and desire for God, not slavery to and fear of God. He writes:

> This is true perfection (τελειότης): not to avoid a wicked life because like slaves we servilely fear punishment, nor to do good because we hope for rewards, as if cashing in on the virtuous life by some business-like and contractual arrangement. On the contrary, disregarding all those things for which we hope and which have been reserved by promise, we regard falling from God's friendship (φιλίας ἐκπεσεῖν τοῦ θεοῦ) as the only thing dreadful and we consider becoming God's friend the only thing worthy of honor and desire. This, as I have said, is the perfection of life.[137]

In this way, he defines perfection as an intimate relationship with God that is uncoerced and toward which one's desire should be oriented.[138] This desire, when fulfilled, is constantly enflamed with greater desire for participation in God.

Anagogy is an ascent accompanied by the joy of one's new "status," in which a reminder of one's previous state functions as a cause for delight: "The bridegroom imparts to the soul ascending to him an intensity in her enjoyment of goodness. Not only does he manifest his own beauty (κάλλος) to the bride, but he reminds her of her horrible beastly forms that she may delight in her present enjoyment, by comparing them with her former state."[139] Ludlow summarizes the theanthropic relational aspect of this participatory ascent when she writes that "it is not about soul abstracted from human life rising to a pure principle of good, but about the relationship of a human person with the God who has revealed Himself in personal form."[140] Thus, one's joy is compounded in a number of ways: from one's satisfaction in deeper participation with God, from one's progress in virtue, from the potential for new growth, and from the recollection of previous, less-desirable levels of joy and goodness. In order to embark on this journey, one must turn from evil and orient oneself Godward with one's entire being with a singularity of purpose: one eye and one soul looking to the One God in the Trinity.[141]

THE STAGES OF GODWARD SPIRITUAL STRUGGLE

The emphasis in this chapter thus far has been on understanding what it might mean for an ethics to be Godward. We have at least concluded that this Godward ethics is (1) a perpetual progression (*epektatic*) that begins now through spiritual struggle and continues eternally in an immutable and infinite God; and (2) is an anagogic ascent of intimacy and joy with God who is Goodness, Virtue, and the τέλος of human nature. In both dimensions of Godward progress, the spiritual struggle presented in the previous chapter persists, ranging from simple, low-order, fleshly detachment to high-order, apophatic experiences with God. In an effort to further consolidate Gregory's theory and the ethics of this book for its application to embodied practices, I suggest three intermittent stages by which to organize the bishop of Nyssa's vision of the spiritual life.[142]

The purpose of locating the three origins of struggle in chapter 2 was to understand what it is humans have to struggle against and why it is we have to struggle. This discussion helped shape what spiritual struggle entails. In a way, the discussion was one of anthropology—who is the human being, why does she have to struggle, and how should she struggle—and one of theodicy—the need for spiritual struggle is a result of separation from God, even when the struggle is with God Himself. Our task here in delineating the three stages of Godward spiritual struggle requires a reintegration of the concept of spiritual struggle and of Godward progress, unnaturally separated in these two chapters. One cannot make sense of spiritual struggle apart from spiritual progress in God, and vice versa. In fact, in the very definition of spiritual struggle, orientation to God is explicit. When recombining our insights from the previous chapter regarding *what* one ought to do (who or what to struggle against, and why) and the *epektatic* and anagogic dimensions of journey from this chapter, the stages of this ethics might be best arranged within the purview of transformation: *how* is one transformed in embodying Godward spiritual struggle?

Terminologically, many scholars of Gregory use his theory of *epektasis* as synonymous with his general view of the spiritual life. I agree that Gregory might not be systematic enough for a differentiation here. However, I have been using "spiritual progress," the "spiritual journey," or the "spiritual life" in this chapter as overarching terms, whereas *epektasis* refers to a perpetual progress or striving and anagogy refers to a perpetual ascent. Other than potentially capturing his theory more accurately, it helps to categorize the different components of his theory. At the risk of minor misrepresentation of some authors below, I will stick to my categorizations for consistency and clarity.

At the outset, it seems most needful to determine the exact pattern, if any, that Gregory is proposing in the sources above. Are there specific stages that he is suggesting, and do these stages have implications for the pursuit of virtue? Though there is no overwhelming consensus regarding the most appropriate consolidation and explication of Gregory's theory, a basic three-tiered model is often proposed in order to understand the spiritual journey. Some have suggested patterns in which purification and illumination fall in the first stage, followed by a second stage of depreciation of worldly values, and concluding with union with God.[143] Thomas Bohm suggests that in Gregory's theory, human beings never arrive at any sort of union with God. Instead, spiritual advancement consists only of intellectual contemplation of God.[144] Hui Xia notes that Jean Daniélou, Andrew Louth, and Warren Smith all propose stages of purification, illumination, and union, though Gregory himself did not suggest these categories explicitly.[145]

Xia goes on to offer her analysis of the stages of divine ascent specifically in the "De vita moysis," arguably the work in which Gregory's theory is most developed. She suggests two larger stages—the preliminary stage and the mystical stage—with which Boersma agrees.[146] The first stage consists of human sensory experience and is best characterized by light—that is, what humans can sense and describe. In this stage, one's understanding is enlightened through the "light of virtue," mentioned in the "De vita moysis" and in Gregory's commentaries on the Psalms and the Beatitudes.[147] This stage requires constant effort in order to achieve a certain level of virtuosity.[148] A person must be focused with a constant drive to live in accordance with the word of God. This constant drive, however, is grace-enabled in all its stages because it does not ignore the reality of human fickleness and frailty. It is in this stage that the purification of the soul begins in a process of continual self-formation until a personal relationship with God is formed.[149] Next is the mystical stage, best characterized by darkness. At this stage, sense perception is no longer needed.[150] There is a sort of material likeness, says Xia, but it is not a stage that can be articulated through regular sensory description.[151] It is here that union with God is achieved, best described as a "constant communication or exchange of love."[152] This communication has no end because of God's infinitude.

Andrew Louth, in a similar way, understands Gregory's pattern as a progression from light to deeper and deeper darkness, in contrast to Origen's pattern, which increases in light.[153] Louth points to a lack of systematization in Gregory's writings, in which the three supposed stages blend into each other.[154] Moreover, *epektasis* describes the *soul's* encounter with the inexhaustibility of God. One can experience God's presence in what Gregory calls "the mirror of the soul, the spiritual senses, and the indwelling Word."[155] It is not enough to know *about* God and His infinitude but positive experiences of God, such as seeing Him in the inner person and participating in His divine attributes,[156] are also essential in making progress.[157] Yet choosing to characterize Gregory as a mystic, Louth ultimately attributes the experience of God (beyond a simply knowledge-based understanding of God) to the mystical realm beyond sense perception.[158] Participation in God is felt but not perceived by the senses.[159] It is curious, however, in a process in which "the soul becomes like God as it is purified by increasing in virtue," that sense perception would not overlap with an intimate experience of and even unity with God.[160] Gregory's mystical experience of God in the darkness might not so readily welcome a wedge between that which is consciously sensory and that which is unconsciously embodied.[161]

Ronald Heine, in his interpretation of Gregory's commentary on the Psalms, points to a reason it is so difficult to systematize the Cappadocian's model. The starting points of the spiritual journey detailed in Gregory's writings are all different. In his commentary on the Song of Songs, Gregory describes a soul already united to God. It is in a spiritually mature state, and for this reason it skips some concepts Gregory would include for spiritual novices. In the "De vita moysis" and his commentary on the Psalms, he instead covers the entire spectrum, which Heine describes as consisting of a beginner stage, an intermediate stage, and a mature stage.[162] Yet to complicate matters more, Gregory, in his commentary on the Psalms, speaks of five stages, which turn out to be different from the stages mentioned in his commentary on the Song of Songs.[163] Heine concludes that Gregory's goal, as noted above, was not to be precise or systematized but instead to offer a theory in which he made clear that the Christian life is a continual process of the soul's ascent to God.[164]

I suggest an interpretation of Gregory's theory that combines several claims noted above, namely, the general tripartite structure, the process of purification preceding a more intense experience of God, the constancy of grace-enabled struggle, and the infinitude of the God who is the orienting principle of this journey. Ultimately, my suggestion might fall most in line with Herbert Musurillo's breakdown of the *epektatic* journey, who, similar to those of others, offers three stages in his interpretation of Gregory. The first includes a struggle against the passions, which leads to ἀπάθεια—detachment from worldly distractions. In the second stage, as the soul becomes more like God in the denouncement of evil and growth in the good, one grows in knowledge of God. The third stage is a continuation of growth in knowledge of God but this time in the darkness. Based on Musurillo's stages and the assessment of Gregory's primary texts given above, if I were to offer a suggestion for three categories, they would include (1) material and bodily detachment; (2) the strengthening of the soul in a process of increasing similitude to God; and (3) intimacy or union with God that is felt and experienced in ways beyond the intellect's capacity to articulate.[165] To be clear, these stages are not the same as the three origins of spiritual struggle categorized in the previous chapter. All three origins of spiritual struggle exist within each of these stages below, constituting what can be labeled as the nonlinear nature of the spiritual spectrum.

Regarding the first stage of Godward spiritual struggle, to be freed from enslavement to bodily cares and desires is critical in the ability of the soul to grow in deeper relationship to its spiritual Creator. This first stage is a primer of sorts for the second stage. It is in this stage that a virtue such as self-control is acquired through grace-filled self-denial. Consider Gregory's treatise on perfection, where he focuses on the name of Jesus Christ and how Christians ought to imitate Him, orient themselves toward Him, and unite with Him. The Christian is to imitate the perfection found in Christ, and if this is impossible regarding certain qualities, characteristics, or virtues, then what is unattainable should be worshipped.[166] Put into practice, the Christian is to get rid of all evil and all attachment to bodily passions.[167] Gregory calls Christ the author of detachment (ἀρχηγὸν τῆς ἀπαθείας) and asserts that those who are detached from the mire of passion (βορβόρου τὰ πάθη) that smears the brightness of the soul are able to properly orient themselves toward participation in and union with God.[168] Thus, fighting against sin, living a life of struggle, and freely choosing the good life are continual tasks of those who wish to call themselves Christians.[169] A Christian, according to Gregory, "necessarily demonstrates in himself the power of the other names (ἄλλων ὀνομάτων) by which Christ is known, becoming a partaker (κοινωνὸς) of every calling throughout life."[170] In other words, those who orient themselves toward Christ by first detaching from the passions will exhibit the virtues of Christ—His "other names."[171]

In Homily 12 of "In Canticum Canticorum," Gregory emphasizes a theme especially important to the connection between Godward progress and spiritual struggle. He asserts that the perpetual ascent toward God is simultaneous with the process of purification through bodily senses.[172] In Homily 10, he draws on this same point—it is through sensory experience, or more accurately through detachment from bodily passions, that one's soul is able to draw closer to God.[173] The journey is a movement of the soul—the dwelling place of God—and the disposition of the soul is dependent on a person's interaction with material. In this way, the concept of spiritual struggle developed in this project is central to the way Gregory envisions the implementation of this ethics. In order for God to dwell within a person, she must first be purified through a redirection of bodily impulses, in which the death of passion enables the ascent of the soul.[174] This "mortification" (νέκρωσιν) is not an obliteration of desire altogether but an orientation to God through the body—the locus of diachronic moral transformation.[175] The soul "never ceases moving forward nor standing still but is always entering into what lies beyond through progress" (οὐδέποτε οὔτε τοῦ εἰσιέναι λήγων οὔτε τοῦ ἐξιέναι παυόμενος, ἀλλὰ πάντοτε διὰ προκοπῆς εἰς τὰ ὑπερκείμενα) through this purgative mortification of bodily passions coupled with a perpetual orientation of the soul toward its unattainable end—God.[176]

A positive reorientation of one's passions can even originate from God's own strikes and blows. In chapter 2 of this book, one of the three origins of spiritual struggle was God, and though it seemed in Kierkegaard's understanding that God is only the source of spiritual struggle when higher levels of spirituality are reached, the Cappadocian finds it possible for God to incite struggle even at the lower, more base levels of spirituality—detachment from bodily passions. "The divine scepter, the Spirit, is a comforting rod whose blow effects healing and whose fruit consists of those other goods that Paul recounts, especially self-control (ἐγκράτεια), the tutor of a virtuous way of life (ἐναρέτου πολιτείας)."[177] In the same breath, he points to Isaiah who was struck with coal and thereby purified, insisting that the goal of spiritual struggle in any light is purification.[178] Purification and ascent occur simultaneously, and both are contingent upon a person's orientation toward God.[179] Gregory does recap his theory toward the end of this homily, though without much insight distinct from his previous excurses.[180] What seems instead to take his attention is that in order for the soul to "always move forward and never stand still," two things are necessary: purification through mortification of bodily passions (which at the same time purges the soul) and an orientation of the soul toward its unattainable end—God.[181]

In the second stage, as one begins becoming like God, one begins to experience real character change—central to any ethics of virtue. This second stage is characterized by a more profound internal transformation of the person who has already achieved a significant amount of detachment from bodily passions. Though again there can potentially exist struggle from all three origins of spiritual struggle, in the second stage, a person can focus less on shedding the negative and more on acquiring the positive. God is Virtue, Goodness, and the perfection of human nature, and growth in these virtues is a process engaged with more clarity in this stage. The sojourner is less encumbered, able to see with more lucidity who God is and what the path toward Him entails. It is for this reason that this project serves to (re)unite ethics and theology explicitly. What a person believes about God and His character through His self-revelation becomes central to the pursuit of semblance to God. One becomes what one worships. The task of dogmatic theology, in this light, goes hand in hand with the task of moral theology. God in this model cannot be replaced with a list of virtues. The principle governing the second stage is that it is through focus on and a relationship with God that one becomes like God. It is the experience of God, not the struggle to acquire virtue, that is inherently transformative.

The third and final stage is the stage in which a higher form of union with God is experienced. Often described as mysticism, this stage includes any experience of God for which words fall short of expression; it is sensed but not expressed. The romanticized notion of mysticism that may be associated with notions such as luminosity, levitation, telepathy, teleportation, and the like, is not the purpose of this stage. It can be argued that Orthodox Christians have been labeled in the West as possessing more of a mystical theology for this reason, but a closer look reveals that this mysticism is not, or at least should not be, understood as separate from the mundane, the sensual, or the perceivable.[182] This is evident in an overemphasis on the question of Gregory's mysticism, which might also arise from historical discrepancies in the understanding of mysticism between East and West.[183] The question of whether he presents a mystical theology proper seems to have occupied a good deal of scholarship surrounding the theory of *epektasis*,[184] recently being called his "philosophy of spiritual consciousness."[185] However, though acknowledging that this line of inquiry has its merits, for the purposes of constructing an ethics reflective of contemporary Orthodox Christians, one's experience in this stage can simply include moments in which a person prays so deeply, gets lost in God's Scriptural words so immensely, or experiences God in a way that is so transforming that all other sensory experiences in those moments seem to dissipate. It is such a keen and sharp experience of God's presence that the presence of anything and everything else becomes insignificant or altogether absent. After all, more than one might like to admit, there may exist a thinner division between experiences of sensory overload and those mystical experiences deemed beyond perception.

Gregory often mentions bodily passions as the basest of impediments to embarking on this journey. Passionlessness, or *apatheia*, through spiritual struggle is the most fundamental requirement in Gregory's theory.[186] The clarity with which the Cappadocian delivers these basic but unambiguous requirements is helpful. Yet it is precisely after this first stage that Gregory seems to lack a strict systematization—a supposed ambivalence by which he is often characterized.[187] As a complement to these stages, I suggest further nuance in interpreting Gregory of Nyssa's theory of *epektasis*. The journey is best envisioned as a *nonlinear spectrum*. The latter part of this suggestion—its spectral character—is not far from the observation by Louth that Gregory's categories blend together. Those who have suggested stages, myself included, do not necessarily mean to imply that the reality of Gregory's spiritual journey is not spectral in nature. It would be difficult to claim otherwise in light of his "De vita moysis" and commentaries on the Psalms and Beatitudes.

Conceiving of Godward spiritual struggle as both a spectrum and as consisting of stages are not mutually exclusive. The latter serve as markers or points within the former. That is, the greater the number of stages or details within each stage that one is able to point out in the journey, the more points along the spectrum are defined. Balthasar describes this spectrum as one on which there is one type of knowledge of God that differs in degrees of elevation. What propels one further along the spectrum is an increase in this knowledge, yet even the lower levels of the spectrum are participating in this knowledge, albeit in lesser degrees.[188] Although I agree that the differences between elevation are differences in the knowledge of and intimacy with God, I am suggesting that this spectrum is often nonlinear. What this means is that a person does not necessarily always have to make progress through the spectrum sequentially. Instead, it is possible for occasional "jumps" between stages or between different parts of a single stage.

For example, one who has been deemed sufficiently detached from bodily passions (stage 1) has not necessarily been tested by every temptation possible. Seldom has it been a prerequisite, for Gregory or anyone else for that matter, to undergo all temptations that are humanly possible before successfully considering a person detached, and thus able to grow strong spiritually. One can have already acquired a general spirit of detachment—allowing one's soul to be strengthened (stage 2)—while at the same time, or even intermittently, struggling with base temptations that are either new or have been reignited (stage 1). Another example of the nonlinear nature of the spiritual journey can be seen among those who claim to experience God in ways that cannot be articulated (stage 3) but are still expected to interact with their surrounding communities in the rich and complex tapestry of human existence. Such people are not expected to reflect perfection in a way that allows for no human errors, disagreements, or weaknesses.

Take, for example, Saint Paul, who describes experiences with God for which language is insufficient yet describes weaknesses and disagreements both in his ministry and personally.[189] Paul's "third-stage experiences" did not entirely diminish the importance of unrelenting struggle within the first two stages. In fact, Paul, in Philippians 3:13, is Gregory's very model for the spiritual struggler. In the "De vita moysis," he writes, "For that divine Apostle, great and lofty in understanding, ever running the course of virtue, never ceased *straining* (ἐπεκτεινόμενος) *toward those* things *that are still to come.* Coming to a stop (στάσις) in the race was not safe for him; . . . stopping in the race of virtue marks the beginning of the race of evil."[190] Even Paul, according to Gregory, was not in a position in which he could cease his struggle.

Instead, straining onward for eternal life and unity with God—"those things that are still to come"—was the only way to safeguard against participation in vicious deeds. Later in his work, Gregory uses the same Pauline verse to make the explicit connection between the ascent of the soul and the need for continuous struggle: "If nothing comes from above to hinder its [the soul's] upward thrust, the soul rises ever higher and will always make its flight yet higher—by its desire of the heavenly things *straining* (συνεπεκτεινομένη) *for what is still to come.*[191] Thus, striving for eternal life, for Gregory, was required even of a soul that has already ascended to great heights.

Examples of the nonsequential reality that characterizes the Godward spiritual progress are found all throughout Scripture. Similar to the discussion of flawed saints and the unity of the virtues in chapter 1, there are a number of examples of those deemed kings, prophets, righteous, saints, and martyrs historically, whose temporary lapses can only be explained through a nonlinear pattern. A good example for the topic at hand is Moses's disobedience at the waters of Meribah in Numbers 20 that prevented him from entering the Promised Land even after speaking with God in the depths of the darkness (stage 3). Similar examples include David the prophet and king who committed vile acts of adultery and murder, though he was described by God as a man after his own heart.[192] Likewise, Peter in the New Testament is seen denying Jesus Christ and even being referred to as Satan when he refuses to accept the necessity for the Messiah to be crucified. Yet both these events occurred after Christ told Peter, "On this rock I will build my church, and the gates of Hades will not prevail against it."[193] Thus, it seems that a perfectly linear and sequential spectrum might not be at play in an ethics of Godward spiritual struggle, which in turn might be better construed as a sort of upward spiral ascent that oscillates between a variety of struggles, sometimes even among different stages.[194]

I am not suggesting that this is the plan that Gregory details but that it is the pattern that most accurately captures and depicts his theory that seemed to be developing as his writings matured. It is at the same time an underemphasized yet critical component of the nature of the journey. Understanding the spiritual journey as nonlinear might provide insight into Gregory's seeming lack of systematization. His aim is not, nor is it within his ability, to propose an ethics in which all the complexities of life and the multitude of circumstances therein are addressed. His aim, instead, is to encourage his readers in the struggle that is the spiritual journey, and this he repeats a number of times, especially in his "De vita moysis." Godward spiritual struggle as an ethics that in its essence points to a reality in which there is always more for which to strive, encourages this forward and upward motion toward

God, who is Virtue, Goodness, and Perfection. It is an ethics that bridges the temporal with the eschatological and captures the essence of Christianity in its imitation of and assimilation to divine goodness—a restoration of humanity's broken image.[195] If a person who has been growing in likeness to God demonstrates weakness of a lower stage, that person should not lose hope because this is typical of the journey. No one can claim perfection, and yet perfection—as redefined by Gregory—is accessible to any and all who desire it and pursue the end of that desire—God.

CONCLUSION

By this point, I hope to have made space for and developed the skeleton of an Orthodox Christian ethics as one of Godward spiritual struggle. Godward spiritual struggle is an ethics of divine–human synergy that is at once exertive and grace-enabled. As an embodied ethics located within the anthropological tension of human frailty and strength, the pursuit of intimacy with and participation in God as the paragon of virtue, as goodness, and as the fulfilment of human nature renders the human being a locus for the extirpation of evil.[196] It is within the human person that the suffering of this world is confronted through a bodily and spiritual purgation of the evil originating from human separation from God, individually, extrapersonally, and communally. Perfection in this ethics is redefined as progress toward God, effectively closing the chasm between the human and divine, whereby ethics are necessary in the first place. Godward spiritual struggle initiates a Christian's eschatological fulfillment as a perpetually progressive ascent that is a dynamic and ever-unfolding journey to God, always experienced afresh.

As an ethics of progress, there exists a spectrum that, while nonlinear experientially, is nonetheless hierarchical. Pursuing the higher "stages" of this ethics, and God as the highest of these, is part of the transformative process of Godward spiritual struggle. My thesis might encompass an array of embodied practices that extend beyond what might classically be considered the sacramental life. However, I confine the application of the ethics to two embodied practices—asceticism (Godward spiritual struggle applied to the body) and sacred reading (Godward spiritual struggle applied to the practice of reading Scripture) that are different enough to cover some ground in envisioning the applicability of the ethics proposed, an accusation not seldom waged against an ethics of virtue.[197]

I have not entirely detailed in explicit terms exactly what participation in God might mean for Gregory of Nyssa.[198] He is clear *that* participation is growth in God's likeness through assimilation to His known characteristics and in virtue. However, the means by which to assess one's level of participation in God and the details therein are not immediately obvious. This may have been intentional for Gregory because it was not his primary goal; assessing one's participation in God is not critical to actually participating in God; and the task itself may be impossible in light of apophatic limitations. Still, J. Warren Smith's interpretation of Gregory does help shed some insight onto this question. Presenting Gregory's basic anthropology with specific attention to the existence of body and soul, Smith sees Gregory's emphasis as one in which the body's role is crucial to the transformation of the soul. Similar to Coakley's comments above, Smith describes this relationship as one in which the soul and body co-originate and require each other in order to successfully develop and mature. In fact, "rationality is an acquired power that comes from nothing but the transformation of the soul in accordance with the body's development."[199] In this way, the human soul is predisposed for dynamic maturation, but not without the body.[200] It seems, then, that Gregory does not leave us entirely without answers to the question of participation. Participation in God is through the transformation of the body, which at the same time transforms the soul. Brian Daley describes this transformation of human nature in God as one from a changeable and fleshly state to a stable and luminous one—a transformative process that will help make sense of the practice of asceticism as a spectral progression of Godward spiritual struggle applied to the body.[201]

NOTES

Epigraph: "De vita moysis," ed. Herbertus Musurillo, in *Gregorii Nysseni Opera* VII, pars I, ed. Jaeger and Langerbeck (hereafter *GNO* VII/I), 213.26–214.1.

1. Boersma, "Gregory of Nyssa," 167.
2. Boersma, "Becoming Human in the Face of God," 151.
3. Meredith, *Gregory of Nyssa*, 1.
4. Keenan, "De Professione Christiana and De Perfectione," 174.
5. Balthasar, *Presence and Thought*, 171–72.
6. Coakley, "Gregory of Nyssa," 38.
7. Coakley, 44, 47.
8. Ludlow, "Christian Formation."
9. Zdenko Sirka finds Nyssa's distinctiveness and effectiveness in his application of the lives of Christians to the texts he explicates. See Sirka, "Role of Theoria."
10. Cadenhead, "Corporeality and *Askesis*," 285.
11. As Gregory put it, the "De vita moysis" is written as an allegorical interpretation of Moses's life for the purposes of spiritual edification: *GNO* VII/I, 1.6.24–7.3; 33.6–10.

The purpose of his text was to help his readers understand the life of Moses in a way that allows them to pursue and benefit from a virtuous life.

12. Louth, *Origins*, 7.
13. Gregory's goal is to remind his reader to wisely use every moment of temporal existence for the purposes of ascending the *epektatic* journey. See Boersma, "Overcoming Time and Space."
14. Rowan Greer and J. Warren Smith put forward a reading of Gregory that insists that his texts were never intended only for Christians in advanced levels of spirituality. See Greer and Smith, *One Path for All*. Godward spiritual struggle, the "one path for all," is a journey on which to embark at any point by pursuing God amid any and all circumstances. This one path, I think, captures the universalism attributed to Gregory's use of ἀποκατάστασις. See Ludlow, *Universal Salvation*, 21–111. Despite the reality that all people are on *different parts* of the spectrum, they are on the *same* spectrum; none have reached a final destination of virtuousness, categorically disparate from any others. No one is to boast oneself above another. None have secured complete virtue, and so all must strive for the continuous pursuit of God-likeness by which virtue will at the same time be acquired. An inherent ethics of exertion, Gregory's is a call to action not in spite of the salvation granted by Christ's incarnation, crucifixion, and resurrection but *because* of this salvation—i.e., as a response to the salvation granted by God.
15. Ludlow, "Divine Infinity and Eschatology," 237. Most scholars of the Nyssen agree that his theory of *epektasis* developed most prominently toward the end of his life. See also Meredith, *Gregory of Nyssa*, 22.
16. Coakley, "Gregory of Nyssa," 55.
17. Coakley, 51.
18. Coakley, 52.
19. Coakley, 53.
20. Coakley, 54.
21. Gregory of Nyssa, *De Anima et Resurrectione*, 66.9–71.11. Gregory admits that humans are led to God by desire in a process that is inherently dynamic. However, the soul *can* be satiated; it *can* stop desiring, though this satiety does not cut off the attachment to love. There is no limit to the love and beauty experienced by the soul when it detaches from the flesh and attains the heavenly. Gregory's ambivalence regarding the notion of satiety or a lack thereof, which eventually becomes central to his theory of *epektasis*, could be the reason Sarah Coakley sees Gregory of Nyssa's *De anima et resurrectione* as a break or shift in Gregory's writings. See Coakley, "Gregory of Nyssa," 52.
22. *GNO* VII/I, 1.3.16, VII/I 2.112.19. See also Phil. 3:13, which Gregory is referencing.
23. Daniélou, *Platonisme et théologie Mystique*.
24. See Coakley, "Gregory of Nyssa," 38.
25. A more recent reading of Gregory offered by Mark Edwards finds the Cappadocian more Platonic than Origen, given certain qualification. See Edwards, "Origen and Gregory of Nyssa." In the same volume, Johannes Zachhuber files the Nyssen's views on the νοῦς as less Platonic and more Christian. See Zachhuber, "Soul as *Dynamis*."
26. Meredith, *Gregory of Nyssa*, 7–8.
27. Meredith, 11.
28. See Gregory, Daniélou, and Musurillo, *From Glory to Glory*, 46–56.
29. Heine, *Perfection*, 57.

30. Heine, 55–56, 59.
31. Gregory of Nyssa, *Opera Ascetica*, 192.15.
32. *GNO* VII/I, 1.4.5–6.
33. *GNO* VIII/I, 192.20–22.
34. *GNO* VIII/I, 194.5–205.14.
35. *GNO* VIII/I, 213.17–214.1.
36. Heine, *Perfection*, 52.
37. Gregory and Heine, *Gregory of Nyssa's Treatise*, 72–73, 79. Heine sees Gregory as having adjusted some of Origen's thoughts so that by the time he wrote his later, more mature writings, *epektasis* was the theory that provided this redressing. This is also made clear by Heine, *Perfection*, 8–9; Meredith, *Gregory of Nyssa*, 18; and Smith, *Passion*, 125.
38. Meredith, *Gregory of Nyssa*, 13.
39. Heine claims that Gregory did not just develop the theory of *epektasis* in response to Origen's belief that God is finite but also because of Eunomius's belief that the nature of God can be fully understood by humans and that the Son is not the Same as the Father. See Heine, *Perfection*, 8–9.
40. Origen's Commentary on the Gospel of Matthew, XIII.1; translation from Heine, *Perfection*, 73–74.
41. Heine, 8–9.
42. Meredith asserts that Plato and Gregory agreed that imitation of God was the aim of life. However, the latter believed He was infinite, while the former believed He was finite; Meredith, *Gregory of Nyssa*, 22. Further, Andrew Louth points out another departure of Gregory from Platonism and neo-Platonism. For Gregory, there is no ecstasy, i.e., no way to pass from the created nature of humans to the uncreated nature of God since humans were created ex nihilo; Louth, *Origins*, 79. Smith agrees on this point, to which Gregory's discussion of *diastema* is important, to which this book will turn below; Smith, *Passion*, 132. On Gregory's Platonism in relation to that of Origen, see Edwards, "Origen and Gregory."
43. For a fuller discussion of Origen's theory of satiation, see Smith, *Passion*, 106–15.
44. Smith, 115–16, 123–25.
45. Gregory of Nyssa, "In Canticum Canticorum," 158.12–160.10; See also Gregory, Daniélou, and Musurillo, *From Glory to Glory*, 567–71.
46. *GNO* VII/I, 2.114.5–17.
47. *GNO* VII/I, 2.112.21–113.2.
48. Gregory of Nyssa, "De Oratione Dominica De Beatitudinibus," ed. Callahan, in *Gregorii Nysseni Opera VII*, pars II, ed. Jaeger (hereafter *GNO* VII/II), 125.9–10, 129.1–131.8.
49. *GNO* VII/II, 111.11–22, 117.2–26; see also *GNO* VIII/I, 213.14–17.
50. *GNO* VII/II, 124.2–5; translation from Graef, *St. Gregory of Nyssa*, 130.
51. *GNO* VII/II, 124.16–125.8.
52. *GNO* VI, 252.9–253.3. ἐπειδὴ γὰρ βούλεται ἡμᾶς ὁ λόγος τρεπτοὺς ὄντας κατὰ τὴν φύσιν μὴ πρὸς τὸ κακὸν διὰ τῆς τροπῆς ἀπορρέειν, ἀλλὰ διὰ τῆς ἀεὶ πρὸς τὸ κρεῖττον γινομένης αὐξήσεως συνεργὸν τὴν τροπὴν πρὸς τὴν τῶν ὑψηλοτέρων ἄνοδον ἔχειν, ὥστε κατορθωθῆναι διὰ τοῦ τρεπτοῦ τῆς φύσεως ἡμῶν τὸ πρὸς τὸ κακὸν ἀναλλοίωτον, τούτου χάριν ὥσπερ τινὰ παιδαγωγὸν καὶ φύλακα πρὸς τὴν τῶν κακῶν ἀλλοτρίωσιν τὴν μνήμην τῶν ποτε κατακρατησάντων θηρίων ὁ λόγος προήνεγκεν, ἵνα τῇ ἀποστροφῇ τῶν χειρόνων τὸ ἀκλινές τε καὶ ἀπαράτρεπτον ἐν τοῖς ἀγαθοῖς κατορθώσωμεν οὔτε ἱστάμενοι τῆς ἐπὶ τὸ κρεῖττον τροπῆς οὔτε πρὸς τὸ κακὸν ἀλλοιούμενοι.

53. Meredith, *Gregory of Nyssa*, 19.
54. Boersma, *Embodiment*, 1–3.
55. Coakley, "Gregory of Nyssa," 54.
56. Robert Fortuin makes a good argument for why the essence/energy distinction popular in contemporary Eastern Orthodoxy might be problematic. Gregory uses "analogous predication" as the "language of mystery" to describe God, without overstating a distinction between essence and energies. See Fortuin, "Analogy." In my discussion, I am making the simple observation that God is both knowable and unknowable and that this combination is an important factor in propelling the journey to God.
57. Geljon, *Philonic Exegesis*, 128.
58. Geljon, 129.
59. See O'Leary, "Divine Simplicity," 326; and Williams, *Wound of Knowledge*, 118.
60. O'Leary, "Divine Simplicity," 326, 337.
61. Williams, *Wound of Knowledge*, 130.
62. "Epektasis," 265.
63. Abecina, *Time*, 217.
64. "Epektasis," 265.
65. Smith, *Passion*, 127.
66. Balás, *[Metousia Theou]*, 22–23; Louth, *Origins*, 79.
67. Ludlow, *Divine Infinity*, 221–22.
68. See Boersma, *Embodiment*.
69. *GNO* VII/I, 2.129.14–130:9.
70. *GNO* VII/I, 1.3.22–23.
71. *GNO* VII/I, 2.43.3–4.
72. *GNO* VII/I, 2.61.7–9.
73. Gregory of Nyssa, "In Inscriptiones Psalmorum," ed. McDonoughand Alexander, in *Gregorii Nysseni Opera V*, ed. Jaeger (hereafter *GNO* V), 124.11–175.25.
74. *GNO* V, 129.22–130.4.
75. *GNO* V, 174.2.
76. *GNO* VI, 137.4–171.7.
77. *GNO* VI, 149.
78. *GNO* VI, 164–68.
79. *GNO* VI, 149.
80. *GNO* VI, 158.
81. *GNO* VII/I, 2.68.22.
82. *GNO* VII/I, 2.68.22.
83. *GNO* VII/I, 2.87.10.
84. For a good argument as to why Gregory's mysticism of darkness is no less a mysticism of light, see Laird, *Gregory of Nyssa*.
85. *GNO* VII/I, 2.89.15–95.9.
86. *GNO* VII/I, 2.97.16–21.
87. *GNO* VII/I, 2.96.20–21.
88. *GNO* VII/I, 2.97.7–10.
89. *GNO* VII/I, 2.97.3–5.
90. *GNO* VII/I, 2.45.131–9.
91. *GNO* VII/I, 2.98.10–11.
92. *GNO* VII/I, 2.99.9–10.

93. *GNO* VII/I, 2.88.6, 102.8.
94. *GNO* VII/I, 2.38.14–15.
95. *GNO* VII/I, 2.39.24–40.1.
96. *GNO* VII/I, 2.55.5–23, 138.11–13.
97. *GNO* VII/I, 2.82.4–86.10, 141.20–142.5.
98. *GNO* VII/I, 2.62.9–17.
99. *GNO* VII/I, 2.112.7–16.
100. *GNO* V, 151.14–21.
101. *GNO* V, 25.11–26.29.
102. *GNO* V, 25.15–17.
103. *GNO* V, 26.29.
104. *GNO* V, 26.10–11.
105. *GNO* V, 45.9–17, 116.18–117.6.
106. *GNO* V, 25.22–26.29.
107. *GNO* V, 115.22–118.1.
108. *GNO* VII/I, 2.141.19–20.
109. *GNO* VII/I, 2.121.3–122.3.
110. *GNO* VII/I, 2.124.3–7.
111. *GNO* VII/I, 2.112.25–113.2.
112. *GNO* VII/I, 2.118.20.
113. *GNO* VII/II, 121.16–29.
114. *GNO* VII/II, 121.28–29.
115. *GNO* VII/II, 145.13–18.
116. *GNO* VII/II, 122.14–17.
117. *GNO* VII/I, 1.4.5–6.
118. Williams, *Wound of Knowledge*, 57.
119. *GNO* VI, 158.8–11.
120. *GNO* VII/II, 125.9–16; *GNO* V, 26.2–29; "Epektasis," 264.
121. Smith, *Passion*, 136.
122. Balás, *[Metousia Theou]*, 56–60, 64–71, 75.
123. Balás, 161.
124. Balás, 75.
125. Balás, 154.
126. Silvas, *Gregory of Nyssa*, 194–95.
127. See Boersma, *Embodiment*, 211–50. In this chapter, Boersma describes how growth in Christ is at the same time growth in virtue, yet not moralism.
128. *GNO* VII/I, 1.3.12–14: ἐπὶ δὲ τῆς ἀρετῆς ἕνα παρὰ τοῦ ἀποστόλου τελειότητος ὅρον ἐμάθομεν τὸ μὴ ἔχειν αὐτὴν ὅρον. *GNO* VII/I, 1.4.18: τῆς δὲ ἀρετῆς εἷς ὅρος ἐστὶ τὸ ἀόριστον.
129. *GNO* VII/I, 1.4.25–5.4, 2.138.21–139.6.
130. Gregory does affirm the unity of the virtues (e.g., *GNO* VII/II, 118.16–119.13), but this unity resides in God. Gregory's theory sheds some light on why there has been some disagreement concerning the unity of the virtues. On one hand, in theory there exists a unity of the virtues because God—the Paragon of Virtue—is their source in whom resides the perfection of all goodness and virtue. In this sense, virtue indeed necessitates a unity, as God possesses this perfect unity. The departure of any virtue from its ideal perfection would imply a deficiency in another virtue. Humans, on the other hand, embark on the journey toward God, growing in virtue along the way. The human journey, in

Gregory's design, is always short of complete and perfect virtue. Any one single virtue, no matter how perfectly it seems to have been acquired, is always necessarily short of the perfect form found in the Paragon Himself. However, the closer one gets, the more the complementarity is made obvious and the more it seems that there is a unity. Humans can progress so far along this path that compared with other humans, they may appear to possess virtues indefinitely, as parts of their transformed selves. This transformative process, in a sense, is the goal of virtue ethics in creating virtuous agents, and is at the same time a result of Gregory's model.

131. Heine, *Perfection*, 70.
132. Matt. 5:48.
133. Smith, *Passion*, 133; Smith, "John Wesley's Growth," 353.
134. *GNO* VII/I, 2.117.20–24.
135. *GNO* VII/I, 1.5.2–4.
136. *GNO* VIII/I, 214.1–6; translation from Heine, *Perfection*, 59 (Greek removed).
137. *GNO* VII/I, 144.20–145.4; translation from Ferguson and Malherbe, *Gregory of Nyssa*, 137 (emphasis theirs; Greek insertions mine).
138. For a helpful discussion on the relational character of assimilation to God in Gregory of Nyssa, see Maspero, "Deification."
139. *GNO* VI, 164, 252.1–8.
140. Ludlow, *Gregory of Nyssa*, 130.
141. *GNO* VI, 259.17–260.1.
142. See Vigorelli, "Soul's Dance," for the Platonic origins and Clementian resemanticization of this general tripartite model in Gregory of Nyssa. Pseudo-Dionysius the Areopagite and Evagrius of Pontus also had similar models that can be implemented as models for contemporary asceticism. The former was of the first to suggest a tripartite structure of purification, illumination, and union. See Pseudo-Dionysius, Heil, and Ritter, *De Coelesti Hierarchia*. The latter presented a model of *praktike, theoria physike*, and *theoria theoligike*. See Stefaniw, "Exegetical Curricula"; and Ramelli, "Origen to Evagrius." Though any of these models could generally suffice, to present all these models would be redundant. I chose Gregory of Nyssa's because *epektasis* and anagogy carry with them a concomitant and more explicit emphasis on spiritual struggle and perpetual progress in God who is Himself eternal. Gregory's model is certainly less explicit in its tripartite structure but is more explicit in its Pauline basis on perpetually striving forward. See these works by Gregory: "De Perfectione," "Commentary on the Beatitudes," "Commentary on the Inscriptions of the Psalms," "Commentary on the Song of Songs," and "De vita moysis." See also "Epektasis."
143. This is actually Heine's assessment of Daniélou. See Heine, *Perfection*, 2–3.
144. Xia, "From Light to Darkness," 541.
145. Xia, 540.
146. Boersma, "Becoming Human," 157.
147. Xia, "From Light to Darkness," 546.
148. Xia, 543.
149. Xia, 544.
150. Xia, 547–48.
151. Xia, 549.
152. Xia, 551.
153. Louth, *Origins*, 81.

154. Louth, 83.
155. Louth, 88.
156. The language of God-likeness and participation, intimacy, growth in, and assimilation to God's characteristics has been used throughout this book instead of the terminology of *theosis* or deification. The latter risks denying the unbridgeable chasm that Gregory asserts is fixed between creation and the Uncreated God, unknown in His nature and essence. Gregory used the concepts of *diastema* and *adiastema* to make sense of how humans can participate in God without becoming God and how the *eschaton* will be distinguished from the present through the absence of time and space. For a full and pertinent discussion of this term, see Boersma, *Embodiment*, 19–52. Also see Abecina, *Time*, 26; Ludlow, *Divine Infinity*, 19-44; and Smith, *Passion*, 132. Ultimately, it seems the concepts of *diastema* and *adiastema* can be used exegetically for the curious language found in 2 Peter 1:4 and can be used to address the polemics surrounding the concept of *theosis* between Eastern and Oriental Orthodox churches in recent times.
157. Louth, *Origins*, 88–89.
158. Louth, 93.
159. Louth, 94.
160. Louth, 90.
161. The categorizations of "consciously sensory" and "unconsciously embodied" will not be emphasized here. These are uncommon characterizations, more often referred to as the sensible and the intellectual. At the heart of any formulation of these categories is a sensibility that can be articulated versus a knowledge that is felt or perceived but that evades articulation. This latter reality might instead be called the spiritual—knowledge of the *nous*, which can indeed be an embodied experience that the mind has yet to decipher adequately. Raphael Cadenhead points to the difficulty of making sense of the knowledge of God through the portals of the body and the mind (νοῦς): they mature at different rates. See Cadenhead, "Corporeality and *Askesis*," 292–93. This is what I mean by unconsciously embodied—that knowledge of God can be known before grasped and articulated in intellection. See also Ramelli, "Gregory of Nyssa."
162. Heine, *Psalms*, 75.
163. Heine, 54.
164. Heine, 78–79.
165. Morwenna Ludlow points out that it is not entirely clear whether Gregory understands the realm beyond articulation as accompanying or surpassing the intellect. What is clear, however, is that language is always insufficient to express the experience. See Ludlow, *Gregory of Nyssa*, 231.
166. *GNO* VIII/I, 173.15–178.19.
167. *GNO* VIII/I, 178.2–181.15.
168. *GNO* VIII/I, 212.1–4.
169. *GNO* VIII/I, 183.4–186.7, 378–79.
170. *GNO* VIII/I, 209.23–210.4.
171. *GNO* VIII/I, 210.2.
172. *GNO* VI, 360.2–361.15.
173. *GNO* VI, 313.1–16.
174. *GNO* VI, 343.9–344.6.
175. Cadenhead, "Corporeality and *Askesis*."
176. *GNO* VI, 354.5–7.

177. *GNO* VI, 365.17–366.2.
178. *GNO* VI, 368.7–369.13.
179. *GNO* VI, 361.2–4.
180. *GNO* VI, 366.10–370.13.
181. *GNO* VI, 350.19–352.5.
182. Lossky, *Mystical Theology*, 7–11, 20–21. Lossky defines mystical theology as "no more than a spirituality which expresses a doctrinal attitude." Spirituality, discussed as being in harmony with and inseparable from action, is at the same time united with doctrine. The East has not typically fragmented these three, and with such an understanding, has never divorced mysticism from theology, despite opposing opinions. Dogma and doctrine express revealed truths, which despite often being presented as mysteries, do not escape the realms of contemplation and experience. Interstingly, Lossky places Saint Paul's out-of-body experience from 2 Corinthians 12:2–4 within what would contemporarily be more accurately presented as a case for a sort of mystical psychology. This allows him to point to the discrepancy between East and West. In the Eastern tradition, this is not a text that comes to mind when discussing mystical theology, but it would certainly fall into this category in the West. This is not to say that the East discredits or minimizes this Scriptural account, but there is a *banality* to mystical theology in the East, as will be discussed below, that is very much in connection with the material, the spiritual, and the dogmatic. The development of this disparity between definitions of mystical theology can also be attributed to a concomitant hyperindividualization within Western mystical writing, which is almost entirely absent in the East.
183. Lossky, 38–39, 42, 221, 238. The mystical theology of the East holds that spiritual realities are never to be overshadowed by philosophical endeavors. While this Eastern mystical theology does function under the title of the metaphysical and does not seek to deny that, it remains true that what is denounced by Western phenomenologists, such as Jean-Luc Marion, in metaphysical mystical theology is not existent in the Eastern equivalent. See Marion, *Visible and the Revealed*. Instead, both Eastern mystical theology and phenomenological concepts, like Marion's saturated phenomenon, point to realities that are experienced but cannot be entirely articulated or reduced to the sum of its parts. E.g., the mystical experience of beholding uncreated light is not a philosophical exploration into the nature of an Uncreated Being; it is an experience that is presented as real and available to the senses but is not reducible to the intellect or simple expression of the experience.
184. To cite a few contributors to this debate: Laird, *Gregory of Nyssa*, 174, understands Gregory's mysticism of darkness as no less a mysticism of light. Heine, *Perfection*, 104–5, sees in Gregory's thought no basis for mysticism but instead a response to Origen's theme of satiety. Meredith, *Gregory of Nyssa*, 87–88, 100, believes that Daniélou's assessment of Gregory's mysticism is overstated, preferring instead to think of it as "sublime moralism." Others—such as Louth, *Origins*, 79—interpret Gregory's theology as mystical despite opinions to the contrary.
185. McGuckin, "St. Gregory of Nyssa," 22.
186. See Cochran, *Protestant Virtue*, for an interesting analysis of *apatheia*—a fundamental doctrine of Stoic moral thought—and how it relates to the Christian, and more specifically, the Protestant ethics of virtue. She ultimately does not see *apatheia* as being at odds with a Christian virtue ethics. Instead, the Stoic ethics of assent is one directed toward a higher divine character. I also suggest the language of "passion" instead of "emotion," at

least to grasp more accurately the type of Christian *apatheia* suggested in this project and in Gregory's theory.

187. Ludlow, *Gregory of Nyssa*, 135–47.
188. Balthasar, *Presence and Thought*, 97, 175.
189. Acts 15; 2 Cor. 12:7–10; Gal. 2:11–14.
190. *GNO* VII/I, 1.3.14–17; translation Ferguson and Malherbe, *Gregory of Nyssa*, 30 (emphasis theirs; Greek insertions mine).
191. *GNO* VII/I, 2.112.16–21; translation Ferguson and Malherbe, *Gregory of Nyssa*, 113 (emphasis theirs; Greek insertions mine).
192. 1 Sam. 13:14; Acts 13:22.
193. Matt. 16:18, 23, 26.
194. Heine, *Psalms*, 71, 79.
195. Keenan, "De Professione," 178.
196. Gregory affirms the Orthodox Christian anthropology discussed at the outset of this book, noting that humans do not only have an inclination toward evil but toward good also: οὐδὲ γὰρ μόνον πρὸς τὸ κακὸν ὁ ἄνθρωπος τῇ τροπῇ χρῆται· ἢ γὰρ ἂν ἀμήχανον ἦν αὐτὸν ἐν ἀγαθῷ γενέσθαι, εἰ πρὸς τὸ ἐναντίον μόνον τὴν ῥοπὴν εἶχεν ἐκ φύσεως. *GNO* VIII/I, 213.14–17.
197. For good discussions of the accusation against virtue ethics' inapplicability (and defenses against such an accusation), see Begley, "Practising Virtue." A direct example of this accusation is given by Truscott and Crook, *Ethics*, 8, of the impracticality of applying virtue ethics to the contemporary assessment of psychologists. Authors who have defended against such an accusation include Oakley, "Virtue Ethics," 197–99; Vardy and Vardy, *Ethics Matters*, 77–78; and Swanton, "Practical Virtue Ethics." Jiyuan Yu, "Practicality," demonstrates that ancient Greek and Chinese virtue ethics help the modern reader remember that the issue of practicality is more than asking what does moral philosophy tell us to do. Finally, Baker, "Virtue," offers a fuller picture of how virtue ethics can be rendered most practical.
198. There is no extant text of Gregory's that specifically takes up the task of describing what participation in God is. See Balás, *[Metousia Theou]*, 121.
199. Smith, *Passion*, 146.
200. Smith, 147.
201. Daley, "Divine Transcendence," 500–503.

PART III

Applying the Ethics

4

Asceticism as Godward Spiritual Struggle Applied to the Body

> So *we are* always confident, knowing that while we are at home in the body we are absent from the Lord. For we walk by faith, not by sight. We are confident, yes, well pleased rather to be absent from the body and to be present with the Lord. Therefore we make it our aim, whether present or absent, to be well pleasing to Him. For we must all appear before the judgment seat of Christ, that each one may receive the things *done* in the body, according to what he has done, whether good or bad.
>
> —2 Corinthians 5:6–10

This chapter functions at two levels. At the macro level, asceticism is analyzed as a case study, or instantiation, of the ethics of Godward spiritual struggle applied to the body. Placing asceticism within this ethical framework helps to unpack the essence of this practice. Vice versa, I contend that an analysis of Christian asceticism should lead to an ethics of struggle-laden, grace-filled progress in God similar to the structure of this book's ethics. Godward spiritual struggle is at the same time a lens through which to make sense of common Christian practices *and* an ethics that when applied to any component of life renders that practice an opportunity for divine union (and thereby virtue). At the meta level, this chapter is organized into the three spectral and intermittent (though still progressive) stages of Godward spiritual struggle.

First, in line with the first stage of Godward spiritual struggle, this chapter describes one dimension (that of sexual purity) of detachment from bodily pleasures central to early discussions of Christian asceticism. Many of these ancient Christian views tend toward an extreme and distorted view of sexuality, but the exploration is necessary nonetheless to make progress regarding this chapter's thesis. Next, this chapter explores the second stage of asceticism: ascending to an angelic state or restoration to humanity's primordial state. It is a state in which one's soul is strengthened to be no longer encumbered excessively by bodily attachments. The third stage elucidates asceticism's ultimate goal—allowing the body to become the place of the presence of God. This section delves more deeply into the significance of the body as an instrument of Godward ascent. The significance of the body as locus resides in the process of internalization of a number of Old Testament, Second Temple, apocalyptic, and apocryphal concepts, images, archetypes, and rituals. This internalization—or interiorization, as it will be referred to in this chapter—most notable in early Syriac Christian authors, provides further insight into the understanding of sexuality, purity, and asceticism in the early Church period. Both monastic and nonmonastic communities, by internalizing their religious ancestral heritage, were alerted to the importance of the purity of the body temple. It is for this reason that they soon came to be associated with angels, as they acquired the status of the dwelling place of the Presence of God.

In conceiving of asceticism as Godward spiritual struggle applied to the body, at the micro level the explication serves as a recovery of an ancient Christian mode of (re)orienting the body to God for contemporary appropriation. In appealing to resources on asceticism from the Patristic era in which this practice takes on its most recognizable and most frequented form, I hope to extract the essence of Christian asceticism for its modern application. In this way, this chapter is the first of two that demonstrate the practical import of this ethics: when Godward spiritual struggle is applied to different components of life, it renders an otherwise normal practice transformative and opens a portal to unity with God.

THE FIRST STAGE: CONTROLLING IMPULSES GONE AWRY

If an ethics of virtue were constructed in the early Church, whose influence on Orthodoxy cannot be understated, asceticism would constitute its foundation. Scholarly attention to and ecclesial emphasis on asceticism have waned contemporarily. Yet it remains true that ancient Christianity strongly attested to the ability of asceticism (contrary to some beliefs) to (re)orient one's focus onto God and neighbor, and away from one's self. Christianity certainly cannot claim asceticism as unique to itself, but in differentiating between asceticism undertaken for the self and asceticism as a form of Godward spiritual struggle, the former is encumbered with notions of self-improvement and self-centeredness that risk counterproductivity to essential facets of virtue. By contrast, Godward asceticism is focused on the self only paradoxically; it is an improvement of oneself for the purpose of actualizing love of God and neighbor.

Asceticism in the early Church served as a focal point for the acquisition of virtue among monastics and nonmonastics alike. In fact, the monastic movement originated as a movement among laity who saw themselves as embodying the Christian Gospel.[1] Asceticism has always been associated with some level of sexual renunciation, but this level varies widely, from periods of abstinence within marriage to complete rejection of sexual behavior on the grounds that it is intrinsically impure. Sexual purity was only one of the many facets of Godward spiritual struggle applied to the body. Other components included watchfulness (struggle against torpidity in sleep) and fasting (struggle against gluttony), among other general activities aimed against the slothfulness of the body. Yet sexual continence took pride of place in the discussions of asceticism, and this might signal the power sexual activity held over those in pursuit of detachment and the difficulty of observing sexual activity in moderation—realities not difficult to observe contemporarily. Because of the potential dangers associated with sexual impulses, and the inherent difficulty of controlling them, many early theologians and monastics commented on sexual purity in the context of Christian asceticism. As such, it is an essential component of the first stage of Godward spiritual struggle applied to the body.

Among the most extreme views on sexual continence were those of Methodius of Olympus, a third- to fourth-century bishop and martyr. In his "Symposium on Virginity," spoken through the mouths of a number of different characters, Methodius lauds virginity and its benefits. Sexual intercourse ought to be avoided at all costs,[2] and even those who are married must be chaste if they want to "adorn their tabernacles" (κοσμήσαντες τὴν σκηνὴν).[3] Methodius includes lawful or legitimate intercourse as an obstacle to chastity, expecting those who marry to attain a chastity that includes sexual abstinence, because this is the only way for them at least to produce little sprouts if not the large branches of the trees of virgins.[4] Methodius, in his epilogue, makes room for procreation as a (lesser) good, later describing virginity as sent to humankind from heaven, the embodiment of which was likened to having one's head in the heavens while still walking on Earth.[5]

Methodius asserted the light airiness of those detached from the passions of this world because of their chastity, which is superior to all other advantages of virtues. Though chastity, according to Methodius, did include the control of sexual desire, it was not limited to this control but instead encompassed all the virtues.[6] Those who are chaste have "wings," allowing them to fly above the concerns of mortals and see the immortal realm, which consists of indescribable beauty. Moreover, "a magnificent array of lights bathes them in the glow that God pours down on them like water, making the world beyond bright with mystical illuminations."[7] The body is a temple that is to remain pure and undefiled; thus virgins represent the altar or the ark within the Holy of Holies, where sacrifices and libations are forbidden.[8] As such, according to Amy Brown Hughes, it is through virginity that a person ascends to greater levels of likeness to God in a process that is both active in needing to carve out space for and accepting Christ and passive in its need for Christ's transformative mediation in the ascender.[9] It is through virginity that one participates in Christ and grows in virtue.[10]

In fact, in the *Acts of Thomas*, purity, which is associated with virginity, is depicted as the virtue par excellence for Christians. Purity is the thread that pieces together much of the narrative found in the *Acts*, at times exaggerated and unbalanced: the apostle is found breaking up a number of marriages, contrary to what canonical Scripture witnesses.[11] Still, strong favor is given to sexual purity—a recurring theme in these ancient texts. The focus on bodily purity when coupled with a belief in an imminent eschatology rendered a Christian, in Thomas's narrative, able to let go of one's attachment to the world with ease.[12] A Christian who believed that Christ would return soon and that the world to come would be established imminently found little reason to hold on to material matters, be they fleshly desires, relational problems, or polemics of any sort. In the same vein, the virtue of women is exalted through a depiction of longing for Christ in the world to come instead of longing for their husbands. Promises of the kingdom were realities to believers in Christ, and this provided the thrust needed to resist the impurity noxiously portrayed in this text and in others.

Similarly, for Methodius, virginity is an emulation of the "Archvirgin" (ἀρχιπάρθενος)—Christ Himself, who leads the chorus of the virgins.[13] Virgins come second only to Christ's very Bride, who Methodius maintains is His own undefiled flesh. At times, this exaltation of virginity seems overextended in Methodius's thought, warranting disagreements. On this point, Peter Brown compares Porphyrius, a pagan philosopher and follower of Plotinus, with Methodius. Porphyrius rejected the Christian ideal of complete virginity and celibacy and was more in line with Clement's ideology.[14] He held abstinence from food much more highly than he did celibacy. In response to this current, Methodius's *Symposium*, in obvious emulation of Plato's famous work, consisted of virgins who were able to access the unfallen primordial state of Adam.[15] Methodius asserted the following: Marriage was permitted as a concession to human frailty; human sexuality pointed to a higher and better reality, a spiritual one; human history was the gradual taming of sexuality; the bridge between God and man was through virginity; and the virgin body was lifted up above earthly matter.[16] In all this, through gradual development, Christianity came to associate virginity with purity. It was not obvious to Christianity's Jewish ancestors that celibacy implied purity. In fact, in the texts of Aphrahat, a third- to fourth-century Syriac ascetic and sage, the opposite is suggested: it was procreation that was given the upper hand in Jewish conceptions of purity.

In "Demonstration 18," Aphrahat makes a strong case for the preeminence of celibacy above all other lifestyles, presenting his case in opposition to the Judaic critique of celibacy that claims that procreation is better than celibacy and that the latter is in a sense impure.[17] Against this, Aphrahat maintains that it is celibacy that is most pure, citing a number of examples of righteous celibates in the Old Testament, including Moses, Joshua, Jeremiah, Elijah, and Elisha.[18] Naomi Koltun-Fromm picks up on Aphrahat's conflation of holiness with celibacy, or licentiousness with marriage. Only those who observe sexual abstinence exhibit purity in its greatest capacity.[19] However, this is in tension with another string of interpretation—that of rabbinic Jews in Aphrahat's time, the fourth century AD. Many posited the exact opposite—that only those who procreate are pure and are fulfilling God's command to the fullest.[20] Aphrahat is aware of their interpretation and think they have it wrong, at least according to "Demonstration 6." However, in "Demonstration 18," as Fromm points out, Aphrahat gives room for procreation and Christian marriage, admitting that they are good as ordained by God, but they are not as good as celibacy.[21] Nonetheless, he maintains that if Moses in Exodus 19 commands the Israelites to observe celibacy for three days in order to see God for one hour, a person would have to be celibate all their lives to be with God all the time.[22]

Koltun-Fromm demonstrates that the tannaitic Jews and Aphrahat recognize this tension and agree on these three points: (1) Both Aphrahat and the tannaitic Jews agree that because Moses spoke to God mouth to mouth, he could not concern himself with earthly matters such as marriage and children.[23] (2) Rabbinic interpretation of this text does indicate an association between sexual abstinence and holiness, but this did not affect how the rabbis thought life should be lived generally; it applied only to Moses's case.[24] (3) The rabbis hold an ambivalence toward Moses's life: they respect and admire his celibacy but still are aware that God ordered procreation. One of their solutions included the possibility of exhibiting particular attributes of Moses *after* one has procreated, just as Moses procreated with Zipporah.[25] All this, for Koltun-Fromm, shows that Aphrahat and the Jews were not using entirely different methods of interpretation. For example, they are both using Moses, whereas Christian schools of thought, according to Fromm, had tendencies to use Abraham as a more universal character. Each school of thought reveals the other's ambivalences.

In the same vein, both assert the necessity for Moses's constant celibacy in order to be in God's presence for so long on so many occasions.[26] However, Aphrahat reveals the struggle of rabbinic studies with sexual abstinence's appeals and offenses. At the same time, Aphrahat's discourse with the rabbinic stance reveals his own ambivalences regarding marriage. It was not to be taken for granted that what may appear to be a ubiquitous stance on sexual abstinence among early Christian ascetics did not have its opposition, and more than that, Scripturally based opposition.[27] It would be very rare to find an early Christian writer making an argument for which biblical support is not provided. The discussion of sexual continence was not an entirely straightforward one, complicated by texts such as 1 Corinthians 7:1–9, 32–35,[28] in which Saint Paul gives concession to marriage primarily as a means of countering uncontrolled sexual appetite, recommending continence if possible, and Luke 20:34–36, where Jesus Christ asserts that there is no marriage in the afterlife after the resurrection of the dead. Clearly, there are challenges in interpretation and reasons for such strong opinions on sexual continence in the early Church. But not all accounts of asceticism were as unbalanced as those of Methodius and Aphrahat.

Clement of Alexandria, a mid-second- to early third-century theologian who gained notoriety in the early Church, offers only a slightly milder perspective.[29] Familiar with the Stoic and Pythagorean ethics that rejected pleasure as a viable basis for sexual intercourse, Clement presented an austere and influential Christian sexual ethics.[30] Peter Brown and Ilaria Ramelli elaborate on Clement's position toward sexuality and virginity. Though there existed circles of Encratitic Gnostics in Syria who believed they could bypass the moral and intellectual discipline required of Christians through a moment of instant redemption,[31] Clement embraced a different view. For Clement, the true gnostic was formed through a gradual, steady life of goodness.[32] All aspects of this life were supposed to be composed, calm, and peaceful, and the Stoic doctrine of *ἀπάθεια* set parameters for this realization.[33] Those who exhibited this life were seen as "stretching upwards in soul, loosed from the world and our sins, touching the Earth on tiptoe so as to appear to be in the world."[34]

However, as Ilaria Ramelli points out, in "condemning excessive asceticism in general," Clement actually held a more positive outlook on sexuality than did the Encratites.[35] For the Encratites, sexual intercourse was a mark of fallen humanity. Clement, by contrast, considered sex appropriate within marriage, albeit only for the purposes of procreation; neither pleasure nor unity were legitimate reasons.[36] In this way, Clement was preserving the sanctity of sexuality in marriage, pushing back against those in his time who considered sex always a bestial act. He ultimately lauded virginity as the best option,[37] but required it only of monks and not of those living outside the confines of monasticism.[38] Clement did well to uphold the possibility of Christian perfection for married noncelibates,[39] but he would soon be drowned out by third- and fourth-century bishops (like Methodius) and clergy who were keen on advocating for virginity.[40]

Perhaps the most balanced of these views on sexual continence in asceticism in the early church is found in the *Shepherd of Hermas*, the most circulated noncanonical writing before the fourth century,[41] even considered as a potential book of the developing New Testament corpus but eventually not included in later codices.[42] One selection in particular deserves special attention: mandate 4.1 on chastity and adultery. Although this mandate primarily describes prohibitions and suggestions for different circumstances surrounding adultery, the way it defines chastity is noteworthy. In contrast to the rigidity with which chastity is defined by Aphrahat and Methodius, the *Shepherd* clearly refers to chastity as *fidelity*, not as celibacy.[43] Within the bounds of chastity lies the man who refrains from thinking of other men's wives but thinks only of one's own. Within these wide parameters, "you will never sin."[44] This is in stark contrast to Methodius, who recommends celibacy even within marriage. Only those who are celibate can "decorate their tabernacles" with the fruit of the chastity tree. The *Shepherd* here seems to give the most lenience within marital relations relative to the other ancient texts mentioned here. However, even the most lenient of these only acquiesces to permit marriage and procreation as a lesser evil than adultery; it remains a less virtuous alternative to celibacy.

Other than this perspective found in the *Shepherd*, one cannot deny the encouragement in the early centuries of Christianity of complete abstinence from sexual intercourse.[45] It is specifically *not* the suggestion of this section to encourage such a stringent view of sexuality, but it is often the case that behind extreme views lies a lesson to be learned, albeit in a less extreme form. Some, such as Clement, found room for a more lenient view on sexuality. Hermas focused on fidelity instead of celibacy. But many others did not, and the rigidity of their positions is stark. Moreover, even Clement—though progressive in his own right, arguing against those who maintained that sexual behavior is inherently evil—did not acquiesce to the utilization of sex as a means for pleasurable or unitive purposes. Asceticism promoted the control of any appetitive desires to which one could become attached or reliant. These included the pleasure of food, sleep, and certainly sex, among other things. Yet this only explains why Clement may have refrained from permitting sex for pleasurable purposes. It seems more stringent to prohibit sex even for unitive purposes between spouses. The other texts noted in this section elucidate why early Christian ascetics, like Clement, advised for control of sexual appetites even among the married.

The disdain with which sexual intercourse was viewed seemed to be more reflective of the society of these authors than it was of sexuality itself. For example, Aphrahat clearly conflates sexuality with bestiality, as though there were no choice for a middle ground. It was hard for him, as it was for others in his time, to imagine a temperate, controlled, responsible exercise of sexuality. This is not far from the *Acts of Thomas,* which conflates virginity with purity—the virtue par excellence.[46] Complete abstinence was the only solution to the bestiality that these writers saw in sexuality, though this may not strike the modern reader as the most obvious of solutions. Similar to other fleshly desires, which in this pattern for Godward spiritual struggle must be fought against and controlled, it seems that sexual urges should be under a person's control.

Even within the confines of marriage, sexual intercourse was not always appropriate, but this does not imply, at least not for all early Christian texts, that sexual intercourse was deemed intrinsically malignant. The severity with which some sexual prohibitions are made signal the ease with which the impulse can become habitual and on which a person can become obsessed, addicted, or reliant, in effect misaligning one's orientation, causing it to veer away from God. To be under the power of any bodily desire or material item is categorically antithetical to the detachment that is required in the pursuit of God.

The addictive quality of sexuality is not an insight to be glossed over, especially considering all the contemporary issues about sexual crimes, abuse, and misconduct. To deem these Patristic voices irrelevant or anachronistic because of their extreme nature would be to ignore an issue in sexual ethics that lies at the root of its impropriety. Sexual perversion has proven problematic throughout much of human history, and the regaining of control over one's disorderly sexual impulses through the concept of spiritual struggle applied to the body (i.e., asceticism) could be an important means to the virtuous flourishing of any community. The same conclusion applies to other realms of asceticism, which are not taken up here. Obviously, some of these authors describe extremes that are neither practical nor appropriate in a contemporary context. However, fundamentally, they envisioned the application of autonomous bodily control for their entire communities, calling for asceticism beyond the bounds of the monastic garb and in their anticipation of Christ's παρουσία, struggling toward fleshly detachment, the first stage of Godward spiritual struggle.[47]

THE SECOND STAGE: ANGELIFICATION AND RESTORATION

Bodily purity, which involved struggling against one's sexual desires, was one aspect of the first stage of the journey to God. Although bodily purity—along with its requisite sexual continence—was the most desirable of virtues, it did not alone constitute asceticism. Indeed, asceticism sought a return of humanity to its original state before Adam and Eve's Fall in the Garden; it was also a transformation into the likeness of angels. At first glance, these two statements appear to be in opposition: is one restored to a sort of ideal human nature, or is one transformed into an angelic nature? The answer is both.

Texts from Saints Clement of Alexandria, Athanasius the Apostolic, and Gregory of Nyssa help demonstrate that a restoration of primordial nature is the same as a transformation into angelic nature. Both expressions describe ascending above or conquering *fallen* human nature, and both are essentially the fulfillment of God's will and the response of God to humanity's Fall.[48] Most important is that the second stage (the strengthening of the soul) of Godward spiritual struggle applied to the body in asceticism is manifested in a transformative progression from that which is fallen in humanity to that which is risen in God. These concepts of restoration or transformation (the second stage of asceticism) prepare one for the ultimate goal (and third stage) of asceticism: becoming a dwelling place for the presence of God.

More than just his teachings on purity and sexuality, Clement of Alexandria's protomonastic theories had a far-reaching impact on Christendom.[49] These theories are extant primarily in his *Eclogae propheticae, Adumbrationes,* and *Excerpta ex Theodoto,* all of which shed light on his understanding of asceticism. Clement, among other early Christian writers, sees humanity's destiny as a constant progression from image to likeness, so much so that even if humanity had not fallen, the Word would have incarnated to give humans heavenly rebirth.[50] Humans are made for constant progression that, for Clement, begins with baptism (ἀναγεννῆσαι δε ὕδατι), progresses from a common image (εἰκόνα) between all humanity to growth in likeness (ὁμοίωσιν) as a sort of heavenly being, and reaches fulfillment through the ascetical life.[51] In his "Stromates," Clement describes these earthly angels as having reached gnostic perfection (γνωστικῆς τελειότητος) through detachment (ἀπάθεια). They are equal to angels and luminous, shining like the sun.[52]

Bogdan Bucur's reading of Clement insists that this process consists of stages in which the human does not merely mimic the state of angels through metaphorical change but also in fact experiences a sort of real ontological change.[53] The human being moves from abstention from evil to active beneficence, embodying the goodness of God and divine providence while acquiring "the unchanging habit of well-doing after the likeness of 'God.'"[54] Clement continues describing this angelic transformation: "Such an one has already attained the condition of "*being equal to the angels.*" For he who has come to this state is in a condition to be holy, falling into none of the passions in any way, but as it were already disembodied and already grown holy without this Earth."[55] The ascetic is able to reach a state of perfection through levels of cosmic hierarchy: angels, archangels, the seven-created first angels (*protoctists*), and the Logos. The governing principle of this hierarchy is the "Face of God," which the *protoctists* can see and contemplate because of their proximity to God. These *protoctists* provide a model for perfected souls and function as high priests lifting the prayers that come from below.[56] The ascent through this hierarchy is dynamic and fluid. Clement held that every thousand years there would be a promotion of ranks beginning with humans and ending with the *protoctists*.[57] Although Origen, Evagrius, and Clement thought that becoming angelic was only a distinction of degrees and not necessarily one of nature, Christians eventually understood this to be only metaphorical; humanity will be "christomorphic" at the end of times when Christ comes, but they will not actually become angelified.[58] Clement's process of angelification was developed from prominent notions in Jewish apocalypticism and certainly shaped the Christianity that followed, while eventually losing its ontological thrust.[59] Even by the time of Gregory of Nyssa, as seen below in his description of his angelic sister, he maintains that she keeps her human essence while exhibiting angelic proclivities and desires.

The perpetual progress to angelic perfection, moreover, was not a journey to be taken alone; this process through the cosmological hierarchy required eldership and discipleship. It is through the gnostic ascetic that humans connect to the angelic realm. "I would venture to propose that, for Clement," writes Bucur, "a perfected Christian—one who is 'living as an angel on earth, already luminous,' having 'already attained the isangelic condition'—embodies in his very being and offers to those with whom he interacts a foretaste of the 'rest' in God to which the seeker aspires."[60] The perfected Christian—that is, the gnostic leader—has trod the path of angelification and as a result is able to channel the Logos to human beings: "Eldership and discipleship are thus sine qua non conditions for the ascetic reshaping of the believer."[61] Prodding ever so slightly at the tendency for the modern reader to approach a text with a kind of moral detachment, Bucur asserts that Clement's call, then, is for his readers to engage this transformative process, not to concoct merely theoretical analyses of his propositions. In other words, the vocation of all humans has been ordained even "pre-primordially" to embark on the perpetual journey of angelification, first through baptism and then through ascetical adherence to an angel elder.[62]

Clement likely influenced Gregory such that, as the goals and functions of early Christian monasticism continue to unfold, asceticism was often understood as a microcosm of Gregory's *epektatic* ascent. In other words, it was the goal of the ascetic to observe the commands of God in Scripture to aspire to perfection; it is in the same vein that Gregory understands *epektasis*. As noted above, early Christian monastics did not see themselves as part of a clerical body but rather as a movement of lay people who wished to embody the words of Christ in the Gospel.[63] Though some understood this calling as a solitary one, the majority came to find that communal or coenobitic monasticism was the best way to adhere to Christianity's chief commandments to love God and neighbor. Clement, as early as the second century, presents a number of concepts vital to the exploration of asceticism in the early Church: control over sexual desire as a means to (angelic) purity and freedom from compulsory desires (ἀπάθεια); the centrality of community in order to love God and neighbor, thereby progressing toward perfection; and the goal of asceticism as a continual ascent *to* God and *through* God in order to become *like* God.

Next, Saint Athanasius's *Vita Antonii* takes its reader through Antony's ascetical journey from his early life, to his encounter with the word of God during liturgy, to the beginnings of his solitary life, and through what would later be appropriated as a monasticism that would have widespread influence in the East and to all corners of Christendom. More than this, Athanasius's account of the father of monasticism's life and struggle highlights a dimension of virtue that speaks much to the concern of contemporary readers. Regarding debates on grace versus works that would continue to develop in much of Christianity's reception history after Athanasius's time, he developed a clear conception of the cooperative or synergistic relationship between God and humans, though of course his language differs.[64] The cooperation between Antony and God was central to his renown as a man of God and father of monasticism.[65]

It is clear in the *Vita Antonii* that exhibiting grace-enabled exertion allowed the human who struggled for virtue in concert with God's grace to enter a sort of ethereal life. The more one progressed on this path, the more primordial one became. Athanasius described this as the "natural" condition that Antony acquired.[66] This natural condition is that of virtue and is the condition that God intends for humanity; thus, "in accordance with nature" (κατὰ φύσιν), one becomes fully human. Athanasius's description of Antony in this state was a man who appeared polite, calm, cheerful, and graceful, all resulting from the detached disposition attained by Antony's denunciation of worldly pleasures.[67] What is even more astounding is his description of Antony at 105 years old, just before his death and after decades of strenuous asceticism and a diet of only bread, salt, and water: "Indeed, maintaining even undiminished eyesight and with perfectly healthy eyes, he had good vision. Not one of his teeth fell out, though they had been worn down beneath the gums on account of the old man's advanced age. His feet and his hands also remained healthy. In short, he appeared more radiant, stronger, and more energetic than all those people who enjoy a wide variety of foods and baths and different types of clothing."[68] Earlier in the biography, when Antony emerges from his cave after twenty years of solitude, he is described as one "having been initiated into divine mysteries and inspired by God," and neither fat nor emaciated, grieved nor frantic, stressed nor lax.[69] In a word, he had made progress toward restoration of his human nature.

However, in the Syriac version of the *Life of Antony*, this very same scene is described differently. Antony is described as an "angel of light" upon his emergence from the cave.[70] There are a number of interpretations of this textual variance (among others) between the Greek, Coptic, and Syriac versions of this text.[71] The point here, however, is to note that the descriptions of "angel of light" and "restored human" are used to describe the same process of transformation in Antony. The bodily struggle of asceticism rendered Antony detached, which allowed him to live a life unencumbered by the weight of habitual sin that carries with it death. Instead, he lived a life of lightness and freedom, a life intended by God in which restored humanity mimics angelic life despite, or more accurately *because of*, his intense struggle against and rejection of fleshly desires.

In this way, Athanasius documents the means to, effects of, and reasons for the cooperative journey to virtue through which one can attain true humanity, as intended by the Creator. The steps for Antony were clear: weaken the body to dispel its desires and attachments, which in turn will strengthen the soul; the soul's strengthening implies greater intimacy with one's spiritual Creator; and finally, this intimacy ensures that one's humanity reaches its greatest potentiality and is restored to its intended primordial state. The irony of asceticism comes to the fore: what appears as suppression of the body is actually intended for its ultimate perfection. Asceticism, as presented in the *Vita Antonii,* is not hatred of the body but a spiritual struggle applied to the body in order to expel the parts of humanity (fleshly tendencies, proclivities, attachments, etc.) that are affected by the Fall in the Garden of Eden.

Finally, in unpacking the second stage of asceticism, we turn to Gregory of Nyssa. The *Vita Macrinae* is a work of notable ancient Christian figures: Gregory of Nyssa himself; his brother, Basil the Great; their brother, Peter, a presbyter; their sister, Macrina; and their mother. Gregory in this work shows how highly Macrina prioritized purity. She was unwilling to be married, especially after her betrothed died, and she refused to uncover her body to physicians even when she fell very ill.[72] Gregory's approval is clear when he holds her virginity and purity in high regard. He observes that the more trials she endured, the more she was purged of impurities, as is metal in a furnace.[73] These included difficult life events, such as deaths of close family members, as well as struggles against the flesh in the asceticism she exhibited.

Gregory applauds Macrina's serious devotion to ascetical struggle, for her aim was toward Christ *and* virtue. He explains, "For it was really towards her beloved [Christ] that she ran, and no other of life's pleasures ever turned her eye to itself away from her beloved."[74] Her relentless focus significantly affected her mother and brothers. One example Gregory cites is Basil's pompous return from his rhetorical training. Macrina brought him back to the life of renunciation of all worldly cares in order to continue "without impediment towards virtue."[75] Gregory sees a strong link between ascetical struggle, the focus on Christ, and the acquisition of virtue. Austere asceticism in this light, describes Gregory, allows one to progress toward angelic nature, though not ontologically (contrary to Clement's assertions above). Still, Gregory presents human nature here as something to be resisted and conquered. Gregory describes Macrina and her mother as follows:

> For to have freed nature from human passions (ἀνθρωπίνων παθημάτων) was a feat beyond human strength, while to appear in body, to be encompassed by bodily shape and to live with the organs of sense was thereby to possess a nature inferior to that of the angelic (ἀγγελικῆς) and the incorporeal (ἀσωάτου). Perhaps one might even go so far as to say that the difference was minimal, because, although they lived in the flesh (σαρκὶ), by virtue of their affinity with the incorporeal powers they were not weighed down by the attractive pull of the body (σώματος), but their lives were born upwards, poised on high and they took their souls' flight in concert with the heavenly powers.[76]

Gregory describes in different ways the same journey. To acquire virtue, one must be sincere in one's ascetical struggle, which is at the same time directed toward Christ. Transformation through bodily detachment and inner purity initiates a journey toward that which is incorporeal and angelic.

In his *De virginitate*, Gregory explicitly links virginity to this incorporeality. He writes: "Virginity is exceptional and peculiar to the incorporeal nature (ἀσωμάτου φύσεώς), and, through the kindness of God, it has been granted to those whose life has been allotted through flesh and blood, in order that it may set human nature (ἀνθρωπίνην φύσιν) upright once more after it has been cast down by its passionate disposition (ἐμπαθοῦς διαθέσεως), and guide it, as if by the hand, to a contemplation of the things on high."[77] Virginity, in its dispassionate disposition, is participation in God Himself. It is a way of life that resembles the angels, that is, those who have transcended worldly pleasures. In the same text, Gregory asserts that angelification occurs as a result of virginity. He asks, "How could anyone fly up to heaven unless, equipped with heavenly wings, he be borne upwards because of his lofty way of life?"[78] Ilaria Vigorelli demonstrates that in the Nyssen's text, virginity serves as the link between humanity and God, since this virginity belongs to God and since in the Virgin Mary, God descends and unites. So too those who rid themselves of fleshly desires in a life of virginity accept the descent and subsequent unity with God.[79]

Similarly, Hans Boersma describes Gregory's understanding of virginity as participation in God through the acquisition of the divine characteristics of purity, blamelessness, holiness, and incorruptibility.[80] Bodily virginity functions as "an initial embodied manifestation of the defeat of death."[81] Although virginity, for Gregory, is more than only sexual renunciation, "he clearly regards the latter as the initial participation in genderless, angelic existence, and so as participation in divine purity, incorruptibility, and impassibility."[82] Importantly, however, in his later writings, this bodily virginity came to refer to moral purity generally, not to sexual continence specifically.[83] Though Gregory does not mention *epektasis* explicitly here, his emphases on orientation to and participation in God when discussing asceticism and virginity are reflective of the broader *epektatic* model.[84] Despite his lack of an explicit reference to what might be a modern rendering of the theory of *epektasis*, the directive of the ethics proposed remains unchanged: struggle for angelic detachment against the passions, lay hold of Christ and acquire virtue, and He will lay hold of you.

The connection between asceticism and the recovery of primordial human nature is a common theme in early Christian texts, not as disdain for the body, nor only with a focus on sexual purity, but also as transformation to angelic nature. Asceticism in this sense is a fulfillment of God's plan for salvation. That is, in Jesus Christ's incarnation, He restored humanity while calling humans to participate in this restoration. Asceticism is the physically exertive aspect of this participation, and the concept of angelification most notably captures the second stage of the strengthening of one's soul, though definitive categorization can be difficult. As outlined in the previous chapter, distinctive lines between stages do not necessarily exist. More than simply confirming the stage of angelification, it remains that asceticism, understood as a process of humanity's restoration, points to the fruitfulness of applying the concept of spiritual struggle to the various dimensions of Christian life within a framework of perpetual progress to God. This paves the way for the final stage of Godward spiritual struggle: union with and a similitude to God.

THE THIRD STAGE: LITURGICAL TRANSFORMATION AND DIVINE INDWELLING

The climax, so to speak, of asceticism is the transformation of the body into a locus for the presence of God. Making room for God's indwelling is the chief concern for the apparent obsession with notions of purity and angelification and their associations with asceticism. Yet, as with any conceptual development, these associations did not arise in a vacuum. Instead, the idea of the human as a locus for the presence of God resulted from numerous literary and ritualistic strands, including the Old Testament, Second Temple literature, apocalyptic literature, and the New Testament, taking its most developed form in the Patristic era.

C. R. A. Morray-Jones documents the progression of the communication of the Holy of Holies, the Divine, and the Glory before it is later adopted into Christianity. First, according to the Old Testament, the heavenly temple is a copy of the archetypal heavenly palace and throne room—the dwelling place of God. At its center God dwells, with surrounding layers (initially three; and by the second century AD, seven) throughout the temple.[85] The closer one gets to the center of the temple, the closer one gets to the Divine. In later Second Temple literature, cosmological significance gets assigned to this temple imagery in which the levels of the temple become celestial levels through which the visionary in this literature ascends and encounters God and His throne.[86]

Jones is particularly interested in using the Sabbath songs of Qumran, which form a liturgical cycle, to connect this Second Temple literature with Christian conceptions of and assimilations of temple and cosmological archetypes. The ritualization of these liturgical songs functioned as a sort of communal mysticism that produced an intense experience of being present in the heavenly temple and participating with heavenly angels.[87] In other words, ritual functioned as a journey of ascent toward the Glory. Jones maintains that the descent within and ascent without are two dimensions or aspects of the same process; they are not mutually exclusive alternatives.[88] Just because they are structural opposites does not mean they are functional opposites. As such, a celestial ascent functions as a temple descent, or as an entering into it. The work of the community and its angelic counterparts are the substance that constructs the temple. The community itself is also identified with the temple; the hierarchy embodies the living structure of the cosmic temple.[89] The interior of the temple functions concomitantly as the primordial garden as well as the eschatological place of the righteous.

It is all this imagery that eventually becomes interiorized, and this is seen clearly in Aphrahat's "Demonstrations." For Aphrahat, the ideal Christian is the "place" of the presence of God, "the heavenly temple, the throne within it, the radiance, and God Himself, together . . . with God's eschatological manifestation." This ideal Christian, which he refers to as the sage, ascends to the presence and the Throne through knowledge of the creation. Aphrahat successfully captures in this sage a thread of theology clear in Second Temple literature. Third Enoch's Metatron exhibits a number of similarities to the sage, including the recovery of Adam's divine image, which was lost.[90] But Aphrahat has taken the Second Temple literature's apocalyptic seer and understood him in light of the risen and transfigured Christ of the New Testament.[91]

For Aphrahat, Christ is the wisdom and Glory of God, the Eucharistic presence, and the true tabernacle of Worship.[92] It is love for Christ, imitation of Him, and the reception of baptism and the Eucharist that transform the apocalyptic seer into this sage. The sage interiorizes all the Second Temple imagery described and becomes a god in the likeness of God.[93] Just as Christ humbled Himself and became incarnate, so too is the ideal Christian to acquire humility in the likeness of God. One must make oneself small in humility, as Christ did; God gave up what was His, so humans may become like Him.[94] The theophanic presence of the sage is not only eschatological but is also something experienced here and now. He "is the presence of God for those who come to him. His gifts, his experience of the presence, and his wisdom are to a purpose, and that purpose is to make God present, manifest, and visible."[95] He functions as the proof and living image of hope in Christ—the divine and the humble.

Pseudo-Macarius also helps elucidate the process of the interiorization of this literature in the formation of the Christian as a locus for the divine presence. His language is strong in describing the magnificence of the soul illuminated by Christ, who mounts the soul as His throne. In homily 1, Macarius writes,

> For that soul that is deemed to be judged worthy to participate in the light of the Holy Spirit by becoming his throne and habitation, and is covered with the beauty of ineffable glory of the Spirit, becomes all light, all face, all eye. There is no part of the soul that is not full of the spiritual eyes of light. . . . For the soul has no imperfect part but is in every part on all sides facing forward and covered with the beauty of the ineffable glory of the light of Christ, who mounts and rides upon the soul.[96]

Some, however, have accused Macarius of overemphasis in describing spiritual experiences. In what turns out to be a defense of Juana Raasch's analysis of Pseudo-Macarius, Alexander Golitzin describes recent developments in the study of apocalyptic literature that clarify Macarius's discussion of the experience of the divine light in this life. The accusation against Macarius was his mystical overemphasis on experience and feelings.[97] Golitzin addresses the latter portion of that accusation—the feelings—as reflective of the internalization of the experience of the visions of light, pointing out that Macarius was not as systematic in his discourses as someone like Evagrius.[98]

The Macarian language of vision, light, and glory, shining within a purified temple of the heart or intellect, draws on ancient Christian and pre-Christian Jewish literature, with deeper roots in the liturgy of the First Temple and prophetic revelations.[99] This literature holds the revelation of transcendent realities highly. What Macarius did was take the main components of this transcendence—the glorious visions, ascents to heaven, and transformation and participation in the liturgy of heaven—and internalize them without ridding them of their believed realities. He held that the share of the divine glory was promised in the Old Testament, fulfilled in the New Testament, and experienced now through the Holy Spirit. For example, he makes the connection between the temple of God and the indwelling of the Holy Spirit when he writes, "For the King of Glory, ardently desiring her beauty, has deigned to regard her, not only as temple of God, but also as the daughter of the king and also the queen. Indeed, she is the temple of God, since she is inhabited by the Holy Spirit."[100]

For Macarius, it is this same Holy Spirit that left the physical temple, leaving it for destruction. He writes, "The Holy Spirit left them when the veil of the Temple was rent in two. And so their Temple was handed over to the Gentiles, destroyed and made desolate."[101] According to Golitzin, the Gospel for Macarius was summed up as follows: There was limited accessibility to the Glory of God in Israel through the cultus and the high priest; the Glory of God came veiled in the flesh in New Testament; and now (i.e., after the New Testament), the heart or the inner man of the baptized Christian becomes the locus of theophany.[102]

Continuing the theme of interiorization, in another work, Golitzin analyzes aspects of apocalypticism that are sometimes overlooked—the ascents to heaven, visions of angels, and "direct revelation of heavenly mysteries."[103] In particular, he points to the works of Niketas Stethatos, a disciple of the tenth-century Symeon the New Theologian. Niketas was not unaware of these aspects of apocalyptic literature; his writings reflect a profound understanding of the interiorization of ascent, transformation, and participation. Golitzin refers to this approach as "interiorized apocalyptic," "the transposition of the cosmic setting of apocalyptic literature, and in particular of the 'out of body' experience of heavenly ascent and transformation, to the inner theater of the Christian soul."[104] Niketas describes witnessing this out-of-body event when Symeon was permeated by the immaterial divine light and transformed inwardly as a result.

Internal transformation is an experience attested by a number of spiritual elders in ancient Christian monastic communities. Elders would be seen as transfigured through the purification of the heart. They are described in a number of texts as ascenders to the Throne of Glory. They were earthly angels or heavenly men. This is also apparent among others aforementioned, including Pachomius and Macarius. Furthermore, Golitzin points to a number of fourth-century Christian writers—including Ephraem, Evagrius, and Pseudo-Macarius—who describe the same process of interiorization as Niketas.[105] What he wishes to demonstrate is that Niketas, writing in the tenth century, was aware of the implications of apocalyptic and Old Testament pseudepigraphy and incorporated this apocalyptic interiorization in continuity with many of his fourth-century predecessors, despite the spatial and geographical discontinuities. By responding to those who understood visions and ascents as literal, Niketas, as one of a number of condemners between the fourth and fourteenth centuries of those who took visions and ascents literally, saw himself as *affirming* the teaching of the Apostles of Christ, not as *straying* from that tradition.[106]

Thus, the process of interiorization, taken from all the genres presented, understood the person, and more specifically the ascetic, as the locus of God's presence. The fact that this interiorization was influenced by so many different literary strands only emphasizes the importance of the body as temple. Yet, as history demonstrates, asceticism among Christians generally, and Christian monastics specifically (except in the case of a few exceptions), took on a communal form—a liturgical form. In fact, the Christian liturgy served as an indispensable vehicle by which the process of interiorization was accomplished. Even among the "exceptions," which included hermits and solitaries living isolated lives in deserts, liturgy was often the one communal activity that was not neglected.

Liturgy as Interiorizer

The liturgy has long remained a central component to Christian life. Though the liturgy, from its inception, took on various forms among different regions, the liturgy, in addition to the initiation rites that were also pluriform and developing, became associated with a Christian's very identity.[107] The emphasis on the liturgy was at the same time an emphasis on the power of liturgy to transform its participants into dwelling places of the Divine.[108] This was a fitting outlook on the rite because many associated the bread and wine with God's body and blood—an association supported by Scripture's accounts of the Last Supper.[109] God was present *in* and *at* the meal from the earliest of Christian Eucharistic accounts. Andrew McGowan writes: "In the fourth century as in the first, a diverse group of believers gathered around a table to share simple food, and the Christians prayed and gave thanks to God for the life and work of Jesus remembering his own acts of eating as they performed their own, affirming his presence in and at their meal."[110]

This real presence—distinguished by McGowan from a medieval and modern metaphysical understanding of what it might mean for God to be present in the Eucharistic elements—is the source of the transformative nature of the Divine Liturgy. The transformation offered through the liturgy was twofold—one had to struggle to purify oneself in order to be made worthy of receiving the Eucharist, but one also received a purifying grace *through* the mystery or sacrament in order to aid in further purification of the participant.

Saint John Chrysostom, a late-fourth-century monk and archbishop of Constantinople, notes both these junctures in the process of transformation. In his first instruction to the catechumens, he writes,

> One who is about to approach those sacred rites and awesome mysteries ought to be alert and wide-awake, cleansed of every earthly care, abundantly filled with temperance and zeal. He should banish from his mind every thought which is foreign to the mysteries and should make his house clean and ready in every respect, just as if he were about to receive the emperor under his roof. That is the way to prepare your mind, such are the thoughts you should think, such should be the purpose of your will.[111]

Similarly, in Homily 46 on the Gospel of Saint John, he warns his reader of the dangers of approaching the body and blood of Jesus Christ without purity of body and conscience. Otherwise—he maintains—that person would be just as guilty as those who nailed Christ to the cross.[112] If this were not extreme enough of an expression, in section 6 of Homily 82 on the Gospel of Saint Matthew, he asserts that partaking of the mysteries while openly and unrepentantly in sin is worse than demonic possession.[113] He goes on to claim that he would rather give up his own life than have someone receive the mysteries in this manner.[114]

Such intensity of language is a direct reflection of the transformative nature of participation in the Eucharist. Chrysostom exclaims: "This blood is the salvation of our souls, by This the soul is washed, by This is beautified, by This is inflamed, This causeth our understanding to be more bright than fire, and our soul more beaming than gold; this blood was poured forth, and made heaven accessible."[115]

He continues, "They who share this Blood stand with Angels and Archangels and the Powers that are above, clothed in Christ's own kingly robe, and having the armour of the Spirit. Nay, I have not as yet said any great thing: they are clothed with the King Himself."[116] It is through the liturgy that one attains the purity that is needed in order to reach the ultimate stage of the spiritual journey—unity with God.

Pseudo-Macarius's writings, dated to the fourth century, also demonstrate an awareness of the liturgy as a vehicle to the soul's ascent to God. He wished to "reconcile the individual mystical longings of his correspondents with the liturgical and sacramental life of the Christian Church."[117] In this way, asceticism as a function of the *epektatic* journey becomes a communal, not an individual, activity. It is through the work of the people (λειτουργία) that any part or individual of that community is transformed. Macarius continues by asserting that the liturgy shapes the soul for encounter with God.[118] The liturgy, for Macarius, functions as a double icon: the Eucharistic assembly as an icon for the heavenly liturgy and as an icon for the soul.[119] The ritualization of the Church order and hierarchy assists the ascent to heaven—that is, the journey to God—and the locus of the ascent is the individual body that has acquired the extraordinary significance of the temple.

As the understanding developed, especially notable in Pauline literature, of the individual body as a microcosm of the temple and, of course, the cosmos, the ascent into the heavens began to be understood in light of the descent within the temple of the body.[120] This carries with it a transformative power, because the vision of the Glory transforms the visionary into an angelic likeness of that Divine Image.[121] As Christianity came to assimilate the functions of temple imagery, cosmological archetypes—and liturgical ritualization of these images and archetypes, Christ, His Church, and its members—became one. The middle wall of separation was abrogated; the purity laws were no longer needed because Christ abolished the distinction between sacred and profane, given that He fills all in all. What this ultimately means is that the momentum that the Old Testament, Second Temple literature, and New Testament carried in light of this research continues, and should continue, to function as a transformative operation for those who inherited all this—namely, Christians. Christ is the temple; He "belongs to the people" (λειτος) gathered for liturgy; and He is the Glory of God that fills the temple and the cosmos. Christians are thus cast in a new light: they are temples and microcosms who receive the Body and Blood of Christ, the mediation of the Divine Glory through a process of interiorization.

The liturgy is the vehicle of interiorization, and Niketas Stethatos realizes this in an analysis of the genre of interiorized apocalyptic. The liturgy was understood as concelebration with the multitudes of angels surrounding the Throne of Glory and hymning His praises.[122] The spiritual father celebrating the liturgy was seen as the mediator of the divine presence. He was the vehicle through whom God made Himself available to the people and through whom the people had access to God, both literally in the Eucharist and metaphorically through interior transformation.[123] But in order to experience this effect fully, one must be purified internally, because there can be no discord between good and evil, virtue and vice, within a person who desires to be transformed:

> So long as the nature of the powers within us is in a state of inner discord, we do not participate in God's supernatural gifts. And if we

> do not participate in these gifts, we are also far from the mystical liturgy . . . of the heavenly altar, celebrated by the intellect through its spiritual activity . . . [but, once the intellect has been purified through askesis and prayer] we participate in the ineffable blessings of God, and worthily, together with God and God the Word, offer up the divine mysteries of the intellect's spiritual . . . altar as initiates . . . and priests . . . of His mysteries.[124]

Thus, the liturgy absorbs the images and archetypes of apocalyptic literature and makes sense of purification through spiritual struggle, expressed here through asceticism and prayer. Golitzin notes that preparations for visionaries in Old Testament pseudepigraphy included a good deal of *askesis*. In Golitzin's conclusion that "Niketas could easily have read these much older texts as testimonies to the same experience of the light and liturgy of heaven that both he and especially Symeon claimed as their own," he marks medieval Byzantium as participating in an awareness of interiorized apocalyptic's importance.[125]

To conclude, Golitzin makes two important notes regarding the process of interiorization. First, there is a seriousness of the struggle and its depth in the soul of a visionary. War must be waged because the cosmic struggle has now become internalized. Second, the Eucharistic liturgy and ecclesiastical assembly are revealed as an allegory or iconography of the soul's life in grace.[126] In other words, the Church is the macrocosm, and the soul is the microcosm. Just as work is done liturgically in the Church yet is nothing without the grace of the Holy Spirit, so too does the struggle of the soul toward virtue function in relation to the grace of God. In this way, the grace-enabled struggle, or the model of cooperation between divine and human agencies foundational to the ethics of this book, is unpacked in light of the literary and ritualistic heritage that preceded it. Life in Christ, in this way, becomes interiorized without becoming individualized. On the journey to God, the temple *within* receives the light of the Trinity upon the altar of the heart and through the altar of the Church.[127]

Particular Instantiations of Interiorization

The goal of asceticism presented here, in preparing the body to become the dwelling place of God—that is, uniting with God or assimilating to Him—is not a far cry from reality; it is not, among these authors, intended as a mystified, impractical, or impossible state to reach. It is in fact precisely because of ascetics who exude a sort of aura of peace and fortitude, as a result of their intimacy with God, that asceticism becomes all the more accessible, relevant, and transformative. One such instance is seen in the father of coenobitic or communal monasticism—Pachomius. Mark Burrows does well to present a thesis that instantiates Morray-Jones's embodiment of the divine image alluded to above. Pachomius, most known for his structuring and spreading of coenobitic or communal monasticism, is known as the *apa* of the community he created.[128] What Burrows argues is that he structures this community not necessarily through what he *does* but through who he *is*.[129] Recalling the opening discussion of this project regarding ethical methodology, Burrows is focusing more on an ethics of virtue that flows from Pachomius's being instead of his ability to follow a strict set of prescribed laws, as a deontological ethics would put forth. As a being transformed and outpouring with dynamic virtue, Pachomius represented the invisible God as a visible man; he was God's temple—a vehicle for the divine presence.[130] Moreover, Pachomius was not only to be the agent of the divine for the monastic community—the *koinonia*—but also for the whole world—the *oikoumene*.[131] His task was to be a father who led to the Father—to mediate between heaven and Earth. It was through allegiance to Pachomius as *apa* father that one's allegiance to the Father could be tested and verified in a very real, material sense. His example was to be imitated, as He was the express imitation of Christ in the community. He took up his cross rather literally, standing up in cruciform as he prayed. Moreover, as the lawgiver of the community, he functioned as the image of Moses—the new Moses giving the new law.[132] Pachomius's function as the visibility of the invisible God is demonstrated in the life of his successors. Though many who followed technically assumed his position as *apa*, they were not held to the same esteem as was Pachomius. His successors would refer back to Pachomius's life, because the power did not reside in the title or position of *apa* but in the transformed being of Pachomius.[133]

The examples are by no means trapped in Christianity's early years. Golitzin points out that to Orthodox Christians, the existence of the sage is of no surprise, as they surely meet holy men and women in their lives who seem illumined with the glow of divinity.[134] For Golitzin, one of these illumined elders was Father Aimilianos, who to Golitzin exemplified the very "Presence of the King."[135] Golitzin further emphasizes that Orthodox Christians' common patrimony (of Israel) with non-Orthodox, and the scholarly work that the latter accomplish, contain within them, and deep within the Hebrew Scriptures, an understanding of divine–human union that is very real now and that is an urgent message to all.[136] As a deeply embedded seed of Scripture and a central facet and reality of life with Christ, it has transpired from extrabiblical sources, through the Old Testament, New Testament, and early Christians to our present day.

CONCLUSION

Recall the two levels of this chapter mentioned above. At the macro level, asceticism was presented as the application of an ethics of Godward spiritual struggle to the body. The goal of the ascetic is to become a locus for the dwelling of God Himself—specifically, a fulfillment and interiorization of the ancestral heritage of Christianity; and more generally, the goal of Christianity and the fulfillment of human nature. When applying an ethics of Godward spiritual struggle to the body, asceticism can be seen as being made up of three loosely delineated stages to complement the nonlinear spectrum suggested in chapter 3. The first stage is struggle for purity against one's disordered bodily desires and weaknesses, which include sexual depravity. The second stage is acquiring the likeness of angels or being restored to an elevated or primordial humanity, which is synonymous with the strengthening of the soul. The third stage is to become the dwelling place of God, which is synonymous with uniting with God or assimilating to God. It is the suggestion of this book that Godward spiritual struggle applied to any of the realms of Christian life would proceed in a similar fashion.

The ethics of Godward spiritual struggle in this book is meant to offer the reader a practical ethics that can be embodied contemporarily. As such, at the micro level, the essence of asceticism has been unpacked, begging the question of how it might be implemented as part of mundane, twenty-first-century life.[137] Though this project is certainly atavistic, the thesis is not mainly one of lamenting a mode of the past that has been lost but recovering a Christian mode that is fundamental to the Gospel, that has been overlooked in modernity, that has been largely missing from Christian accounts of virtue, and that addresses concerns within contemporary accounts of virtue ethics. The number of monastics across most, though not all, churches has declined, but this is not necessarily a bad thing, because it is asceticism that is the focus here, not monasticism.[138] Asceticism is not reserved for the nonmarried, a conception that was not foreign to the early Church.[139]

In his discussion on marriage versus nonmarried celibates, John Behr, through many of the authors and texts examined in this chapter, interprets marriage as having an elevated status and virginity as an interiorized disposition of the soul, not an external feat of the body (similar to Gregory of Nyssa's later texts, as noted above).[140] The only author that Behr had difficulty interpreting in this light was Clement of Alexandria. As detailed above, Clement was writing among many who held that all sexual activity was inherently vicious. To this, Clement replied that sexuality with marriage and for the purposes of procreation was permissible.[141]

Nonetheless, Behr takes his argument a step further than Clement and concludes that marriage is not about procreation, nor is it even about the unitive goal between the man and woman (nor is it even about the two combined). Marriage is about manifesting and making Christ present. It is, in a sense, "procreating" Christ.[142] Christian marriage challenges the notion that marriage as an institution or celibacy as an institution is sufficient in and of itself. They are not sufficient; the only sufficiency is in longing for, holding on to, and manifesting the God who is the source of all. Abstinence is not normative, but it can be used to redirect a married couple's focus and attention to God if they have lost this focus.[143] Once this focus is lost, everything is lost. Purity and asceticism are critical for the soul's ascent or in the development of spirituality, that is, the proximity of the soul to its spiritual Creator.

As noted above, sexual intercourse has a special tendency to possess its practitioners, that is, to transform into an obsessive, addictive activity that distracts from Godward spiritual struggle. In assimilating the model of human nature presented at the outset of this book, sexual activities stem from impulses that are at once good and natural to humanity and yet easily distorted as a result of the fallenness of that nature. Humanity is fallen, risen, and rising; it is dynamic, often at a crossroads between opposing pulls, reminiscent of Saint Paul's descriptions of humanity's opposing wills in Romans 7. There might exist the temptation, especially when discussing sexual ethics, to compartmentalize right and wrong, and good and bad, actions. Yet this line of inquiry presupposes a human nature that is given and static, not one that is in flux, on a journey, and in tension. In this book's schema, the proper instantiation of any and all actions (and especially of those that risk compulsiveness, e.g., sexuality) require a fundamental reorientation to God. Only in this turning, this metanoia, can one properly assess the function of a given action or realm of experience, such as sexuality.

The question still remains what asceticism might look like in the twenty-first century.[144] Noted above were the imagery, literature, and rituals that became internalized in those monastics who practiced asceticism. Everything that came before these monastics was fulfilled and encapsulated in those who became dwelling places of God Himself; they became living tabernacles. Paul Evdokimov offers a contemporary Orthodox instantiation of this early Church asceticism, suggesting how asceticism might be understood in modernity among nonmonastics. Interestingly, he appropriates asceticism in a manner analogous to the early Church's appropriation of Old Testament imagery, literature, apocalypticism, and rituals—through what he calls "interiorized monasticism."[145] Just as the early Church's monastics interiorized Old Testament, Second Temple, and apocalyptic literature, so too did Evdokimov interiorize the early Church's monasticism. Ascetic monasticism is a practice that is to be interiorized in the twenty-first century lives of nonmonastic noncelibates. Thus, a double interiorization is rendered (an "interiorization of interiorizations"), because what was interiorized in the early Church's monasticism remains interiorized in his suggestions. The form that this modern asceticism takes, according to Evdokimov, includes calmness, silence, rest, prayer, and contemplation.[146]

In such busy and stressful environments that many find themselves in today, being able to collect oneself and be present for the service of others is a struggle but is vital. This asceticism should lead one to seek humility and purity of heart in order to help others do the same. The precepts of interiorized monasticism must be applied to everyone in their own special way so as to create hearts that love God and neighbor. He insists that this applies to everyone and not just the monk; it is a vocation and identifier for all Christians.[147] The three vows of monasticism—poverty, chastity, and obedience—are to be acquired by all humans if they desire to be truly free.[148] Modern asceticism is the "interior combat necessary for the spiritual person to acquire a mastery over the material world."[149] This internalization of asceticism, however, does not exclude its essential physicality. Traditional ascetical practices that aid in one's control over one's body are as essential contemporarily as they were during the Patristic era. In the end, it is the grace of God that enables, empowers, and sustains, but humans are responsible for the good disposition of a free and unencumbered will.

In exposing the essence of asceticism in the early Church, it is clear the initial goal was to bridle bodily urges that went awry in order to enable people to be transformed into godly persons of virtue. The exploration has brought us to this conclusion: asceticism is the mechanism by which to regain autonomy of the body, thereby enabling the agent to act in accordance with what she knows to be good for the fulfillment of her nature (which in this case is unity with God). Asceticism then is an enabler and manifests itself in any number of ways contemporarily. Asceticism in the twenty-first century is what enables parents to cater to their children when they would rather tend to other pressing matters, demanding the sacrifice of one's own bodily interest for others. Asceticism is what enables those who care for the environment to use their resources more economically, even if it produces otherwise preventable inconveniences. Asceticism is what gives a person the ability to turn their gaze away from a screen toward the eyes of others in order to be present, tend to their needs, and actualize love. Asceticism is what gives a person the control to reserve their sexual proclivities only for the person to whom they have vowed a life of committed love and intimacy, cutting infidelity at its roots, as Christ implores in the Sermon on the Mount. What a lamentable and frequented situation it is when I am presented with an opportunity to love my neighbor but am impeded by an untrained body bridled with attachments. Asceticism is not the knowledge of good and right action in these situations, but it is training the body to act in accordance with that which is good. The concern is not so much whether a person knows what is good (though this is requisite), but more often than not the issue is whether the body has been prepared to willfully enact the good. If the person has struggled in orienting the body to God through *askesis,* the answer is "yes" more often than in the case of untrained, misoriented bodies—that is, bodies that have not undergone a process of Godward spiritual struggle. To be sure that the stages of this ethics were not incidental with the practices of asceticism, especially considering its close proximity conceptually, we now turn to one more instantiation of this ethics: Godward spiritual struggle applied to the practice of sacred reading.

NOTES

1. Kavanagh, *On Liturgical Theology*, 6.
2. Méthode D'Olympe, "Le Banquet," ed. Musurillo and Debidour, in *Sources Chrétiennes* 95, ed. de Lubac, Daniélou, and Mondésert (hereafter *SC* 95), 1.II.21–33, 3.XII.1–36.
3. *SC* 95, 9.IV.55.
4. *SC* 95, 9.IV.46–58.
5. *SC* 95, 1.I.3–32.
6. See Ramelli, "L'inno a Cristo-Logos." See also Hughes, "Legacy."
7. *SC* 95, 8.II.31–34; translation from Methodius, *St. Methodius*, 108.
8. *SC* 95, 5.VIII.10–14.
9. Hughes, "Legacy," 60–63.
10. Hughes, 66.
11. Hughes, 161–251.
12. Hughes, 90–107.
13. *SC* 95, 1.IV.1, 6.
14. Brown, *Body*, 179–81.
15. Brown, 184–85.
16. Brown, 185–87.
17. Neusner, *Aphrahat*, 76–77.
18. Neusner, 77–81.
19. Koltun-Fromm, "Sexuality and Holiness," 375–77, 385–86, 389.
20. Koltun-Fromm, 375–76.

21. Koltun-Fromm, 385–86.
22. Koltun-Fromm, 389.
23. Koltun-Fromm, 390.
24. Koltun-Fromm, 391.
25. Koltun-Fromm, 394.
26. Koltun-Fromm, 389.
27. Koltun-Fromm, 375–77, 385–86, 389. See also Koltun-Fromm, *Hermeneutics.*
28. For a discussion on the relation between the Stoics and this pericope from Saint Paul, see Balch, "1 Cor 7:32–35."
29. Cosaert, *Text of the Gospels,* 5, 11.
30. For an important discussion of Clement's sexual ethics in relation to Stoic and Pythagorean ethics, see Gaca, *Making of Fornication.*
31. Brown, *Body and Society,* 124–25.
32. Brown, 125–26.
33. Brown, 127.
34. Clément d'Alexandrie, *Le Pédagogue,* ed. Marrou and Harl, in *Sources Chrétiennes* 70, ed. de Lubac and Daniélou (hereafter *SC* 70), 140 (1.5.16.3); translation William Wilson. See also Méthode D'Olympe, *Le Banquet,* 202.28–206.30.
35. Ramelli, *Social Justice,* 127.
36. Clement makes this assertion in several parts of book III of the "Stromates." See also Ramelli, "Transformations," 383, 385.
37. Ramelli, 383.
38. Ramelli, 137.
39. The apparent redundancy in language here is to differentiate between the few who were purported to be married and yet still celibate.
40. Ramelli, 138–39.
41. Osiek and Koester, *Shepherd of Hermas,* 1.
42. Osiek and Koester, 4–7.
43. Osiek and Koester, 110. See the commentary portion of this reference regarding the relationship between chastity and fidelity.
44. Osiek and Koester, 109.
45. See Quispel, "Study of Encratism," on the *Acts of Thomas* as proclaiming "the good news of Christian divorce."
46. Klijn, *Acts of Thomas,* 161–251.
47. There existed a culture in Syria that enabled and supported asceticism and celibacy while in regular communities, not hermitic or coenobitic lifestyles. See Griffith, "Asceticism," 220–45.
48. Restoration of primordial nature and the acquisition of angelic nature are also seen in fourth- to seventh-century Syriac clothing metaphors. See Brock, "Clothing Metaphors." Brock begins by outlining the trajectory of clothing metaphors within the four main scenes of salvation history (p. 12). First, before the Fall, Adam and Eve wore clothes with robes of glory or light. They were stripped of these robes at the time of the Fall, with little concern for what replaced them. Syriac writers tended to be focused more on the garments of light then on what replaced them. The third stage was remedial: the Divinity Himself puts on Adam/body by incarnating. The goal is to reclothe mankind with robes of light. When He enters the womb of the Jordan, He deposits the robes of glory/light in the waters, making it accessible for all in the waters of baptism. The final stage, then,

is when the waters at baptism through prayer become the same waters as Christ's Jordan River in sacred time. The baptized put on the robe of glory that Christ left there. Baptism in this way is reentry to Paradise, and that not just of the beginning of time, but an eschatological Paradise. The robe of glory is only partially received in baptism but is perfected at the end of times, when humans will be even more glorious than mankind was at the beginning of time (13). Examining the thread of clothing metaphors as it runs through salvation history provides an insightful way to make sense of humanity as a whole and how God, the Creator of that humanity, related and relates to the various states in which humanity has found itself. These clothing metaphors provide a framework to understand the telos of humanity: to become angelic, godlike, to wear divine garments only as a gift resulting from the Divine One putting on human garments.

49. Bucur, "Hierarchy," 4.
50. Bucur, 8–9.
51. Clément, *Pédagogue*, 1.12.98.2–3 (*SC* 70, 284).
52. Clement, "Stromates," ed. Descourtieux, in *Sources Chrétiennes* 446 (hereafter *SC* 446), 270, 6.13.105.1.
53. Here, "ontological" is used to distinguish real from metaphorical transformation. Clement is thinking of a change—albeit a real and spectacular one—in *degree*, not *kind*.
54. Bucur, "Hierarchy," 15.
55. Clement, "Stromates," 7.10.57.5 (*SC* 428, 186); "Stromates," 7.14.86.7 (*SC* 428, 266); translation from Clement, *Extracts*.
56. Bucur, "Hierarchy," 24.
57. Bucur, 27–28.
58. Bucur, 33–35.
59. For a discussion on the features of apocalypticism and mysticism and the former's (sometimes oppositional) relationship with notions of eschatology among so-called Jewish and Christian Middle- and Neo-Platonists and in imperial and late antiquity, see Ramelli, "Mysticism."
60. Bucur, "Hierarchy," 43.
61. Bucur.
62. Although Clement does not explicitly use the language of perpetual progress, in his parallel between the various glories in heaven and church hierarchy in "Stromates" 6.13, he gives room for a similar model: "Since, according to my opinion, the grades here in the Church, of bishops, presbyters, deacons, are imitations of the angelic glory, and of that economy which, the Scriptures say, awaits those who, following the footsteps of the apostles, have lived in perfection of righteousness according to the Gospel. For these taken up in the clouds, the apostle writes, will first minister [as deacons], then be classed in the presbyterate, by promotion in glory (for glory differs from glory) till they grow into 'a perfect man.'" He then continues in his description of the various states of glory in heaven. *SC* 446, 270; translation Philip Schaff, *Ante-Nicene Fathers*, vol. 2.
63. Kavanagh, *On Liturgical Theology*, 6. See also Athanasius, John of Shmun, and Serapion of Thmuis, *Life of Antony*, 59, 61, where Antony is not described as going through a ritual of consecration or tonsuring, but was moved by God's word in Scripture. He saw himself as embodying the command to sell what he has in order to follow God and to be perfect. Though monasticism became formalized and came to be seen as a community distinct from lay communities, adhering to the Gospel remained central to the practice. *SC* 400, 132, 134; translations of the life of Antony are taken from this source.

64. Athanasius, *Vie D'Antoine*, ed. Bartelink, in *Sources Chrétiennes* 40 (hereafter *SC* 400), 150: "This was Antony's first contest against the Devil; or, rather, through Antony it was the triumph of the Saviour"; *SC* 400, 240: "And by these prayers, these demons were turned away by the Lord"; and *SC* 400, 352: "Antony healed people not by issuing orders but by praying and calling on the name of Christ. As a result, it became clear to everyone that it was not he who was doing these things but the Lord, who through Antony was demonstrating his love for humankind and healing those who were suffering."
65. For another and potentially fuller account of cooperation or synergy—as the term is popularly referred to in Orthodox Christian circles—see Cassien, "Conference XIII."
66. *SC* 400, 174.
67. *SC* 400, 172, 174.
68. *SC* 400, 374.
69. *SC* 400, 172.
70. Barnes, "Angels," 360.
71. For more on this debate, see Athanasius and Draguet, *La Vie Primitive*; and Barnes, "Angels," 353–68. Another helpful source in this conversation is Rubenson, *Letters of St. Antony*, 128.
72. *SC* 178, 242, 244, 246.
73. *SC* 178, 188, 190.
74. Translations from Gregory and Corrigan, *Life of Saint Macrina*, 39; *SC* 178, 216.
75. Gregory and Corrigan, 25; *SC* 178, 162.
76. Gregory and Corrigan, 29; *SC* 178, 178, 180 (Greek insertions mine).
77. *GNO* VIII/I, 254.11–16; translation from Gregory, *Ascetical Works*, 11 (Greek insertions mine).
78. *GNO* VIII/I, 294.8–10; Gregory, *Ascetical Works*, 40.
79. Vigorelli, "Soul's Dance," 72–73.
80. Boersma, *Embodiment*, 117–22.
81. Boersma, 117.
82. Boersma, 144.
83. Cadenhead, *Body and Desire*, 123–37.
84. I have only engaged Gregory's ascetical theology briefly here. For a fuller discussion, see Cadenhead, *Body and Desire*.
85. Morray-Jones, "Temple Within," 404–5.
86. Morray-Jones, 424.
87. Morray-Jones, 420.
88. Morray-Jones, 428.
89. Morray-Jones, 421.
90. Golitzin, "Place of the Presence of God," 424.
91. Golitzin, 435, 438.
92. Morray-Jones, "Temple Within," 402.
93. Golitzin, "Recovering the 'Glory of Adam,'" 297.
94. Golitzin, 300–301.
95. Golitzin, "Place of the Presence of God," 428.
96. Pseudo-Macarius, *Fifty Spiritual Homilies*, 37.
97. Golitzin, "Temple and Throne," 108–9.
98. Golitzin, 125–29.
99. Golitzin, 117.

100. Pseudo-Macarius, *Fifty Spiritual Homilies*, 257.
101. Pseudo-Macarius, 59.
102. Golitzin, "Temple and Throne," 122–23.
103. Golitzin, 128–29.
104. Golitzin, 141.
105. Golitzin, 143–48.
106. Golitzin, 150–51.
107. For good discussions on early Christian identity and the pluriformity that characterized early Christian worship and initiation rites, see Bradshaw, *Search for the Origins*, where Bradshaw debunks numerous assumptions that have colored the last several decades of liturgical scholarship, opening a path for the ten principles he suggests for interpreting early Christian liturgical evidence; also see Bradshaw and Johnson, *Eucharistic Liturgies*; Bradshaw, *Reconstructing Early Christian Worship*; and McGowan, *Ancient Christian Worship*. In my assessment, McGowan's work is the most helpful in painting a picture of the development of ancient Christian worship from its predecessors into some of its most common forms. Still, all these authors at the fore of the conversation point to the regional variety that was typical of early Christian liturgical practices.
108. For a good article on the ethical formation of congregants in early Syriac Christian liturgy, see Harvey, "Liturgy."
109. Spinks, *Do This in Remembrance of Me*, 27–29, 67. Spinks sees Christology and the presence/association of identity as an important concept in early Christian liturgy, even from the very beginning. He writes: "The interpretative words of Jesus regarding the bread suggest some prophetic identity of the bread with himself. In the narratives that have a command to repeat the rite, for the Christian communities the saying quite naturally associates the identity with some sort of presence of the Risen Lord. The Emmaus meal suggests that the elements are a means of divine disclosure of the Risen One."
110. McGowan, *Ancient Christian Worship*, 64.
111. Chrysostom, *Baptismal Instructions*, 134.
112. Chrysostom, *Homilies . . . on the Gospel of St. John*, 401.
113. Chrysostom, *Homilies . . . on the Gospel of St. Matthew*, 1093.
114. Chrysostom, *Homilies . . . on the Gospel of St. Matthew*, 1094.
115. Chrysostom, *Homilies . . . on the Gospel of St. John*, 400.
116. Chrysostom, 401.
117. Golitzin, Recovering the 'Glory of Adam,'" 292.
118. Golitzin, 293.
119. Golitzin, 294.
120. Morray-Jones, "Temple Within," 426.
121. Morray-Jones, 427.
122. Golitzin, "Earthly Angels," 136–38.
123. Golitzin.
124. Golitzin, 136.
125. Golitzin, 149.
126. Golitzin, "Temple and Throne," 126.
127. Golitzin, 129.
128. Burrows, "On the Visibility of God," 12, 16.
129. Burrows, 11.
130. Burrows, 15–28.

131. Burrows, 18.
132. Burrows, 19–24.
133. Burrows, 26–28.
134. As noted in the previous chapter, and as is discussed further in the final chapter, I have tended away from the language of "theosis" because of its polemical charge between Eastern Orthodox and Oriental Orthodox. Here, it is the language Golitzin uses, so I include it to stay true to his own presentation.
135. Golitzin, "Place of the Presence of God," 444.
136. Golitzin, 446–47.
137. On this point, Petre Maican makes a notable argument as to how holiness is available in personal distinctiveness in Christ, not just in sterotyped depictions of holiness shrouded in the monastic garb. See Maican, "Holiness."
138. See King, *Thomas Merton*, 26. He writes, "Christian monasticism flourished throughout the Middle Ages and produced some of the most profound mystical writings of all times, but then it began to decline." Eastern Christian monasticism seems to have declined as well (though the statistics remain unavailable). However, because monks have remained the main source for Eastern Christian bishoprics and because monasticism is still often viewed in the East as the source for a paradigmatic Christianity, it could be that the decline has been less drastic in the East.
139. Examples of asceticism among lay people have been noted above in Aphrahat's lay ascetic community.
140. Behr, "Marriage," 25–26.
141. Behr, 37–38.
142. Behr, 49.
143. Behr, 50.
144. Lisa Cahill offers a perspective on this question reflective of an early Christian focus on solidarity with the poor. See Cahill, *Sex*.
145. Evdokimov, *Ages*, 133.
146. Evdokimov, 64.
147. Evdokimov, 135–39.
148. In my analysis of ancient Christian monasticism and asceticism, I focused on only one of three monastic vows—chastity. Yet much can be gained by examining the other two pillars of monasticism—poverty and obedience—within the same tripartite spiritual model offered in this project. Ilaria Ramelli demonstrates that the practice of asceticism, even in its ancient Christian form, expands beyond matters of sexuality. With an eye to voluntary poverty as requisite to asceticism, she demonstrates the link, spearheaded by Gregory of Nyssa, between philosophical asceticism and the rejection of slavery and social injustice. See Ramelli, *Social Justice*. For a fuller picture of contemporary asceticism, it would indeed be fruitful to examine each pillar within the framework of God-ward spiritual struggle.
149. Ramelli, 159.

5

Sacred Reading as Godward Spiritual Struggle Applied to Scripture

We shall sketch out the manner in which holy Scripture is to be understood. . . . One who had devoted himself to studies of this kind, with all chastity and sobriety and nights of watching, might perhaps through these means be able to trace out the sense of the Spirit of God hidden in profundity, . . . because the soul cannot come to the perfection of knowledge otherwise than by being inspired with the truth of divine wisdom, . . . in order that, by entering upon a narrow path, it might unfold, as a loftier and more sublime road, the immense breadth of divine knowledge.

—Origen

In this chapter, as well as in chapter 4, there exist macro and micro levels of analysis. The former, in this chapter, develops when the three stages of Godward spiritual struggle are envisioned for the practice of reading Scripture. What emerges is a mode of spiritual reading of Scripture typical of ancient Christian exegesis aimed at the transformation of the reader. The latter—the micro level—is a direct corollary of the structure of this book's ethics: applying the ethics of this book to any practice helps elucidate the essence of that practice. The micro level, then, in effect serves as a suggestion for the modern divide between Scripture and ethics. There have been a variety of different opinions as to the proper place of sacred reading in ethical formation. These discussions have often taken place among Catholic ethicists, whose conceptions of ethics have experienced some degree of separation from Scripture. This has been clear at least since Vatican II admonished moral theologians to be "nourished more by the teaching of Scripture" (*doctrina S. Scripturae magis nutrita*).[1] I suggest that placing the practice of reading Scripture within the ethics of Godward spiritual struggle creates a practice that can mine Scripture more deeply and holistically to tap its formative power for creating virtuous agents.

The term "sacred reading," rendered from the Latin *lectio divina*, gained its prominence in the medieval West as a systematized method for prayerfully reading Scripture in order to participate in God's very self.[2] *Lectio divina* names one particular method of sacred reading, but other methods exist. This chapter's discussion concerns sacred reading as a general practice and not simply the particular method of *lectio divina,* which suggests that one read, meditate on, pray, and contemplate on the words of Scripture.[3] Most manuals on *lectio divina,* in giving brief synopses of its history, mention three stages of its use: early Christian Patristics, Benedict, and Guigo II. It was not until the twelfth century that Guigo II named and ordered the four steps of the ladder of *lectio divina* that bring one from Earth to heaven. Before then, similar tenets had been in place but not necessarily in this particular order or with these specific systematizations.[4] In fact, the early second- to mid-third-century Alexandrian theologian and scholar Origen is responsible for coining the term, which was originally in Greek.[5] This chapter, then, is an exposition of the "sacred reading" that came before Guigo II and even before Benedict, focusing heavily on (as has been the case throughout this book) the first four centuries of Christianity.[6]

In attempting to reconstruct what may be a Patristic exegetical methodology, the task to present any monolithic or harmonious *consensus patrum* with regard to Scripture, even if possible, may be counterproductive to the pluralities that decorated early Christian thought and that continue to characterize our time.[7] Such an endeavor is also beyond the scope of this chapter. Here, instead, I attempt to place the entire discussion of methodology—both modern and ancient—into the three stages of the model of Godward spiritual struggle. The first stage includes a detachment from one's own preconceptions with a willingness to be transformed by the text—that is, to read the text as sacred Scripture. This stage presupposes a Christocentric reading of Scripture that is wholistic and that humbly submits one's personal reading, or "private interpretation," to that of the community. One embarks on the second stage when the words of Scripture begin their embodiment in the "sacred reader." Typical of the second stage of Godward spiritual struggle, character formation and the acquisition of virtue ensue, in this particular case in a prayerful reading of Scripture. Finally, what has begun in the first two stages continues until unity with God perpetually reaches its fruition in a person who is entirely subsumed in the Word of God, putting on the "mind of Christ." Ultimately, the transformative power of Scripture remains largely untapped in methodological discourse, and tapping into this transformative depth will allow Scripture to become a good guide to a Christian ethics. Godward spiritual struggle applied to Scripture reading unveils this latent transformative power of Scripture and makes an appeal to the ethical model of this book.

THE FIRST STAGE: VULNERABILITY, CHRIST, AND COMMUNITY

In the first stage of sacred reading, the struggle entailed often seems to include hermeneutics qua methodology, but this is true only insofar as these exegetical suggestions extend from *spiritual* exegesis.[8] In this stage, detachment can take many forms, but three of the more relevant "methodological" incarnations of this detachment in relation to an ethics of Godward spiritual struggle are vulnerability, Christocentricity, and communal exegesis.

Vulnerability

Detachment begins with trust that what is being read is indeed Scripture.[9] To be formed by Scripture requires detachment from the idea that my own point of view is superior to those of all others, instead trusting in and being vulnerable to the text as the Word of God in the context of the Church community. One ought to approach the text as though it has something to offer beyond its immediate historicity and hermeneutical and textual analyses. Brian Brock puts it well when he writes, "Attempts to dismiss the Bible's moral relevance with the claim that its authors 'couldn't have known' about our moral dilemmas or conceptual distinctions are sure signs that the Bible has ceased to be Scripture for that interpreter, for whom some other text or group of texts has become Scripture, against which the Bible must now be justified."[10] The starting point to which Brock is referring is one of openness to the possibility of transformation, not seeking opportunity for textual interrogation.

A sacred reader approaches the text not with the intent to debunk its contents but with humility to learn from what it offers. To approach Scripture antagonistically is to be ready to dispose of any texts that appear contradictory on the surface or to lose faith in the inspiration of Scripture as a result of these apparent contradictions. Instead, as Patristic exegetes would have it, textual difficulties are opportunities for growth through struggling with the text to expose and access its hidden messages. At every turn, sacred reading requires struggle, which is inherent in the process of moral formation.

Scripture should function to form a person's thoughts *and* actions. Both are important in their own respects and should feed into each other; one's thoughts, opinions, beliefs, and worldviews should shape one's actions and ethics. In the same vein, attempts to unveil the ethics of Scripture through the Decalogue, the Sermon on the Mount, Pauline list-ethics, and other passages of clear ethical instruction fall into this stage. In fact, the majority of contemporary biblical and ethical scholarship falls into this category, in which the text is studied in order to unveil historical accuracies, to suggest models for direct application of a text or group of texts, or to develop themes from the text for their subsequent application. These attempts are not unwarranted; they are tremendously insightful. They are necessary yet insufficient on their own. It is in this first stage that many biblical ethicists have begun and ended their attempts to marry Scripture and contemporary ethics. To be sure, the further stages that will be suggested rely on this first stage, but it is in the latter two stages that sacred reading becomes a true ethics or ethos—that is, Scripture becomes an embodied and transformative way of life.

For example, in this stage, spiritual exegesis would include the use of allegory (and typology, as discussed in the next section) when engaging the text seriously and closely. Communally, Scripture is to be read, reread, and interpreted with a spiritual sense that looks not only to the immediate literal meaning of the text but also to ways in which God may be communicating a deeper reality—a "spiritual" reality, as the Fathers often refer to it. In this vein, John Breck writes,

> At the same time, it is evident that the literal sense in itself is incomplete. A further step in the hermeneutic process has to be taken, to translate the results of exegesis into a living and life-giving witness for people of today. Our study of the Bible, in other words, should lead us from the literal sense to the spiritual sense: from the original meaning of a passage to its significance as the Word of God for the salvation of those who receive it with faith. It is with this concern that I found myself moving from a purely historical-critical approach to the Bible to one based more specifically on the methods and insights of the ancient Church Fathers.[11]

Though there is debate as to the proper place of allegory in biblical hermeneutics, to read allegorically is not the same as reading imaginatively or phantasmally.[12] To read allegorically is to read spiritually, that is, with an aim to grow in knowledge of and intimacy with God.[13] Allegorical reading of Scripture is fundamentally an encounter with the text that is humble and vulnerable to the direction of the Author Himself. Scripture is to be engaged in its particularities, remembering that each word is deliberate and requires due attention. One is not to remain a distant reader of Scripture or follower of Scripture only through extracted themes and ideologies.

There can exist multiple layers and multiple spiritual senses, each underscoring truths that the author of the text is conveying. These different meanings are not different or opposing truths, but, according to John Breck, certain layers are fuller or higher senses of the truth. That Scripture is inundated with allegorical potential implies a requisite serious, struggle-laden, attentive study. The emphasis on vulnerability and an expectation of transformation should by no means interfere with the rigor of deep biblical study. Historically, Origen and the Alexandrian School he so clearly affected have been credited with propagating the allegorical approach to Scripture.[14] At first glance, it might seem that allegory should be discounted as "exegetical heresy" or "allegorical fantasy" in the face of modern, scholastic academia, because the former seems to bypass a post-Enlightenment emphasis on historicity.[15] Understanding the historical backdrop of any text is indispensable in accurately interpreting that text. Yet allegory urges the reader not to stop at that initial interpretation but to dig deeper and ask what might be meant by the text, not just what the text means. That is, a reader ought to take each word seriously, examining what the author of the text intends to communicate beyond what the text seems to immediately convey. Thus, it is not necessary that the literal be pinned up against the allegorical.

Modern readers who find the allegorical method of reading Scripture distasteful and unsophisticated might hold fundamentally disparate beliefs from those of premodern authors. The first might be that premodern readers *really* believed in God as Creator of all things, and in His Son, and that God is the author and inspirer of Scripture.[16] To believe that Scripture is inspired by the breath of God is to believe that there exists a message that promotes human flourishing universally and fundamentally, at a person's core, not just through intellectual consistency or historical accuracy.[17] A presupposed disbelief in God and His authorship often leaves a person with few options besides historical and literal readings of a text, and these ought to be recognized clearly when analyzing Patristic exegetical methodology.[18] The early Fathers are insistent that (literally) every sentence—in fact, every word—carries a profound, spiritual, and transformative message; allegory helps uncover this message. Allegorical reading requires a Christocentric orientation shrouded in humility. One must submit oneself to an encounter with the text, interpreting the text—even historically distant texts—in light of the incarnate, crucified, and risen Christ.[19] This is how, for example, Origen was able to interpret the Song of Songs as a spiritual relationship of love with God, not an erotic relationship between sensual lovers.[20] This exegetical suggestion does not encourage inaccurate readings by any means but a struggle for spiritual enlightenment, acquisition of virtue, and character formation, detailed in the following section. Through a Patristic lens, exegesis ought to be an encounter of the text in order to attune its reader to God's voice, to unite its reader with God, and to move its reader toward closer semblance of God, thereby transforming persons and communities, locally and globally.

Further, and in concert with the opening chapters of this book, this stage requires detachment from a post-Enlightenment approach to Scripture that often honors reason as the sole arbiter in the interpretation of Scripture.[21] One must detach from a notion that limits Scripture to a singular interpretation whose accuracy hinges only on an accurate understanding of the Bible's historicity.[22] This is not to denigrate the importance and possible preeminence of reason and historicity when reading Scripture, but it is a caution not to resist other modes of interpretation that are necessary for transformative readings of Scripture. Just as the reliance on the first stage of detachment from bodily passions was essential to reaching the further stages of asceticism, so too must a person detach from absolute self-trust when practicing sacred reading. There exists a temptation to limit Scripture to human reason that can potentially lead to the same conclusions as those reached had one never read Scripture at all. In a refusal to approach Scripture vulnerably, one will instead choose to overlay preconceived conclusions onto the text instead of allowing the text to reveal its embedded truths.

Christocentricity

The early Church Fathers saw Christ as the interpretive key to the entirety of Scripture's canon, which placed Christ at the center of all domains of life, as λόγος. "The notion that the church fathers were smug and complacent, using their doctrinal commitments to oppress open-minded and liberal adversaries, is a lamentable anachronism."[23] Scriptural and doctrinal commitments, instead, were a matter of adherence to the rule of faith lived out dynamically. Allowing Scripture to take a position of preeminence at the same time calls attention for doctrinal commitments that naturally develop therefrom. The Church Fathers wanted to achieve a total reading of the Bible by exposing the implications and depths behind every single word. They read intensively, looking out for any signs and clues amid the most minute of details and for contradictions—which, when resolved, would result in deeper understanding of the God of Scripture.

In asserting Christ to be the interpretive key of the whole corpus of Scripture, the early Church also relied heavily on its typological interpretation. Typology is a connection between Scriptural texts, not on the basis of particular images or words, but with larger, unifying patterns therein. Typology transcends the particularities of time and space, connecting characters to Christ, the "Master type" in which all other types, before and after, are fulfilled.[24] Any sense of participation between the reader and Jesus Christ requires typology, thereby rendering Christ's actions authoritative. Moreover, to understand the Old Testament readings in light of Christ is to read typologically—or, as Bogdan Bucur would suggest, as "Christophanic exegesis."[25] Without typology, few connections, and thus little sense, can be made intrabiblically.

Allen Verhey maintains that approaching Scripture as a whole is a methodological necessity.[26] It is what Frank Matera's popular twentieth-century work refers to as a synchronic method of reading Scripture as a unity.[27] One risk of not employing a holistic reading of Scripture is that of proof-texting—a problem noted by many biblical scholars and ethicists alike.[28] It is likely that if a holistic interpretative method is not employed, the method of proof-texting will be utilized to some degree—that is, portions of texts and conclusions abstracted from singular events will be taken in isolation from other related parts of Scripture and from the context within which they are found. This, then, naturally leads to a circular logical deduction, in which preconceived ideas seek out support from Scriptural texts, which in turn support and intensify the initial claim. Instead, a holistic interpretation allows for a genuine approach, at least in terms of intent or presumptuousness, to the reality within the biblical canon. This method, which is less susceptible to proof-texting, promises more fruitful results in extracting ethical instruction from Scripture.

Moreover, using a hermeneutic different from a holistic approach risks misconstruing the meaning of one pericope as a result of neglecting other pericopes. This problem is more subtle and has more cumbersome consequences than what first glance offers. Similar to proof-texting, neglecting parts of Scripture, even those not clearly or directly related, is the root cause of the insufficiency of any biblical method that does not employ a holistic hermeneutic. If a part of Scripture is segregated from the whole, it is easy to overemphasize the importance of that segregated portion. The disproportionate focus given isolated texts creates a sort of literalism by providing more (and in some cases less) meaning to those isolated words than would normally be attributed. The words of Scripture can be viewed, in a sense, as a human network. Humans become who they are as a result of their interactions, whether it be with other humans, nature, the environment, and so on. Isolating a human being from the interactions that constitute the very fiber of his or her being is not appreciating the person for her or his true self or complexity.

To read Scripture Christocentrically, for and in another, detached from the service of one's own polemical agenda, is at the same time to read it holistically, and this is meant on at least two levels. First, what is meant by wholeness is that the Old and New Testaments are to be taken as a united canon. The Scriptural canon was formed against a false theology that saw a dualism between the Old Testament and the New Testament.[29] It is not uncommon to promote this false dichotomy today by emphasizing the importance of one testament to the neglect of the other or by imagining a tyrannical Old Testament God in contradistinction to a beneficent New Testament God. The latter, instead, is unlocked by the former and is insufficient and incoherent on its own.[30] The opposite—that the Old Testament can only be fully understood in light of the New Testament—holds true for Christians, an assertion that is not without its complications in the face of the Old Testament's historical and contextual particularities.

However, part of a premodern, Patristic approach to Scripture was understanding Jesus Christ Himself as the interpretive key to the entire canon, which was still solidifying in the early Church. The Church Fathers, as John O'Keefe and Russell Reno point out, saw a coherence in the Bible that was the "Christ-centered unity of Scripture."[31] According to Ignatius of Antioch, Christ is the "archives" (ἀρχεῖά),[32] the "original documents."[33] According to Irenaeus, it is the economy of the Son of God—Jesus Christ—that provides the logic (λόγος) and framework through which Scripture should be interpreted.[34] In this way, the Old Testament cannot be interpreted outside the logic of Christ applied to the text. To put it another way, to understand Genesis's "In the beginning" (ἐν ἀρχῇ), one must first understand John's "In the beginning was the Word" (ἐν ἀρχῇ ἦν ὁ λόγος) not as supercessionism but as a key feature of ancient *Christian* hermeneutic.

The second sense of the wholeness of Scripture is that Scripture unlocks Scripture. An obscure pericope is elucidated by another less-obscure pericope, elucidating both (or several) portions concomitantly. In this sense, one text cannot be understood apart from the rest of the cohesive canon. This is not only to say that the Old and New Testaments cannot be separated, but that inner biblical exegesis, even within the same testament, is necessary for an accurate and transformative reading of Scripture. This intertextuality, for someone like Origen—a third-century scholar whose influence on the Patristic corpus cannot be overstated—could be summed up aphoristically: "Scripture unlocks Scripture."[35] John Breck labels this intertextuality as a Patristic exegetical method: "Scripture, according to the patristic vision, is uniformly and integrally inspired by the Holy Spirit. Therefore, it can be interpreted according to the rule of exegetical reciprocity. This holds that any obscure biblical passage can be interpreted in light of another biblical passage which is clearer, irrespective of the author, date of composition or historical circumstances represented by the writing(s) in question."[36] He goes on to cite Saint John Chrysostom's homily on Romans 16:3, in which he identifies partial readings of Scripture—that is, proof-texting—as a reason for the weakening of faith: "This is why we have become so tepid in our faith: we no longer read the Scriptures as a whole. Rather, we select certain passages as being more clear and useful, and we say not a word about the rest. This is just how heresies are introduced: we have refused to read the entire Bible; we have declared certain parts to be essential and others secondary."[37]

Brian Brock articulates a concept similar to that of Origen. He writes, "Christian biblical exegesis as meditation on Scripture is grounded in learning the unique connections between passages of Scripture, thereby discovering the biblical topography."[38] He continues by making a loose reference to premodern biblical exegesis that would not exclude Patristic methods: "Until the intervention of modern concepts of reading, biblical interpretation was defined as a very particular facility of enriching the understanding of a given passage by making connections, and quite often novel connections, with other passages in a way that brings added theological density and explanatory power to both."[39]

The use of metaphors in Scripture informs our understanding of God. Scripture offers many metaphors to describe God. Metaphors such as Shepherd, Eagle, Rock, Fire, Mother Hen, Groom, Lover, Friend, and others all aim to name characteristics and experiences of God.[40] Each description pushes against the other, adjusting and adding to the insufficiency of each. No single metaphor offers a comprehensive understanding of God, and the paradigmatic assimilation of one will necessarily be detrimental because all metaphors must work in congruence if the most satisfactory, accurate description is to be attained. But if one of the metaphors is missing, a less accurate depiction will be deduced, and the center to which all these metaphors *should* point will be unsatisfactorily shifted. Despite the inability to ever describe God in a comprehensive manner, this analogy helps communicate the limitations that result from an incomplete knowledge and use of Scripture. Each piece of Scripture pushes and adjusts all other related pieces to pinpoint clearer images. The more a portion of Scripture is held in isolation, the less faithful the interpretation and the less apt the moral implications deduced.

Communal Exegesis

Similar to the discussion in chapter 2 of the communal nature of spiritual struggle, the emphasis on communal reading was a mark of Patristic exegesis. Accurate and transformative biblical interpretation is incumbent on the practice of reading within community.[41] To let one's guard down and allow oneself to be guided and formed without inhibition requires trust in the guidance of others within the community of the Church. Interpretation is accomplished only in and through the discourse of the Church, the place for communication, implementation, correction, and service. One's own individual "righteousness" must never be seen as separate or distinct from the larger Christian community. This ethics is one that "aims to situate individual moral agency within a community of formation," despite what may seem to be an attention to personal spiritual struggle.[42]

It would be unthinkable for a Church father to agree that Scripture can be properly interpreted by a person outside the Body of Christ, the Church. Origen, for example, writes, "Foreigners may not [approach certain teachings] unless they have already been enrolled in the Church of the Lord."[43] That is, a person outside the Church may not have the same ability as those within the Church, implying that there exists an inherently communal and Spirit-filled dimension of biblical interpretation. Similarly, Irenaeus, the second-century bishop and martyr, in his treatise *Against Heresies,* is clear regarding the interpretation of Scripture as one ecclesial body of Christ: "We need to view with suspicion those who turn from the primitive succession and assemble themselves together elsewhere," outside the Apostolic Church, perverting matters of truth.[44] He goes on to use much stronger language than claiming that their only error is in misinterpreting Scripture, but the point stands that it is only within the Church assembly that the truth of Scripture is to be interpreted. "The Church treasures such presbyters," he writes, "and they expound the Scriptures to us without danger, neither blaspheming God, nor dishonoring the patriarchs, nor despising the prophets."[45] The nourishing Church forms those who are able to interpret well, who at the same time honor a tradition that recognizes as good guides those sanctified in God.

The Church, in turn, is graced with the gift of interpretation through the Holy Spirit. Origen makes this point when interpreting Leviticus 7:9: "Rather, [let it be] according to the spiritual sense (*spiritalem sensum*), which the Spirit gives to the Church."[46] It is the careful cultivation of this "spiritual sense" (αἴσθησις πνευματική) that is at the heart of transformative exegesis, not the technical application of exegetical strategies, be it allegory, typology, or otherwise. For Origen, the Holy Spirit that aids the community of believers in acquiring the spiritual sense of Scripture at the same time gives the priests the flesh of Christ—the word of God: "The flesh, set aside for the priests of the sacrifices, is the word of God that they teach in the Church."[47] The flesh of Christ in the Eucharist is the locus for early biblical interpretation and dissemination in the early Church. Justin Martyr, a second-century apologist and martyr, provides an early example of the communal nature of reading and hearing Scripture communally in the Eucharistic assembly: "On the so-called 'Day of the Sun,' there is an assembly of all who live in the towns or country, and the Memoirs of the Apostles or the writings of the prophets are read, as long as time permits. When the Reader (ἀναγινώσκοντος[48]) has finished, the presider speaks, admonishing and urging us to imitate these fine examples."[49] The liturgy was the place for Christians to gather, read, and be attentive to the word of God communally, expositing homiletically the riches therein. The Church understood its task as one of embodiment, not mere recitation. The presider's—that is, the bishop's—exhortation and admonition were for the imitation and realization of the words of Scripture by the entire Christian community.

The focus on community becomes especially important when discussing the proper use of Scripture for ethics contemporarily, and many scholars have recovered this realization today. First, interpretation within a larger community ensures a dynamic, ongoing process of interpretation that is embodied, checked, and corrected in that order and in constant cycle. Allen Verhey characterizes the early Church as primarily a place of moral discourse, where personal responsibility was exercised within community:[50] "Judgments rest not so much on an exegetical demonstration as they do on the experience of the authority of Scripture in the context of one's own moral struggles, on one hand, and the believing community and its moral tradition, on the other."[51] In these communities, questions of morality were discussed based on their coherence with the Gospel of Jesus Christ, not on philosophical principles or ethical checklists.[52] Paul Jersild agrees that contemporary Christians ought to practice a similar model of ethical deliberation when reading Scripture: "My conclusion is that the ethical authority of Scripture is expressed with an ongoing process of dialogue and conversation by the community of believers among themselves and with their Scripture and tradition."[53] Such a community shares a common identity constituted by a collective past that lives in them.[54]

Richard Hays does raise an important objection to the communal approach to reading Scripture for ethics: there is no way, according to Hays, to challenge or correct a community's interpretation.[55] However, Hays may be overstating this problem, because there will always exist multiple communities that, when in dialogue, will influence, correct, and challenge each other. Moreover, it is not necessarily true that "unbiased" readings of the text are the most accurate. I do not mean that any interpretation by a community must be correct, but just because an interpretation is made by a community does not mean it has to be checked by some external standard in order to be verified. The verification of an interpretation is accomplished by the incarnation and subsequent impact of the interpretation. In fact, there can be no unbiased reading of a text, even if one intended to perform such a reading. Similarly, the canon is not an unbiased group of texts. It is a deliberate system that came to exist for a reason, as an attestation to the Gospel of Christ and a witness to His resurrection. It has been formative and continues to be formative for a group of people who understand themselves as following through the Holy Spirit the crucified and risen Christ of the Father. In this light, priority in interpretation should be necessarily within this community and with this community's "biases" or predilections.

The emphasis on community in Scriptural interpretation also aids in the hermeneutical problem, which maintains that glaring differences between contemporary culture and those of biblical times are too large a gap to bridge. Instead, as Fowl and Jones note in concert with David Tracy's "analogical imagination," the task of reading in community should be an analogical and dialectic effort of remaining faithful to the God of Scripture.[56] The problem is not only a lack of accurate biblical interpretation, nor is the problem that our time is drastically different from the first centuries (though it is). The problem, instead, is that Christians do not always embody Scripture faithfully in community.[57]

In communities guided by the Holy Spirit, Christians are to undergo an "ongoing process of being formed and transformed through friendships and practices of Christian communities."[58] In this way, they are to manifest the character of the Triune God, which in turn will ripple into the surrounding communities, leading to further transformation. To have this effect requires a keen sense of one's own surrounding communities.[59] Thus, the Christian community must be inherently dialogical. James Gustafson makes the bold claim that the Christian community should determine what God's will for humanity is and make moral judgments in light of this.[60] This transformative power is the primary purpose of Scripture for Stanley Hauerwas, who spurred the contemporary, virtue ethical focus on Christian community. The narrative of Scripture "does nothing less than render the character of God and in so doing renders us to be the kind of people appropriate to that character."[61] Scripture does not describe our world but transforms it through Scripturally shaped communities.[62]

THE SECOND STAGE: EMBODIMENT, PRAYER, AND VIRTUE

In the second stage, a person is thoroughly nourished by the words of Scripture. Sacred reading becomes an essential component of one's daily life and serves to shape one's worldview. It becomes a haven of solace and refreshment. Scripture thus affects its reader at a deeper level, shaping them as a person grounded in and accountable to the words of Divine revelation. The interpretive key in this revelation, as noted above, is Christ, whose self-sacrificing love calls a person to love God and neighbor. Though love is the central command of Christian life, the practice of sacred reading and its formative effects are not reducible to love. Instead, the whole of Scripture (trans)forms a sincere and persistent reader, inculcating virtues like justice, mercy, peace, wisdom, and patience, among others. Furthermore, formation through sacred reading entails more than the development of virtues. Sacred reading shapes one in a worldview that is depicted through stories, actions, characters, and ways of life that feature diverse practices and experiences such as asceticism, feasting, dedications, punishments, and rewards. Scripture contains a breadth of transformative power that is able to reach different persons at different times in different places with different experiences and in different ways, and yet all toward the same goal of union with God. Scripture is unity in diversity. There is a singularity of focus on God as revealed in the Lord Jesus Christ and at the same time a diversity within Scripture that can have an impact on all contexts of life.

Prayerful Embodiment of Scripture

There are, however, certain key characteristics of this second stage worth mentioning explicitly. First, the labor and struggle that is a marker of the first stage continues in the second stage. Stephanie Paulsell highlights reading and studying Scripture as an essential and often untapped ancient spiritual practice: "A long history of reading, writing, learning and teaching as a set of spiritual practices in Christianity lies unremarked upon when it might be recovered and reinvigorated for our own day."[63] She explains that she saw this practice transform her father, who would read six psalms a day as an integral part of his vocation. This work is active and affects "a slow shift of our attachments, a painstaking education of desire," to borrow Tracy's language.[64] This reading is not only an expression of a love for God but also for neighbor, because reading may not be a priority for many of those we encounter every day. Sacred readers are to become carriers of the Gospel message of God, both in word and in action. The spiritual struggle of sacred reading is a perpetual labor of love for which there is no end: "We can swim and swim in the deep pool of Christian faith and never sound the bottom. That mystery, that struggle, belongs to all of us. It is the heart of our life work."[65]

The detachment one achieves by God's grace and through spiritual struggle in the first stage of Godward spiritual struggle enables an approach to Scripture that is less encumbered by preconceptions. When one is detached from the materialistic pleasures of the world, that person should have fewer motives and agendas when reading Scripture. Instead, such a person, to the extent that she is purified of worldly desires, is able not only to be vulnerable to Scripture but also to be attuned to the voice of God in the text. Of the most ancient Christian prayers, still used frequently in all Orthodox churches, is the prayer to the Holy Spirit: "O Heavenly King, comforter, the Spirit of truth, who is present in all places and fills all, the treasury of good, and the life-giver, graciously come, dwell in us, and purify us from all sin, O Good One, and save our souls."[66] It is the Holy Spirit who purifies, and the sacred reader is understood to be more sensitive to the Holy Spirit who guides to the truth. In fact, the *Shepherd of Hermas* mentioned in chapter 4 admits that the more a person is pure, the more spacious of an abode that person becomes for the indwelling of God.[67] Without any emphasis on which comes first, the purer a person becomes, the more that person is able to embody Scripture; and the more Scripture is embodied, the more one is able to pursue deeper purity.

Embodiment of Scripture is critical to the second stage of sacred reading. Sacred reading is not simply an intellectual exercise enacted on an inert text. There exists no Scriptural corpus that is meant to be studied without being lived. If from the first stage a person learns to trust in Scripture as more than a historical text, in the second stage the words are to become life. Scripture is to be brought into one's own context through one's own living expression of the words. This is what Richard Hays calls the pragmatic task of Scriptural interpretation—"embodying Scripture's imperatives in the life of the Christian community."[68] When Scripture is read utilizing all the suggestions mentioned in this chapter—vulnerably, allegorically, Christocentrically, holistically, typologically, in community, and with a focus on character formation—a person brings to life the word of God to those she encounters. The hermeneutical problem is no longer a problem of interpretation but a matter of embodiment. The more Scripture is embodied and lived out in one's context, the more one's interpretation of Scripture becomes illuminated. The more a person is illuminated, the more that person is able to embody Scripture, and so on.

This embodiment of the text is also contingent on reading Scripture *prayerfully*. Allen Verhey describes prayer as a performance of Scripture. It teaches a person humility, gratitude, and hope. Moreover, it serves as invocation, metanoia (repentance, transformation of mind), confession, thanksgiving, and petition.[69] This prayer is twofold: one prays for the ability to read, interpret, and embody Scripture; but one also prays Scripture itself. The words, stories, struggle, commands, and petitions found in Scripture can be offered up as prayer. Praying engages the creativity given to humanity and functions as a means by which to enter into the very history that forms Christian identity. To sing the praises of Moses and the Israelites is to enter into the triumph of victory that a Christian experiences over sin and the evils and injustices of the present world. To ask for the boldness of Abraham amid a difficult trial in life is to participate in a transformation from faith to greater faith. To meditatively pray psalms can encompass the breadth of all human experience.[70] To join the father of a demon-possessed child in his moment of honesty and submission, pleading, "Lord, I believe; help my unbelief!" is to begin a similar journey of honesty, sincerity, and submission to the God who heals from all spiritual and physical infirmities. The examples are endless. What is clear is that prayer is central to the transformative reading of Scripture, so much so that Brian Brock describes prayer as the only constant in the process of reading Scripture.[71] Amid so many different suggestions on how Scripture is to be read, to read Scripture prayerfully is to already understand the transformative nature of the words that are not mere text but are the same breath of God that forms and sustains human life. In a word, prayerfully embodying the words of Scripture moves the reader along a spiritual ascent whose effects are the acquisition of virtue and the formation of character.

Virtuous Reading

The strengthening of the soul in the second stage of sacred reading is manifested by reading Scripture virtuously—that is, as a virtuous person *and* for the acquisition of virtue. In attempting for the past four or five decades to reconnect Scripture and ethics in the modern world, scholars have not always turned to virtue ethics as the most obvious solution. As William Mattison points out, "It is even assumed that a virtue-centered approach to morality is actually non-scriptural."[72] Yet virtue ethicists like Mattison put forward convincing cases for the appropriateness of approaching Scripture with a focus on character formation. One of the significant and recent interventions in the field of biblical ethics is Lucas Chan's *Biblical Ethics in the 21st Century*, in which he offers a hermeneutical proposal for Scripture grounded in virtue ethics. He identifies virtue language in Scripture, signaling four fundamental dimensions of virtue ethics: dispositions and character formation; practices and habits; exemplars; and community and community identity.[73] The first and fourth of these dimensions are especially helpful in illuminating aspects of the overarching, though covert, consensus found in scholarship on Scripture and ethics.

Character formation and the centrality of community have been pivotal in the practice of sacred reading since Christianity's inception, and they have recently begun their slow reemergence into a more prominent contemporary light. The character formation detailed in this section, however, does not focus on virtue theory generally or various virtues specifically as laid out in Scripture, though these are edifying endeavors on their own. Instead, when Scripture is read with attention to and desire for moral formation, the practice becomes innately transformative. Chan notes that Christ and conformity to Him are the ends (τέλοι) in the teleological, grace-filled process of sanctification.[74] This process is similar to, though more general than, the schematics of Saint Gregory of Nyssa's *epektatic* and anagogic process.

At this point, however, the importance of sanctification is reflected in its necessity for a "good," wise, or virtuous reading of Scripture. For many Church Fathers, the virtue par excellence that promoted a wise reading of Scripture was the pursuit of purity grounded in spiritual struggle. The interpretation of Scripture for many of the Fathers required focused exertion to reach a level of sanctified vision whereby one would think in and through the Scriptures. Not only did they know the Scriptures inside and out, but they also maintained that a certain way of life was requisite for properly interpreting the Scriptures. Even with all these strategies in place, purity held potentially the place of highest prominence in the practice of sacred reading.[75]

Gregory of Nazianzus, one of the three heralded fourth-century Cappadocians (along with Gregory of Nyssa and Basil), held that a pure mind was necessary to understand the pure matters of Scripture. Because Scripture is pivotal in discerning theological matters, regarding the discussion of theology, he writes: "It is not for all people, but only for those who have been tested and have found a sound footing in study, and, more importantly, have undergone, or at the very least are undergoing, purification of body and soul (ψυχήν καὶ σῶμα κεκαθαρμένων). For one who is not pure (καθαρῷ) to lay hold of pure (καθαροῦ) things is dangerous, just as it is for weak eyes to look at the sun's brightness."[76] Thus, it is "dangerous" for the impure to study what is pure. Purity and exegetical prowess are positively correlated. Without the virtue of purity, one could rely only on intellect and conjecture, each important in its own right, yet at the risk of rendering a plethora of opinions and hermeneutical impasses—a reality not uncommon today.

Basil similarly highlights the necessity of "cleansing the eye of the soul" when reading Scripture. He writes, "Just as the power of seeing is in the healthy eye, so is the activity of the Spirit in the purified soul" (Καὶ ὡς ἡ δύναμις τοῦ ὁρᾷν ἐν τῷ ὑγιαίνοντι ὀφθαλμῷ, οὕτως ἡ ἐνέργεια τοῦ Πνεύματος ἐντῇ κεκαθαρμένῃ ψυχῇ).[77] The Spirit, that is, the presumed Author of Scripture, is enlivened in the person who has a purified soul. That person is more apt for Scriptural interpretation, not at the neglect of, but in combination with, other necessary hermeneutical tools. Purity is a virtue inculcated through the Holy Spirit, who purifies all creation. Through this unitive harmony, a person pursues a transformative interpretation of Scripture, not passively but through a sort of moral asceticism. In fact, Origen believed that the very difficulty of interpreting the Scriptures points a reader toward the need for this moral asceticism exegetically. He writes, "The aim of the Spirit . . . was pre-eminently concerned with the unspeakable mysteries [ἀπορρήτων μυστηρίων] regarding the affairs of human beings, . . . in order that one who is capable of being taught may, by *searching out* and devoting himself *to the deep things* of the sense of the words, become a participant in all the doctrines [δογμάτων] of the Spirit's counsel."[78] Origen continues by describing sacred reading as an intentionally laborious task that requires attentive harmony with God. Scripture cannot be interpreted superficially; but one must struggle with the text wholeheartedly.[79] He continues, "The Word of God has arranged that certain *stumbling blocks*, as it were, and *obstacles and impossibilities* be inserted into the midst of the Law and the narrative, in order that we may not be drawn away completely by the sheer attractiveness of the language and so we either completely reject the teachings, learning nothing worthy of God, or, not moving away from the letter, we learn nothing more divine."[80]

O'Keefe and Reno make a similar observation about Origen's commentary on Scriptural methodology, writing: "Divine wisdom, he [Origen] argues, has made the Scriptures difficult to interpret for the same reason that the world is set up according to an ascetic logic—so that the project of interpretation might be a properly disciplining exercise of every fiber of the reader's being."[81] Reading is in fact an arduous task so that the reader may enter into a transformative practice, suffering "the dry desserts of incomprehension as so many days of interpretive fasting. Thus disciplined by the body of Scripture, our vision is sanctified and prepared for us to enter into the narrow footpath."[82] Virtue, in this way, serves both as a prerequisite for and a consequence of sacred reading. The ability to read well relies significantly on inculcated virtue, and yet, to be purified in unity with the Holy Spirit serves to further inculcate virtue in that person.

Fowl and Jones are aware of this reality in their work on Scripture and ethics. They maintain that ethical formation both precedes *and* follows Scriptural reading.[83] Interpreting Scripture, according to them, "involves a lifelong process of learning to become a wise reader of Scripture, who is capable of embodying that reading in life."[84] Moreover, sin undermines a person's ability to read Scripture well.[85] At the same time, sacred reading requires other virtues, including humility and practical wisdom. Verhey agrees that there exists an intimate relationship between reading Scripture and the moral life and adds to humility and discernment the virtues of holiness, sanctification, fidelity, creativity, and discipline.[86]

Surely, it would be difficult to assess each person's level of purity or virtuousness in order to determine if any person's interpretation is better than another's, but this would be to miss the point. The emphasis on a virtuous reading of Scripture is a matter of assimilation to God—the τέλος of this "ethical" proposal. When a person becomes united to God through similitude in virtue and open to Him through purification of the soul, that person is more sensitive to and more able to discern the voice of God. This experience is not far from that between a husband and a wife, who better understand each other's words—expressions, tones, tendencies, and the like—the more they grow in unison. At the same time, there is not necessarily an interpretive manual that can provide all the "answers" or interpretations. Just as my intimate relationship with my wife is necessary for me to understand her, so is intimacy with God through assimilation to Him in the virtue of purity necessary to understand His words. For this reason, though there are interpretations outside the bounds of a good reading of Scripture, there is no final interpretation within Scripture's multivalency—one that is bolstered by the allegorical and typological methods noted above, found in Patristic exegeses. Yet at this point, it is clear that sacred reading is transformative both as a process that requires virtue in order to be done well and as a process that itself provides this transformative acquisition of virtue.

THE THIRD STAGE: FULL IMMERSION AND A NEW CREATION

The third stage of Godward spiritual struggle is summarized in this project as union with God. When applied to sacred reading, this stage includes those who have not only seriously grappled with Scripture vulnerably, Christocentrically, and communally (first stage), nor those who have only embodied its words in purity, prayer, and virtue (second stage), but also those who become subsumed in the words of Scripture. In this stage, a person references the words of God constantly, either directly or indirectly, through association or application. Such people cannot help but view the world through a lens crafted by a comprehensive, sincere, and faithful reading of Scripture, exuding a calmness and fortitude that results from their intimacy with the λόγος. They have "put on the mind of Christ" and breathe the breath of God, that is, His inspired words. In a synergy of divine grace and years of close, frequent reading, meditative nights, prayerful days, embodiment, vulnerability, transformation, and struggling for worldly detachment and inner purity, a person makes progress toward this dynamic state.

Jesus Christ Himself is the example of this state par excellence. When tempted by the adversary, He replies with Scripture at every turn. As λόγος, His very words are the Gospel and "the law and the prophets," in the unitive sense detailed above.[87] He quotes the book of Deuteronomy three times, overcoming Satan with the power of the words that flow from who He is: "One does not live by bread alone, but by every word that comes from the mouth of God."[88] Food alone sustains the body, but the word of God sustains the soul, and how powerful it is to encounter one whose soul is sustained by the word of God! Interestingly, Satan himself twisted the words of Scripture to tempt Christ and further his own cause, yet his misuse of Scripture supports the thesis presented here in the three stages. It would be anachronistic to convict Satan of proof-texting, but there remains a fundamental difference between mere knowledge of Scripture and entering into a transformative relationship with Scripture. The former remains solely cerebral, often encouraging a posture of defense, antagonism, and skepticism. The latter, in contrast, requires all the steps mentioned above. To read Scripture without these necessary steps is to misread or to intentionally misconstrue Scripture, as did Satan. To play on a passage in James 2:19, even the demons *read*! Reading alone does not grant access to the transformative power latent in Scripture.

A good example is Saint Antony the Great, the father of Christian monasticism, whose transformational relationship with Scripture affected generations of Christians until this day. From the very beginning of his journey, Antony allowed himself to be transformed by the word of God. He immediately surrendered his livelihood upon hearing the command in Matthew 19:21 to be perfect by selling all possessions, giving them to the poor, and following Christ, thereafter committing himself to the Scriptures. Saint Athanasius offers a glimpse of Saint Antony's intimacy with Scripture: "He was so attentive to [Scripture] reading that he lost nothing [of what he read]; he retained them all, and so his memory took the place of books."[89] His memory of Scripture was so sharp that when monks would visit him for advice, it would be difficult to decipher his own words from those of Scripture.

To this point, Mary Jane Kreidler writes that "in his short admonition, Antony quotes Scripture no less than fifty-nine times" from memory, stating that Scripture is sufficient for the monk's instruction.[90] Similarly, though a lesser feat than Antony's, monks would eventually build habits of memorizing the Psalter—a practice that would propagate, especially among monastics, for dozens of centuries.[91] Interestingly and similar to the example of Christ, Antony describes hearing demons "oftentimes pretend to chant Psalms without appearing, and to recite passages from Scripture, . . . repeating over and again, as though echoing, what has been read."[92] This misuse of Scripture by the demons again serves to emphasize the importance of sacred reading as a means by which not only to prevent Scripture's debased misuse but also to tap into its ultimate transformative power—intimacy and unity with God. The life and works of Saint Antony attest to the power of this transformation to the extent that his body, and not just his soul, was markedly affected, despite his austere asceticism. He was described as a man of beauty, calmness, grace, virtue, and strength of soul *and* body, even until his death at the age of 105.[93]

This third stage of sacred reading is not an unattainable one. I have encountered few that live out this entrenchment in Scripture, evidenced by the transformed life they live and significant impact they have. One such example is that of Father Tadros Yacoub Malaty, an ascetical, married Coptic Orthodox priest who has written extensive commentaries on every single book of the Bible, not leaving a work unanalyzed. His commentaries are full of meditative, prayerful analyses, Patristic commentaries, typology, Christocentricity, historicity, and spiritual allegory. More than this, it is in meeting Father Tadros that one senses the effect Scripture has had on this man of God. His words are seasoned with Scripture, and the peace in his eyes is evidence of his Godward fixation. His very countenance exudes peace and love, despite his old age and weakening body. My purpose here is not necessarily to sing this man's praise but to speak to the accessibility generally of this proposed ethical model and specifically in its application to any component of the Christian life, in this case to Scripture.

I am not alone in singing the praises of other blessed men and women whose illumination transformed those around them. The late Pope Kyrillos VI and the late Pope Shenouda III, 116th and 117th patriarchs of the Alexandrian See of Saint Mark, were pivotal to the modern revival of Coptic Christianity in Egypt and other parts of the world. The former was and is known as a worker of miracles and a man of prayer. A man of few words, he is said to have been one of the few contemporary saints to memorize Scripture in its entirety and to practice those words faithfully.[94] In the same vein, Pope Shenouda III displayed a similar devotion to Scripture, evidenced by an astounding number of sermons, poems, and books, including more than

300 pages commentating on the Song of Songs alone. The late Bishop Athanasius, the Coptic bishop of the region named Bani Mazar whose face always shone, and the luminous "Mama Maggie," lauded as the "modern Coptic Mother Teresa," are also fine examples of the way one can and should allow the power of Scripture to change all that is in and around oneself. These are the same types of men and women I have in mind when describing unity with God. To say that they are united with God is not to exclaim perfection or infallibility but to witness to the obvious connection they possess with God and the transformation that ensues when divine holiness penetrates materiality, evidenced by their luminous, unencumbered, and peaceful lives that had a social, spiritual, and communal impact.

CONCLUSION

In this chapter, I hope to have demonstrated another practical, concrete instantiation of an ethics of Godward spiritual struggle, especially to dispel any coincidental overlaps between asceticism and spiritual struggle and to demonstrate how the transformative power of sacred reading remains largely untapped without consideration to this ethical model. The first stage consisted of vulnerability, allegory, Christocentricity, and typology. This stage includes, but does not end with, the majority of modern scholarship that aids in better understanding Scripture historically and intellectually. In this first stage, however, the reader is urged to go beyond the academic rigor of studying Scripture to a relationship with Scripture as the word of God able to generate transformation. The second stage consists of a prayerful, pure, and virtuous embodiment of Scripture. In this stage, a person by God's grace struggles for inner purity in order to open oneself up for further and deeper interpretation. As a stage of prayerful, meditative, and struggle-laden reading, the more a person embodies God's word, the more that person is able to comprehend.

The final stage of sacred reading is complete submersion into God's word to an extent that a person cannot envision her thoughts or actions apart from their formation in and through Scripture. In this stage, Scripture is not only reserved in one's memory but causes a person to exude an illumination that cannot be denied. Though transformation by God's work has no end or bounds, a person in this stage is rendered a new creation, undeniably different than she was before engaging so wholeheartedly with Scripture; that which is fallen in humanity is en route to the fullness of transformation in the resurrected Christ. In all these stages, one's struggle must be persistent and within the community of Christ's Body, which keeps a person from being self-deceived, prevents gross misinterpretation or implementation, and ensures humility and love in sacred reading. Within these three stages, it would be difficult to imagine what Scripture or ethics each would look like without the other. Though these stages did at times require a person to focus specifically on the acquisition of virtue, the purpose was always the pursuit of God. It is for and from this pursuit that virtue is acquired. That is, virtue is required in order to make progress, and making progress renders greater virtue. In these ways, to place Scripture within an ethics of Godward spiritual struggle is to reintegrate Scripture and ethics for the contemporary Christian and to reorient a person to God and others through a transformative practice that taps into the hidden depths of God's word.

NOTES

Epigraph: Behr, *Origen*.

1. Pope Paul VI, *Decree on Priestly Training*.
2. Paintner, *Lectio Divina*, 3–5.
3. Jones, *Divine Intervention*, 57–91.
4. Jones, 50.
5. Paintner and Wynkoop, *Lectio Divina*, 2.
6. For a good discussion of the relationship between East and West regarding *lectio divina*, see Breck, *Scripture in Tradition*, 67–86.
7. I do not mean that the plurality of Christian reality in the modern world is similar to that in the ancient world. In fact, I praise the latter and denounce the former. The ancient pluralism to which I am referring is that which existed within the bounds of the one Christian Church. An example of this pluralism would be a variety of interpretations on a given Scriptural parable through use of allegorical exegesis. However, when pluralism is discussed contemporarily, it usually implies a difference of fundamental faith and doctrine. While I am not overlooking this glaring difference, my only point is that because neither era can be characterized as entirely monolithic, presenting a monolithic Patristic voice would not only be inaccurate but counterproductive. Further, regarding the notion of a *consensus patrum*, this article falls in Hilarion Alfeyev's camp when he writes: "How is the so-called *consensus patrum*, the 'accord of the Fathers,' to be understood? This concept, borrowed from Western theology, is questionable. Some understand the *consensus partum* as a kind of 'theological summa' or 'common denominator' of patristic thought produced by cutting away the individual traits of every author. Others consider that the 'accord of the Fathers' presupposes their consent on essential matters, with possible disagreement on isolated issues. Personally, I support the second point of view. I believe, as I have said on other occasions, that the many private opinions of the fathers, the fruits of the spiritual quest of men of faith illuminated by God, may not be artificially pruned in order to produce some simplified theological system or 'summa.'" Alfeyev, "Patristic Heritage." Hans Boersma agrees that though distinctions certainly exist between the

fathers and different patristic schools of thought, there still exist shared sensibilities. See Boersma, *Scripture as Real Presence*, 13.

8. Olga Solovieva describes Gregory of Nyssa's "spiritual exegesis" as an "ascetical performance," linking together many of the concepts presented in this book. See Solovieva, "Spiritual Exegesis."
9. The distinction between "Bible" and Scripture" is made by Fowl and Jones, "Scripture, Exegesis, and Discernment," 112, 119. To approach the text as Scripture is to elevate the status of the text from only a historical document to a faith document of potential, and even likely, transformative power.
10. Brock, *Singing the Ethos of God*, 247.
11. Breck, *Scripture in Tradition*, xi.
12. A great deal of effort has been made by modern scholars in determining whether the contemporary use of typology and allegory are accurate representations of the way the church fathers, especially Clement of Alexandria and Origen, used these same terms (τύπος and ἀλληγορία). I tend to agree with the Theological Interpretation of Scripture movement on its conceptual premises but not in its collapsing the distinction between typology and allegory into the category of "figural," upheld by some in this loosely defined movement. David Dawson uses "figural" and "figurative," though this use has not become standardized. See Dawson, *Christian Figural Reading*; and Ayres, *Nicaea and Its Legacy*, 34–38. The modern distinctions between typology and allegory are useful, though not entirely concordant with their ancient analogues. These contemporary debates are in response to Jean Daniélou's influential and overemphasized delineation between typology and allegory. Peter W. Martens identified a broad consensus among scholars concluding that most understand typology as a better (successful and proper) nonliteral exegetical methodology than allegory, while for Origen allegory is in contradistinction to literal exegesis. One might also choose to adopt Bogdan Bucur's helpful language of Christophanic exegesis in this discussion; see Bucur, "Christophanic Exegesis." Ultimately, I maintain O'Keefe and Reno's use of typology and allegory because, in my estimation, their use stays true to the spirit of Patristic exegesis developed and described in this book, while acknowledging that the terminology differs from ancient use to promote modern theological agendas; see O'Keefe and Reno, *Sanctified Vision*, 19–20. It seems that Marten's suggestion for new terminology so as not to conflate ancient and modern definitions of these terms has not been convincingly heeded and thus are unavailable. Consequently, I acknowledge that in maintaining the language of typology and allegory, I am not suggesting that the ancient fathers necessarily used them identically but that the descriptions of the exegetical practices themselves in this book are accurate and respectful of their broader sacred endeavors.
13. Though my use of "allegory" here might differ from, for example, Origen's use, the concept described here is nonetheless helpful in describing a function of ancient Patristic exegesis, though one might benefit from identifying a term that does not conflate with ancient terms used in various manners.
14. Breck, *God with Us*, 126–29.
15. Breck, 129.
16. O'Keefe and Reno, *Sanctified Vision*, 108, 113.
17. Breck, *God with Us*, 129.
18. For a helpful discussion of early Patristic exegesis in relation to modern hermeneutical approaches to the Bible, see Breck, *Scripture in Tradition*, 3, where he writes, "Whether or

not they [the fathers] found a 'spiritual' sense in every phrase of the text, they were convinced that every word was inspired by God for the purpose of guiding the faithful along the way toward life in the Kingdom of Heaven. To their mind, exegesis has one purpose only: to enable the people of God to hear his Word and to receive it for their salvation."

19. O'Keefe and Reno, *Sanctified Vision*, 105.
20. Origen, "Homélies sue le Cantique de Cantiques" (*SC* 37bis, 65–149; Migne, "Exegetica," in *Patrologia Graeca Tomus XII*; hereafter *PG* 13, 37–196).
21. John Breck points to the need, in Patristic exegesis, of submission to the text for proper interpretation of that text: "St John Chrysostom and other Church Fathers insisted that no one can truly interpret Scripture who does not willingly submit to it"; Breck, *Scripture in Tradition*, 44.
22. Joseph Cardinal Ratzinger's (Pope Benedict XVI) assessment of the historical-critical method is helpful here. Although it is not a benefit to get rid of historical-criticism because it has produced much good and we know more than we ever have about the Bible's history, it has at the same time created much confusion. With an increasing concern over "what really happened" as opposed to what the text says and what it is trying to convey, there has been a methodological bracketing out of faith. Instead, we need to get into the conceptual architecture of modern exegesis with goals of synthesis and philosophical and theological renovation. See Joseph Ratzinger, *Biblical Interpretation in Crisis*.
23. Ratzinger, 43.
24. O'Keefe and Reno, *Sanctified Vision*, 69–84.
25. Bucur, "Christophanic Exegesis," 227–43.
26. Verhey, "Use of Scripture," 228.
27. Matera, *New Testament Ethics*, 5–6.
28. To list a few denouncements of the method of proof-texting, see Verhey, *Remembering Jesus*, 74; Chan, *Biblical Ethics*, 1, 50; and Curran, "Role and Function of the Scriptures," 187.
29. Verhey, *Remembering Jesus*, 58–59.
30. Fowl and Jones, *Reading in Communion*, 157.
31. O'Keefe and Reno, *Sanctified Vision*, 25.
32. For a commentary on the scholarly debates surrounding what Ignatius of Antioch may have meant by ἀρχεῖά in Ignatius, *Philadelphians*, VIII 2 (SC 10bis, 116), see Schoedel, *Ignatius of Antioch*, 207. In ANF I 84, the translations offered are "Jesus Christ is in the place of all that is ancient," and "my archives are Jesus Christ." A scholarly consensus seems to understand his use of ἀρχεῖά to refer generally to the Old Testament.
33. O'Keefe and Reno, *Sanctified Vision*, 28.
34. O'Keefe and Reno, 37–42.
35. Origen, *Exeg. in Psalm*, I 3 (PG 12, 1080C). In his commentary on the first Psalm, Origen analogizes Scripture with a house that has many locked rooms, whose keys are not near their own doors but dispersed throughout the house. The keys are the interpretations of different, "distant" passages, dispersed throughout the entire Scriptural corpus for intra-biblical interpretation.
36. Breck, *Scripture in Tradition*, 46.
37. Chrysostom, "Salutate Priscillam" (*PG* 51, 187), 76.
38. Brock, *Singing the Ethos of God*, 258.
39. Brock, 259.
40. Deut. 32:4, 6; 1 Sam. 2:2; 2 Sam. 22:2; Ps. 28:9, 62:2, 78:35, 80:1; Cant. 1–8, Isa. 64:8; Ezek. 34:11–16, Mal. 2:10; Eph. 4:6.

41. John Breck does well summarizing the communal nature of Orthodox religious experience when he writes: "From an Orthodox perspective, every aspect of what can be termed 'spiritual experience' is essentially *ecclesial.* This is because our very identity is defined by our participation, our 'membership,' in the Body of Christ. Any 'personal' reading of Scripture, then, takes place within the Church, as a function of the life of the Church. Like prayer, it draws us into a living communion with the universal Body of Christian believers. Our quest will lead to a *lectio divina* faithful to Orthodox tradition, therefore, only to the extent that it confirms and deepens our commitment to the ecclesial Body of both the living and the dead who constitute the communion of saints"; Breck, *Scripture in Tradition*, 68.
42. Cahill, "Christian Character," 4–5.
43. Origen and Barkley, *Homilies on Leviticus*, V.8, 96.
44. Irenaeus and Payton, *Irenaeus on the Christian Faith*, 125.
45. Irenaeus and Payton.
46. Origen and Barkley, *Homilies on Leviticus*, V.5 (*SC* 286, 228; *PG* 12, 454D).
47. Origen and Barkley, V.8 (*SC* 286, 242; *PG* 12, 459A).
48. A liturgical order.
49. Justin, *Apol.* I 67.3–4 (*SC* 507, 308).
50. Verhey, *Remembering Jesus*, 15–17.
51. Verhey, "Use of Scripture," 228–29.
52. Verhey, *Remembering Jesus*, 19–21.
53. Jersild, *Spirit Ethics*, 81.
54. Verhey, *Remembering Jesus*, 67.
55. Hays, *New Testament* Ethics, 15–18.
56. See Tracy, *Analogical Imagination*; and Spohn, *What Are They Saying*, 50–71.
57. Fowl and Jones, *Reading in Communion*, 80–81.
58. Fowl and Jones, "Scripture, Exegesis," 114.
59. See Cahill, "Christian Character," 3–17. She maintains that because Christian communities do not live in isolation, they must understand the points of intersection between them and other communities of moral identity (p. 4). As noted above, Cahill goes on to cite early Christian communities as good examples of communities that are able to balance between overlapping enough with other cultural communities' conceptions of morality while still maintaining their own distinction and positive contributions. As part of her conclusion, she asserts that Christians should refocus what overlaps in other communities in relation to their experience with Christ (p. 12).
60. Gustafson, "Place of Scripture," 455.
61. Hauerwas, "Moral Authority of Scripture," 260.
62. Hauerwas, 245.
63. Paulsell, "'Inscribed Heart,'" 141.
64. Paulsell, 148.
65. Paulsell, 153.
66. Burmester, *Horologion*, 43–44.
67. "If you are long-suffering, the Holy Spirit dwelling in you will be clear, unobscured by any other spirit of evil. Dwelling in a spacious place, He will rejoice and be glad with the lodging in which He finds Himself. . . . *The Shepherd of Hermas*, Mandate V.I.1–2 (FOTC 1)." Clarke, *Seven Deadly Sins*, 105.
68. See Hays, *New Testament Ethics*, 25; and Hays, *Moral Vision*, 7, 3134–61.

69. Verhey, *Remembering Jesus*, 62, 64–65.
70. See Athanasius's brilliant letter to Marcellinus—quoted by Athanasius and Gregg, *Life of Antony*, 101–30—in which he discusses the function and depth of all the psalms and the vast array of life experiences they cover.
71. Brock, *Singing the Ethos of God*, 269.
72. Mattison, *Sermon on the Mount*, 1.
73. Chan, *Biblical Ethics*, 84–92, 107–12.
74. Chan, 94.
75. This is more a modern rendering, with emphasis on strategy and methodology. It is my contention that ancient Christians were less concerned with methods as intellectual strategies and more concerned with holistic means of life, from which certain tendencies developed in relation to their circumstances. In other words, as noted in the introduction to this section of the text, method was not method only because it was logically sound but also because it is that to which experience in community attested.
76. Gregory Nazianzen, *Oratio* XXVII 3 (*SC* 250, 76; *PG* 36, 13D-16A); translation Gregory and Wickham, *On God and Christ*, 27; Greek insertions mine.
77. Basil, *De Spiritu Sancto* XXVI 61 (*SC* 17bis, 468; *PG* 32, 180C).
78. Origen, *De Princ.* IV 2.7 (*SC* 268, 328; *PG* 11, 372A-B); translation Behr, *Origen*, 509–11; Greek insertions mine.
79. Origen, 376.
80. Origen, IV 2.9 (*SC* 268, 334–36; *PG* 11, 373B–376A); translation Behr, *Origen*, 515.
81. O'Keefe and Reno, *Sanctified Vision*, 137.
82. O'Keefe and Reno, 139.
83. Fowl and Jones, "Scripture, Exegesis," 111.
84. Fowl and Jones, 112.
85. Fowl and Jones, 114.
86. Verhey, *Remembering Jesus*, 56–57, 68–71.
87. Matt. 22:40.
88. Matt. 4:4.
89. Athanasius, *Vita S. Antonii* III (*SC* 400, 138; *PG* 26, 854A); translation from Athanasius, *Life of Saint Antony*, 21.
90. Kreidler, "Montanism," 231.
91. Duggan, "Psalter, 177; Johnson, *Franciscans*, 398.
92. Athanasius, *Vita S. Antonii* III (*SC* 400, 204–6; *PG* 26, 900C); translation from Athanasius, *St. Athanasius: Life of Saint Antony*, translation Meyer, 41.
93. Athanasius, *Vita S. Antonii* III (*SC* 400, 362–64).
94. For an authoritative biography on the life of Pope Kyrillos VI and his ability to create ecclesial revival in his ascetical, prayerful solitude and silence, see Fanous, *Silent Patriarch*.

6

Embodied Ethics and Inevitable Tensions

There is a distinction, but no opposition, between theory and practice; each to a certain extent supposes the other. On the one hand, theory is dependent on practice; practice must have preceded theory. . . . On the other hand, . . . there is no practice without a theory.

—William Hamilton

I must confess my awareness of certain issues in the ethics I have proposed in this book. For example, with the rapid increase in religious pluralism and religious tolerance in the West, the universalism that characterizes Aristotelian-Thomistic ethics is rather appealing. Virtue ethics in the Aristotelian-Thomistic tradition has some real value when it highlights a common humanity and therefore contributes to ethical universalism instead of the particularism that seems to be stressed here. I do not deny the benefits of this ethical universalism, but I also do not deny the potential benefits of the particularism of the ethics of this book. In this project, virtue is defined through a recorded account of a Person and through a continued personal and communal relationship with this Person. To grow in knowledge of Jesus Christ is to embark on the journey toward virtue. Theology becomes ethics, and vice versa. What is universal about this ethics is that anyone who so wishes may enter into a relationship with this Person who is the dynamic guiding principle of this ethics. Further, the specifics of this ethics, because they are located in God Himself, are not entirely determined by the particularities of any given cultural context or social location. This means that certain values and virtues of this ethics are common to all humanity, pervading throughout time, not at the behest of cultural relativism.

The problem of the particularism of this book is also assuaged by the concreteness that this ethics offers. Not only does it locate the Holy Trinity as its orienting principle, but it also defines ethical actions through a specific kind of spiritual struggle applied to certain practices. What may appear as a constraint in this ethics is in fact a more robust directive. This ethics is, before anything, pragmatic. It is an ethics that hesitates to overanalyze every detail of a difficult situation, as often occurs obsessively to a point of despair, preferring instead to act in a way that guarantees an ascent above the situation, if not through it. It is an ethics whose directive is consistent amid life's inconsistencies: find God and strive toward Him; strive toward God and find Him. Aristotle recognizes the importance of putting into action what one philosophizes about, but it is questionable whether his ethics functions as that bridge between the theoretical and the pragmatic. Pragmatism, I am aware, is a double-edged sword, giving rise to tensions when presenting an ethical framework through concrete examples.

Chapters 4 and 5 were attempts to deliver on the promise of providing examples of the implementation of this ethics in order to demonstrate what an Orthodox "virtue ethics" looks like within two of the many components of Christian life. To provide concrete examples is important for any ethics, and especially for an ethics of virtue. It is not difficult to make the argument, which I made at the outset of this book, that a focus on virtue and character formation should take priority to other systems of ethical thought. However, in making such a claim, it is easy to remain only theoretical and to fail to demonstrate the practical implementation of an ethics of virtue. For this reason, I presented two of the many embodied devotional practices that find their roots in Patristics and are common among Orthodox Christians contemporarily. The application of this ethical model to other practices is also not difficult to envision.

For example, a model of Godward spiritual struggle, in which a person is focused on growth in and unity with God, can be applied to the practice of prayer, as is briefly discussed throughout this book. Similar to the discussions in chapters 4 and 5, the first stage would include detaching from certain passions and overcoming any urge to pray lazily, insincerely, mechanically, and so on. The second stage would be a stage full of refreshment, nourishment, and strengthening of a person who perseveres in prayer. The final stage includes those who have "wrestled" with God in prayer, as did Jacob, entrenching oneself in constant conversation with God. In this stage, a person attempts to obey the instruction to "pray without ceasing," with certain techniques—not uncommon in contemporary Orthodox Christianity—and with exercises in which a person practices being present to the perpetual presence of

God.[1] It is a stage in which a person's life becomes a prayer, an offering to God. Again, similar to asceticism, sacred reading, and any other implementation of this ethical model, these stages are not sharply delineated but form more of a spectrum that does not necessarily progress linearly. The implication of a nonlinear spectrum is that a person is never exempt from struggle, despite the deep stage that person may have reached. In all these stages, a transformative process takes place in which a person becomes not only habituated to a good practice but also becomes good in herself. The transformation of one's character is a marker of this orientation to God, and perseverance through the stages taps into the full transformative potential of each practice, including those of repentance, fasting, meditation, and charity, among others.

It seems, however, that the application of an ethics to concrete examples has been a source of tensions in this book, exacerbated by a boldly interdisciplinary approach that has at the same time allowed me to piece together an ethics that incorporates what are otherwise often disjointed pieces of the same puzzle. On the interdisciplinary front, it becomes impossible to sufficiently address all aspects of the various fields brought into conversation. Though I believe I am advancing scholarship in virtue ethics, spirituality, Orthodox Christian studies, and to some extent Patristics, I am at the same time circumspect that in knitting together broad concepts and different disciplines in embodied practices, I do so in a way that is unavoidably embedded in tensions.

One tension in the discussion of asceticism concerns potentially interpreting the discussion of spiritual struggle and the body as an invitation to reinforce existing inequalities by promoting the virtues of grit and resilience. This issue is addressed in the discussion of spiritual struggle in chapter 2; and yet, with the discussion of asceticism in chapter 4, there exists the potential for encouraging asceticism when people occupy different social conditions in which they can be encouraged to "offer up" their suffering as opportunities for spiritual growth instead of working for more just and equitable conditions. Certainly, the intention behind the asceticism presented in this project would never be to promote such a view. The idea behind asceticism, as I have hoped to present it, is not to devalue the body but to bring the body under control so as not to hinder the potential for deeper intimacy with God. The body, when overly indulged, can become distracted from its true fulfillment—God. It is difficult to avoid what may seem like a body/soul dualism when reading some early Christian authors. However, it is *because* the body and soul are so intimately connected that curbing the passions has such a profound effect on the strengthening of the soul. In fact, asceticism in this sense is *elevation*, not devaluation, of the body. To promote asceticism is to admit that the body occupies a profound and central place in the spiritual journey. One is not to neglect the body for the sake of the soul; it would not work. Instead, similar to Saint Gregory of Nyssa's depiction of the soul desiring to rise if only freed from weightiness of the passions, one is to use the body appropriately for the sake of the soul.

To use the body well, in this project, is to allow the body to rise above base, fleshly desires and to orient the body Godward, that is, as an instrument by which to grow in intimacy with God. Inequitable social conditions are never to be encouraged under the guise of asceticism, and the elevation of the entire person—body and soul—in this book is evidence of the need for both in the journey to God.[2] Control over one's body does not imply hatred of the body; on the contrary, it implies love for the health of the body, which is not manifested in situations of oppression, suffering, or unjust social conditions. As mentioned in chapter 4, asceticism manifested as love for the human being, understood as an inseparable integration between body and soul, is seen clearly in Saint Athanasius's *Vita Antonii,* in which Saint Antony emerges from decades of austere asceticism and solitude at the age of 105 with a radiant and healthy body.

This entire book has been characterized as a portrayal of Christian virtue ethics, and the consequences of this distinction are especially pronounced in the discussion of sacred reading in chapter 5. It seems inevitable that tensions will arise in the face of this exclusivity. There are modes of this ethics that can be adopted pluralistically, but it is questionable whether the model works in a framework outside Christianity. Spiritual struggle and striving are concepts certainly not exclusive to Christianity; but never in this project was the intention to divorce this struggle from the principal orientation to the God of Christianity who not only makes progress on this journey possible but who also is the very τέλος of this ethics.

As a book that reclaims the integrity of theology proper and ethics, and as a book that distinguishes itself from other conceptions of virtue ethics with its emphasis on God as the end of the journey and virtue as a means and marker toward this end, it seems that the application of this ethics is limited. However, Lisa Cahill puts it well when she writes, "Irreducible pluralism cannot result in decisive and consistent moral action."[3] Pluralism is good for dialogue, she continues, but sheer pluralism is not an adequate Christian moral response to the injustices in the world.[4] Instead, and as mentioned above, early Christian communities were able to balance between overlapping enough with other cultural communities' conceptions of morality while still maintaining distinction and contribution.[5] An essential task for Christians is to focus on what overlaps between other communities in relation to their own experiences with Christ. Christ is an integral component of this ethics, without Whom the ethics would collapse.

Within the practice of sacred reading, Christ is presented as the interpretive key of Scripture. It is through Christ that Scripture is unlocked, and the layers of the truth embedded therein begin revealing themselves. At the same time, submission to the guidance of the Holy Spirit and in His ability to interpret for and transform the reader is central to this practice. God, as the believed Author of Scripture, an assertion central to Patristic exegetical methodology, is the One in whom a person should grow in order to read Scripture transformatively. Thus, though one could potentially envision extracting notions of spiritual struggle and even of tripartite schemas of detachment, strengthening, and unity with God outside a specifically Christian worldview, when it comes to a particular application such as that of sacred reading, the God of Christianity becomes indispensable. Moreover, as the embodiment of agapic love and incarnational and humble condescension seen nowhere else, Christ transforms certain actions, enlivening an ethos of outward reflection—to Him and others—instead of an inward focus centered on the self. In this way, I acknowledge the tension in this book as a balance between overlapping sufficiently with contemporary conceptions of virtue, goodness, struggle, and fortitude, while offering a distinctly Christian perspective on the experience of God.

Next, regarding religious and devotional practices, there will always exist the risk for a religious practice to devolve into an empty gesture. Though I have not fully developed a detailed account of the concept of sincerity, throughout this book I have hinted at the concept of sincerity in effort and intention in order to counter any tendency toward legalism. Admittedly, a shortcoming of this book's emphasis on pure intention and sustained and sincere effort is that there is no way to measure or gauge any of these concepts. To complicate matters further, sincerity is often relative to circumstances, and there is no way to assess the complexity that lies within the multitude of various circumstances within which any person can find himself. Gauging one's sincerity is a complex, lifelong process, similar to the journey of Godward spiritual struggle itself. It is a process that requires self-awareness, humility, dialogue, and discipleship, among others. Though this tension remains unresolved, it seems, then, that one should be less occupied with trying to gauge the level of one's own or another's sincerity and should instead focus on perpetually "straining forward."[6]

Finally, the overarching methodology here has been a bit strange, and yet I find no alternative. I have located a way of life practiced by a certain group of people (Orthodox Christians); articulated this ethos, or *politeia*, as an ethics proper while devaluing the broader project of Western philosophical ethics; transliterated this ethos from common practices to one with a semblance of an ethics of virtue; and then reapplied the ethical framework proposed to Christian practices. I have sifted this way of life and in the process have risked leaving out essential components for the sake of clarity, organization, and consistency. The truth is this reality is often not clear, organized, or consistent, especially within an anthropological lens that accounts for both the fallenness and risenness of human nature. In a sense, this ethics has been verified before it has been articulated; as described epigraphically, the practice preceded the theory. It could be, then, that the insufficiencies discovered are first my own and only secondarily problems of instantiation or embodiment.

Yet with all the incongruencies, I hope that the potential contributions of the ethics are not overlooked. It is my suspicion that spiritual struggle has been abandoned by the Christian West to a large extent, and the East risks the same. What is more unnerving is that the concept, because it might have been forgotten *somatically*, will take a much longer time to come back into prominence, if it ever does. Could it be that some fifteen centuries of Christianity—namely, the fifteen centuries closest to witnessing the risen Christ—got it all wrong—that the Godward spiritual struggle that formed and informed their practice of Christianity was a gross misinterpretation of the good news? Certainly, many today would answer this question with a resounding "yes!"—and perhaps I have only hinted at how this ethics was embodied beyond the first few centuries of Christianity. But in locating this ethics in a Christian group that embodies this ethics contemporarily, attesting to its transformative effects, I hope to have offered a convincing case for its reasonable appropriation in the twenty-first century.

Still another objection, often waged against any number of religious groups, might be that there exist many Orthodox Christians—some who may even make sizable efforts to abide by this ethical model—who are not recognizably good people to the extent that this ethics purports. To a certain extent, this objection holds water. If an ethics is not affecting its adherents, and if an ethics of transformation is not doing just that, it should be called into question. But can this really be measured? I have been clear in insisting that there can be no absolute scale to measure a person's progress toward God or virtue; the progress is onward and upward in God who is good, but the starting points for each person, in relation to their circumstances, are vastly incongruous. Moreover, the only measure of the efficacy of this ethics is not just the transformation of its adherents, though it might be the most important measure. No one would claim, for example, that if a child grows up to engage in frequent criminal behavior that it is the result of the love, attention, and time given by that child's parents. That it is correct to love, tend to, and give time to your child is irrespective of the malevolent outcome of that child. Certainly those goods given by the parents were actions that in fact should have, and may even in fact have partially, prevented the child from making imprudent decisions that would have led to criminal behavior. To say, then, that love, attention, and time do not "work" because there exist many people who engaged in criminal behavior despite receiving them would be a myopic neglect of the complexities that shape human character, behavior, and decision-making. Similarly, it should not be so alarming to imagine that there can be those who adhere to an ethics of Godward spiritual struggle and resist positive transformation, whether because of legalistic adherence, because of negative external influences, or because of a lack sincerity, dedication, exertion, or penitent submission to God's grace.

This book has also been an attempt to organize aspects of the Christian spiritual journey, especially the Orthodox Christian journey, that might otherwise appear convoluted and disordered, while still leaving space for the complexity that remains an integral part of Orthodox spirituality. The modern renewal of virtue ethics has aptly carved out space for this project as a recovery of and discourse with the ancients, who with facility made sense of their world using the language of virtue. As a retrieval of Patristic thought for contemporary practice, the system described in this book is a "transliteration" of millennia of spiritually formative practices, tested, altered, and developed. In retrieving the concept of spiritual struggle in combination with the centrality of orientation to God, and in suggesting the application of this system as a model for various aspects of contemporary Christian spirituality, my goal has been to offer a small contribution to this ongoing and long-lasting intellectual and spiritual tradition and conversation.

In my estimation (and I hope to have convinced my reader of this, to some extent), there is nothing more effective at exacting change, extirpating evil, and creating goodness in this world than those who have pursued God with their entire beings, whom we might label as sanctified/spiritual intellectuals, or intellectual saints, especially in the West, where the intellectual has been so emphasized. These people have not forsaken the toilsome disciplining of the body, the exercise of which uplifts the spirit. They have not simply labored for clear or "correct" thoughts and opinions amid the chaotic sea of information at their feet, but have acquired sanctified vision, keen spiritual senses, and transformed hearts able to *act* on the love they are convinced is fundamental to human flourishing. They are detached, able to be present to God and to others with singleness of mind and attention. They have put on the mind of Christ; they have pursued a unity with God that continues human nature's present and eschatological restoration, redefining the road to perfection. By engaging an ethics whose τέλος is beyond virtue, they have in the process acquired a virtue decentered from an unhealthy obsession with individual improvement. Their exemplary lives of indisputable bona fide goodness, entrenched in the source of Goodness, have served as illuminations of the road to the restoration of human nature. These persons transformed in the Body of Christ taste an intimation of the life to come, away from fallenness and onward and upward in the risen Christ, affecting all those they encounter in love and witnessing to those hesitant to embark on a journey of Godward spiritual struggle.

NOTES

Epigraph: Hamilton, *Lectures*, 120.

1. 1 Thess. 5:17.
2. I have not been systematic in distinguishing between the soul and spirit. I have conflated the two with terms like "strengthening of the soul" and "increasing spirituality." The distinction between soul and spirit is not foundational to this study, but it might be more accurate to attribute the journey to God as one of the spirit's ascent.
3. Cahill, "Christian Character," 4.
4. Cahill, 11.
5. Cahill, 12.
6. Phil. 3:13.

BIBLIOGRAPHY

Abecina, Alexander L. *Time and Sacramentality in Gregory of Nyssa's Contra Eunomium*. Early Christian Studies, vol. 16. Strathfield, Australia: St. Paul's Publications, 2013.

Adams, Robert Merrihew. *Finite and Infinite Goods: A Framework for Ethics*. Oxford: Oxford University Press, 1999.

———. *A Theory of Virtue: Excellence in Being for the Good*. Oxford: Oxford University Press, 2006.

Alfeyev, Hilarion. *Orthodox Witness Today*. Geneva: WCC Publications, 2006.

———. "The Patristic Heritage and Modernity." *Ecumenical Review* 54 (2002): 91–111.

Amphilochius of Iconium. "Amphilochii Iconiensis Iambi ad Seleucum." In *Patristische Texte und Studien* 9, edited by E. Oberg. Berlin: De Gruyter, 1969.

Annas, Julia. *Intelligent Virtue*. Oxford: Oxford University Press, 2011.

———. "Virtue Ethics and the Charge of Egoism." In *Morality and Self-Interest*, edited by Paul Bloomfield, 205–23. Oxford: Oxford University Press, 2008.

Anscombe, G. E. M., et al. "Modern Moral Philosophy." *Philosophy* 33, no. 124 (January 1958): 1–16.

Antonaccio, Maria. "Contemporary Forms of *Askesis* and the Return of Spiritual Exercises." *Annual of the Society of Christian Ethics* 18 (1998): 69–92.

Aphrahat. *Aphrahat Demonstrations*, translated by Kuriakose A. Valavanolickal. Catholic Theological Studies in India. Changanassery, India: HIRS Publications, 1999.

Aquinas, Thomas. *The "Summa Theologica" of St. Thomas Aquinas, Part I QQ I.–XXVI*. Vol. 1. Literally translated by Fathers of the English Dominican Province, 2nd and revised ed. London: Burns Oates and Washbourne, 1920.

Aristotle. *Athenian Constitution: Eudemian Ethics—Virtues and Vices*, translated by H. Rackham. Loeb Classical Library 285. Cambridge, MA: Harvard University Press, 1935.

———. *Nicomachean Ethics*, translated by H. Rackham. Loeb Classical Library 73. Cambridge, MA: Harvard University Press, 1926.

Athanasius of Alexandria and René Draguet. *La Vie Primitive De S. Antoine: Conservée En Syriaque*. Corpus Scriptorum Christianorum Orientalium. 2 vols. Louvain: Secrétariat du Corpus SCO, 1980.

Athanasius. *Letter to Serapion*, I.28.

———. *St. Athanasius: The Life of Saint Antony*, translated by Robert T. Meyer. 10 vols. Ancient Christian Writers: The Works of the Fathers in Translation. Westminster, MD: Newman Press, 1950.

———. "Vie D'Antoine," edited by G. J. M. Bartelink. In *Sources Chrétiennes*, vol. 40. Paris: Cerf, 1994.

Athanasius of Alexandria, John of Shmūn, and Serapion of Thmuis. *The Life of Antony* [Greek Life and Coptic Life on facing pages], translated by Tim Vivian, Apostolos N. Athanassakis, and Rowan A. Greer. Cistercian Studies Series. Kalamazoo: Cistercian Publications, 2003.

Athanassoulis, Nafsika. "A Response to Harman: Virtue Ethics and Character Traits." *Proceedings of the Aristotelian Society* 100 (2000): 215–21.

———. *Virtue Ethics*. Bloomsbury Ethics. London: Bloomsbury, 2013.

Augustine. *Four Anti-Pelagian Writings: On Nature and Grace on the Proceedings of Pelagius on the Predestination of the Saints on the Gift of Perseverance*, translated by John A. Mourant and William J. Collinge. The Fathers of the Church, vol. 86. Washington, DC: Catholic University of America Press, 1992.

———. "On Nature and Grace." In *New Advent*, edited by Philip Schaff and Kevin Knight. Buffalo: Christian Literature Publishing Company, 1887.

Baker, Jennifer. "Virtue Ethics and Practical Guidance." *Social Philosophy and Policy* 30, nos. 1–2 (2013): 297–313. doi:10.1017/S0265052513000149.

Balás, David L. *[Metousia Theou]: Man's Participation in God's Perfections According to Saint Gregory of Nyssa*. Studia Anselmiana Philosophica Theologica. Rome: I. B. C. Libreria Herder, 1966.

Balch, David L. "1 Cor 7:32–35 and Stoic Debates About Marriage Anxiety, and Distraction." *Journal of Biblical Literature* 102, no. 3 (1983): 429–39.

Balthasar, Hans Urs von. *Presence and Thought: Essay on the Religious Philosophy of Gregory of Nyssa*. A Communio Book. San Francisco: Ignatius Press, 1995.

Barnes, Patrick. "The Orthodox View of Grace." In *The Non-Orthodox: The Orthodox Teaching on Christians Outside of the Church*, 4–12. Salisbury: Regina Orthodox Press, 1999.

Barnes, T. D. "Angels of Light or Mystic Initiate: The Problem of the 'Life of Antony.'" *Journal of Theological Studies* 37, no. 2 (1986): 353–68.

Basil. *Sur le Saint-Esprit*. In *Sources Chrétiennes*, 17 bis, edited by Benoît Pruche. Paris: Cerf, 1968.

Basil and Edward Raymond Maloney. *St. Basil the Great to Students on Greek Literature*. New York: American Book Company, 1901.

Beeley, Christopher A. *The Unity of Christ: Continuity and Conflict in Patristic Tradition*. New Haven, CT: Yale University Press, 2012.

Begley, Ann Marie. "Practising Virtue: A Challenge to the View That a Virtue-Centred Approach to Ethics Lacks Practical Content." *Nursing Ethics* 12, no. 6 (2005): 622–37.

Behr, John. "Marriage and Asceticism." *Sobornost* 29 (2007): 24–50.

———. *Origen: On First Principles*. Oxford: Oxford University Press, 2018.

Bettenson, Henry, and Chris Maunder. *Documents of the Christian Church*, 4th ed. Oxford: Oxford University Press, 2011.

Boersma, Hans. "Becoming Human in the Face of God: Gregory of Nyssa's Unending Search for the Beatific Vision." *International Journal of Systematic Theology* 17, no. 2 (2015): 151.

———. *Embodiment and Virtue in Gregory of Nyssa: An Anagogical Approach*. Oxford: Oxford University Press, 2013.

———. "Gregory of Nyssa: Becoming Human in the Face of God." In *Sources of the Christian Self: A Cultural History of Christian Identity*, edited by James M. Houston and Jens Zimmermann, 146–67. Grand Rapids: Wm. B. Eerdmans, 2018.

———. "Overcoming Time and Space: Gregory of Nyssa's Anagogical Theology." *Journal of Early Christian Studies* 20, no. 4 (2012): 575–612.

———. *Scripture as Real Presence: Sacramental Exegesis in the Early Church*. Grand Rapids: Baker Academic, 2017.

Boettner, Loraine. *The Reformed Doctrine of Predestination*. Grand Rapids: Wm. B. Eerdmans, 1932.

Bouteneff, Peter C. *Sweeter Than Honey: Orthodox Thinking on Dogma and Truth*. Crestwood, NY: St. Vladimir's Seminary Press, 2006.

Bradshaw, Paul F. *Reconstructing Early Christian Worship*. Collegeville, MN: Liturgical Press, 2010.

———. *The Search for the Origins of Christian Worship: Sources and Methods for the Study of Early Liturgy*, 2nd ed. Oxford: Oxford University Press, 2002.

Bradshaw, Paul F., and Maxwell E. Johnson. *The Eucharistic Liturgies: Their Evolution and Interpretation*. Collegeville, MN: Liturgical Press, 2012.

Brakke, David. *Athanasius and the Politics of Asceticism*. Oxford: Clarendon Press, 1995.

Breck, John. *God with Us: Critical Issues in Christian Life and Faith*. Crestwood, NY: St. Vladimir's Seminary Press, 2003.

———. *Scripture in Tradition: The Bible and Its Interpretation in the Orthodox Church*. Crestwood, NY: St. Vladimir's Seminary Press, 2001.

Brock, Brian. *Singing the Ethos of God: On the Place of Christian Ethics in Scripture*. Grand Rapids: Wm. B. Eerdmans, 2007.

Brock, Sebastian, P. "Clothing Metaphors as a Means of Theological Expression in Syriac Tradition." In *Typus, Symbol, Allegorie bei den östlich Vätern und ihren Parallelen im mittelalter*, edited by Margo Schmidt and C. F. Geyer. Regensburg: Verlag Friedrich Pustet, 1982.

Brown, Peter R. L. *The Body and Society: Men and Women and Sexual Renunciation in Early Christianity*. New York: Columbia University Press: 1988.

Brown Hughes, Amy. "The Legacy of the Feminine in the Christology of Origen of Alexandria, Methodius of Olympus, and Gregory of Nyssa." *Vigiliae Christianae* 70 (2016): 51–76.

Bucur, Bogdan G. "Hierarchy, Eldership, Isangelia: Clement of Alexandria and the Ascetic Tradition." In *Alexandrian Legacy: A Critical Appraisal*, edited by D. Costache, P. Kariatlis, and M. Baghos, 2–45. Cambridge: Cambridge Scholars, 2015.

———. "Observations on the Ascetic Doctrine of the *Shepherd of Hermas*." *Studia Monastica* 48 (2006): 7–23.

Burmester, O. H. E. *The Horologion of the Egyptian Church: Coptic and Arabic Text from a Mediaeval Manuscript*. Studia Orientalia Christiana, Aegyptiaca. Cairo: Edizioni del Centro Francescano di Studi Orientali Cristiani, 1973.

Burrows, Mark S. "On the Visibility of God in the Holy Man: A Reconsideration of the Role of Ava in the Pachomian Vitae." *Vigilae christianae* 41 (1987): 11–33.

Burrus, Virginia. *Begotten, Not Made: Conceiving Manhood in Late Antiquity*. Stanford, CA: Stanford University Press, 2000.

———. *The Making of a Heretic: Gender, Authority, and the Priscillianist Controversy*. Berkeley: University of California Press, 2018.

Cadenhead, Raphael. "Corporeality and Askesis: Ethics and Bodily Practice in Gregory of Nyssa's Theological Anthropology." *Studies in Christian Ethics* 26, no. 3 (2013): 281–99.

Cahill, Lisa Sowle. "Christian Character, Biblical Community, and Human Values." In *Character and Scripture: Moral Formation, Community, and Biblical Interpretation*, edited by William Brown, 3–17. Grand Rapids: Wm. B. Eerdmans, 2002.

———. *Sex, Gender, and Christian Ethics*. New Studies in Christian Ethics. Cambridge: Cambridge University Press, 1996.

———. *Theological Bioethics: Participation, Justice and Change*. Washington, DC: Georgetown University Press, 2005.

The Cambridge Companion to Aristotle's Nicomachean Ethics. Cambridge Companions to Philosophy. Cambridge: Cambridge University Press, 2014.

Caputo, John D. *The Insistence of God: A Theology of Perhaps*. Bloomington: Indiana University Press, 2013.

———. *The Weakness of God: A Theology of the Event*. Bloomington: Indiana University Press, 2006.

Cassien, Jean. "Conférences II: Sources Chrétiennes," edited by E. Pichery. In *Sources Chrétiennes* 54. Paris: Cerf, 2009.

Chan, Yiu Sing Lúcás. *Biblical Ethics in the 21st Century: Developments, Emerging Consensus, and Future Directions*. New York: Paulist Press, 2013.

Cherniss, Harold F. *The Platonism of Gregory of Nyssa*. Burt Franklin Research and Source Works Series. New York: B. Franklin, 1971.

Childress, James F. "Scripture and Christian Ethics: Some Reflections on the Role of Scripture in Moral Deliberation and Justification." *Interpretation* 34, no. 4 (1980): 371–80.

Childs, James. "The Eastern Orthodox Doctrine of Grace with a Lutheran Perspective." *Concordia Seminary Scholarship* 84 (1964).

Chrysostom, John. *Baptismal Instructions*, translated by Paul W. Harkins. Ancient Christian Writers. Mahwah, NJ: Paulist Press, 1962.

———. *The Homilies of St. John Chrysostom, Archbishop of Constantinople, on the Gospel of St. John, Translated with Notes and Indices*. Library of Fathers of the Holy Catholic Church, Anterior to the Divine of the East and West, part II, hom. XLII–LXXXVIII. Oxford: J. H. Parker, 1848.

———. "Salutate Priscillam" (Migne, *Patrologia Graeca Tomus* 51, 187). Translation by Breck, *Scripture in Tradition*.

Cicero. *De Finibus Bonorum et Malorum*, translated by H. Rackham. Loeb Classical Library 40. Cambridge, MA: Harvard University Press, 1914.

Clairmont, David A. *Moral Struggle and Religious Ethics: On the Person as Classic in Comparative Theological Contexts*. Malden, MA: Wiley-Blackwell, 2011.

Clark, Elizabeth A. "Women, Gender, and the Study of Christian History." *Church History* 70, no. 3 (2001): 395–426.

Clarke, Kevin M. *The Seven Deadly Sins*. Sayings of the Fathers of the Church. Washington, DC: Catholic University of America Press, 2018.

Clement. *Extracts from the Writings of Clement of Alexandria*, translated by William Wilson. London: Theosophical Publishing Society, 1905.

———. "Le Pédagogue," edited by Henri-Irénée Marrou and Marguerite Harl. In *Sources Chrétiennes* 70, edited by H. de Lubac and J. Daniélou. Paris: Cerf, 1960.

———. "Les Stromates: Stromate VI," edited by Patrick Descourtieux. In *Sources Chrétiennes* 446 (Bd Latour-Maubourg: 1999).

Coakley, Sarah. "Gregory of Nyssa." In *The Spiritual Senses: Perceiving God in Western Christianity*, edited by Paul L. Gavrilyuk and Sarah Coakley, 36–55. Cambridge: Cambridge University Press, 2012.

Cochran, Elizabeth Agnew. *Protestant Virtue and Stoic Ethics*. New York: Bloomsbury / T&T Clark, 2018.

Constantinou, Stavroula. "Male Constructions of Female Identities: Authority and Power in the Byzantine Greek Lives of Monastic Foundresses." *Wiener Jahrbuch für Kunstgeschichte* 60, no. 1 (2012).

Conway-Jones, Ann. *Gregory of Nyssa's Tabernacle Imagery in Its Jewish and Christian Contexts*. Oxford: Oxford University Press, 2014.

Coptic Orthodox Diocese of the Southern United States. *The Divine Liturgy: The Anaphoras of Saints Basil, Gregory, and Cyril*, 2nd ed. Los Angeles: Coptic Orthodox Diocese of the Southern United States, 2007.

Corrigan, Kevin, Dr. Lewis Ayres, and Professor Patricia Cox Miller. *Studies in Philosophy and Theology in Late Antiquity: Evagrius and Gregory—Mind, Soul, and Body in the 4th Century*. Burlington, VT: Ashgate, 2016.

Cosaert, Carl P. *The Text of the Gospels in Clement of Alexandria*. Atlanta: Society of Biblical Literature, 2008.

Curran, Charles E. "The Role and Function of the Scriptures in Moral Theology." In *The Use of Scripture in Moral Theology*, edited by Charles Curran and Richard McCormick. New York: Paulist Press, 1984.

Daley, Brian E. "Divine Transcendence and Human Transformation: Gregory of Nyssa's Anti–Apollinarian Christology." *Modern Theology* 18, no. 4 (2002): 497–506.

Daly, Robert J. *Christian Biblical Ethics: From Biblical Revelation to Contemporary Christian Praxis—Method and Content*. New York: Paulist Press, 1984.

Daniélou, Jean. *Platonisme et Théologie Mystique: Essai Sur La Doctrine Spirituelle de Saint Grégoire de Nysse*. Paris: Aubier & Éditions Montaigne, 1944.

Darwall, Stephen L. *Deontology*. Blackwell Readings in Philosophy. Malden, MA: Blackwell, 2003.

DePaul, Michael R., and Linda Trinkaus Zagzebski. *Intellectual Virtue: Perspectives from Ethics and Epistemology*. Oxford: Oxford University Press, 2003.

Dragutinovic, Predrag. "Interpretation of Scripture in the Orthodox Church." Belgrade, 2018.

Duckworth, Angela. *Grit: The Power of Passion and Perseverance*. New York: Scribner, 2016.

Duggan, Mary Kay. "The Psalter on the Way to the Reformation: The Fifteenth-Century Printed Psalter in the North." In *The Place of the Psalms in the Intellectual Culture of the Middle Ages*, edited by Nancy Elizabeth Van Deusen. Medieval Studies. Albany: State University of New York Press, 1999.

Edwards, Mark. "Origen and Gregory of Nyssa on the Song of Songs." In *Exploring Gregory of Nyssa: Philosophical, Theological, and Historical Studies*, edited by Anna Marmodoro and Neil B. McLynn, 74–92. Oxford: Oxford University Press, 2018.

"Epektasis." In *The Brill Dictionary of Gregory of Nyssa*, edited by Lucas Francisco Mateo-Seco and Giulio Maspero, 263–68. Leiden: Brill, 2010.

Epictetus. "Discourses," translated by W. A. Oldfather. Loeb Classical Library 131. Cambridge, MA: Harvard University Press, 1925.

Evdokimov, Paul. *Ages of the Spiritual Life*. Crestwood, NY: St. Vladimir's Seminary Press, 1988.

Exline, Julie J. "Religious and Spiritual Struggles." In *Context, Theory, and Research*, edited by Kenneth I. Pargament, Julie J. Exline, and James W. Jones, 1:459–76. APA Handbooks in Psychology. Washington, DC: American Psychological Association, 2013.

Exline, Julie J., Kenneth I. Pargament, Joshua B. Grubbs, and Ann Marie Yali. "The Religious and Spiritual Struggles Scale: Development and Initial Validation." *Psychology of Religion and Spirituality* 6, no. 3 (2014): 208–22.

Fanous, Daniel. *A Silent Patriarch: Kyrillos VI, Life and Legacy*. Crestwood, NY: St. Vladimir's Seminary Press, 2019.

Feinberg, John, Norman Geisler, Bruce Reichenbach, and Clark Pinnock. *Predestination and Free Will: Four Views of Divine Sovereignty and Human Freedom*. Downers Grove, IL: InterVarsity Press, 2009.

Flynn, Gabriel, and Paul D. Murray. *Ressourcement: A Movement for Renewal in Twentieth-Century Catholic Theology*. Oxford: Oxford University Press, 2013.

Foot, Philippa. *Virtues and Vices and Other Essays in Moral Philosophy*. Oxford: Oxford University Press, 2002.

Fortuin, Robert F. "Analogy in the Mystical Theology of Gregory of Nyssa: Transcending Negation and Affirmation." In *The Mystical Tradition of the Eastern Church: Studies in Patristics, Liturgy, and Practice,* edited by Sergey Trostyanskiy and Jess Gilbert, 69–83. Piscataway, NJ: Gorgias Press, 2019.

Fowl, Stephen E., and L. Gregory Jones. *Reading in Communion: Scripture and Ethics in Christian Life*. Grand Rapids: Wm. B. Eerdmans, 1991.

———. "Scripture, Exegesis, and Discernment in Christian Ethics." In *Virtues and Practices in the Christian Tradition: Christian Ethics after Macintyre,* edited by Nancey C. Murphy, Brad J. Kallenberg, and Mark Nation. Harrisburg, PA: Trinity Press International, 1997.

Furnish, Victor Paul. *The Moral Teaching of Paul: Selected Issues,* 3rd ed. Nashville: Abingdon Press, 2009.

Gaca, Kathy L. *The Making of Fornication: Eros, Ethics, and Political Reform in Greek Philosophy and Early Christianity*. Joan Palevsky Imprint in Classical Literature. Berkeley: University of California Press, 2003.

Garcia, J. L. A. "Practical Reason and Its Virtues." In *Intellectual Virtue: Perspectives from Ethics and Epistemology,* edited by Michael R. DePaul and Linda Trinkaus Zagzebski. Oxford: Oxford University Press, 2003.

Geljon, Albert C. *Philonic Exegesis in Gregory of Nyssa's "*De Vita Moysis.*"* Providence: Brown University, Judaic Studies, 2002.

Golitzin, Alexander. "Earthly Angels and Heavenly Men: The Old Testament Pseudepigrapha, Nicetas Stethatos, and the Tradition of Interiorized Apocalyptic in Eastern Christian Ascetical and Mystical Literature." *Dumbarton Oaks Papers* 55 (2001): 125–53.

———. "Making the Inside like the Outside: Toward a Monastic Sitz im Leben for the Syriac Apocalypse of Daniel." In *To Train His Soul in Books: Syriac Asceticism in Early Christianity,* edited by Robin Darling Young and Monica J. Blanchard, 66–98. Washington, DC: Catholic University of America Press, 2011.

———. "The Place of the Presence of God: Aphrahat of Persia's Portrait of the Christian Holy Man." In *ΣΥΝΑΞΙΣ ΕΥΧΑΡΙΣΤΙΑΣ: Studies in Honor of Archimandrite Aimilianos of Simonos Petras,* 391–447. Mount Athos: Holy Monastery of Simonos Petras of the Holy Mount; Athens: Indiktos, 2003.

———. "Recovering the 'Glory of Adam': 'Divine Light' Traditions in the Dead Sea Scrolls and the Christian Ascetical Literature of Fourth-Century Syro-Mesopotamia." In *Dead Sea Scrolls as Background to Postbiblical Judaism and Early Christianity,* 275–308. Leiden: Brill, 2003.

———. "Temple and Throne of the Divine Glory: 'Pseudo-Marcarius' and Purity of Heart, Together with Some Remarks on the Limitations and Usefulness of Scholarship." In *Purity of Heart in Early Ascetic and Monastic Literature: Essays in Honor of Juana Raasch, OSB,* edited by Harriet Luckman and Linda Kulzer, 107–29. Collegeville, MN: Liturgical Press, 1999.

Graef, Hilda C. *St. Gregory of Nyssa: The Lord's Prayer, the Beatitudes.* Ancient Christian Writers 18, edited by Johannes Quasten and Joseph C. Plumpe. Mahwah, NJ: Paulist Press, 1978.

Greer, Rowan A., and J. Warren Smith. *One Path for All: Gregory of Nyssa on the Christian Life and Human Destiny.* Eugene, OR: Cascade Books, 2015.

Gregory of Nazianzus. *On God and Christ: The Five Theological Orations and Two Letters to Cledonius.* Translated by Frederick Williams. Edited by Lionel R. Wickham. Crestwood, NY: St. Vladimir's Seminary Press, 2002.

———. *Discours Théologiques.* In *Sources Chrétiennes* 250, edited by Paul Gallay and Maurice Jourjon. Paris: Cerf, 1978.

Gregory of Nyssa. *Ascetical Works,* translated by Virginia Wood Callahan; Fathers of the Church 58, a New Translation, edited by Roy Joseph Deferrari. Washington, DC: Catholic University of America Press, 1999.

———. *From Glory to Glory: Texts from Gregory of Nyssa's Mystical Writings.* Translated and edited by Herbert Musurillo. Crestwood, NY: St. Vladimir's Seminary Press, 1979.

———. *Gregory of Nyssa's Treatise on the Inscriptions of the Psalms.* Translated and edited by Ronald E. Heine. Oxford Early Christian Studies. Oxford: Oxford University Press, 1995.

———. *Gregory of Nyssa: The Life of Moses,* translated by Abraham J. Malherbe and Everett Ferguson. New York: Paulist Press, 1978.

———. "In Canticum Canticorum," edited by Hermannus Langerbeck. In *Gregorii Nysseni Opera* VI, edited by Wernerus Jaeger. Leiden: Brill, 1960.

———. "In Inscriptiones Psalmorum," edited by Jacobus McDonough, SJ, and Paulus Alexander. In *Gregorii Nysseni Opera V,* edited by Wernerus Jaeger. Leiden: Brill, 1962.

———. *The Life of Saint Macrina.* Translated and edited by Kevin Corrigan. Toronto: Peregrina, 1997.

———. "Opera Ascetica," edited by Wernerus Jaeger, Johannes P. Cavarnos, and Virginia Woods Callahan. In *Gregorii Nysseni Opera VIII,* pars I, edited by Wernerus Jaeger. Leiden: Brill, 1952.

———. "De Oratione Dominica De Beatitudinibus," edited by Johannes F. Callahan. In *Gregorii Nysseni Opera VII,* pars II, edited by Wernerus Jaeger. Leiden: Brill, 1992.

———. "Vie De Sainte Macrine," edited by Pierre Maraval. In *Sources Chrétiennes* 95, edited by H. de Lubac, J. Daniélou, and C. Mondésert. Paris: Cerf, 1971.

———. "De Vita Moysis," edited by Herbertus Musurillo. In *Gregorii Nysseni Opera* VII, pars I, edited by Wernerus Jaeger and Hermannus Langerbeck. Leiden: Brill, 1964.

Griffith, Sidney H. "Asceticism in the Church of Syria: The Hermeneutics of Early Syrian Monasticism." In *Asceticism,* edited by Vincent L. Wimbush and Richard Valantasis, 220–45. Oxford: Oxford University Press, 1995.

Gruber, Mark. *Sacrifice in the Desert: A Study of an Egyptian Minority through the Prism of Coptic Monasticism,* edited by M. Michele Ransil. Lanham, MD: University Press of America, 2003.

Guroian, Vigen. *Incarnate Love: Essays in Orthodox Ethics,* 2nd ed. Notre Dame, IN: University of Notre Dame Press, 2002.

———. "Notes toward an Eastern Orthodox Ethic." *Journal of Religious Ethics* 9, no. 2 (1981): 228–44.

Gustafson, James M. "The Changing Use of the Bible in Christian Ethics." In *The Use of Scripture in Moral Theology,* edited by Charles Curran and Richard McCormick. New York: Paulist Press, 1984.

———. "The Place of Scripture in Christian Ethics: A Methodological Study." In *Readings in Moral Theology No. 4: The Use of Scripture in Moral Theology*, 151–77. New York: Paulist Press, 1984.

Gwynn, David M. *Athanasius of Alexandria: Bishop, Theologian, Ascetic, Father*. Oxford: Oxford University Press, 2012.

Haldane, John. "Whither Moral Philosophy?" In *Beyond the Self: Virtue Ethics and the Problem of Culture*, edited by Raymond Hain. Waco: Baylor University Press, 2019.

Hamalis, Perry T., and Aristotle Papanikolaou, eds. "Modes of Godly Being: Reflections on the Virtues in Eastern Orthodox Christianity." In *Studies in Christian Ethics* 26, no. 3 (2013): 271–392.

Hamilton, Sir William. *Lectures on Metaphysics*. New York: Sheldon, 1878.

Hampson, Daphne. *Christian Contradictions: The Structures of Lutheran and Catholic Thought*. Cambridge: Cambridge University Press, 2001.

Harakas, Stanley S. *Wholeness of Faith and Life*. 3 vols. Brookline, MA: Holy Cross Orthodox Press, 1999.

Harper, Demetrios. *The Analogy of Love: St. Maximus the Confessor and the Foundations of Ethics*. Crestwood, NY: St. Vladimir's Seminary Press, 2019.

Harrington, Daniel J., and James F. Keenan. *Jesus and Virtue Ethics: Building Bridges between New Testament Studies and Moral Theology*. Lanham, MD: Sheed & Ward, 2002.

Harrison, Verna E. F. *Grace and Human Freedom According to St. Gregory of Nyssa*. Studies in the Bible and Early Christianity 30. Lewiston, NY: E. Mellen Press, 1992.

Hassan, Sana S. *Christians versus Muslims in Modern Egypt: The Century-Long Struggle for Coptic Equality*. Oxford: Oxford University Press, 2003.

Hauerwas, Stanley. *A Community of Character: Toward a Constructive Christian Social Ethic*. Notre Dame, IN: University of Notre Dame Press, 1981.

———. "The Moral Authority of Scripture: The Politics and Ethics of Remembering." In *The Use of Scripture in Moral Theology*, edited by Charles Curran and Richard McCormick. New York: Paulist Press, 1984.

———. *The Peaceable Kingdom: A Primer in Christian Ethics*. Notre Dame, IN: University of Notre Dame Press, 1983.

Hays, Richard B. *The Moral Vision of the New Testament: Community Cross, New Creation*. Edinburgh: T&T Clark, 1996.

———. *New Testament Ethics: The Story Retold*. J. J. Thiessen Lectures. Winnipeg: Canadian Mennonite Bible College Publications, 1998.

Heine, Ronald E. *Perfection in the Virtuous Life: A Study in the Relationship between Edification and Polemical Theology in Gregory of Nyssa's De Vita Moysis*. Cambridge, MA: Philadelphia Patristic Foundation, 1975.

Herdt, Jennifer A. "Augustine and the Liturgical Pedagogy of Virtue." In *Virtue and the Moral Life: Theological and Philosophical Perspectives*, edited by William Werpehowski and Kathryn Getek Soltis. London: Lexington Books, 2014.

———. *Putting on Virtue: The Legacy of the Splendid Vices*. Chicago: University of Chicago Press, 2008.

Hofer, Andrew P. *Christ in the Life and Teaching of Gregory of Nazianzus*. Oxford: Oxford University Press, 2013.

Holmes, Christopher R. J. *Ethics in the Presence of Christ*. London: T&T Clark, 2012.

Hooker, Brad. *Developing Deontology: New Essays in Ethical Theory*. Malden, MA: Wiley-Blackwell, 2012.

Huang, Yong. "The Self-Centeredness Objection to Virtue Ethics: Zhu Xi's Neo-Confucian Response." *American Catholic Philosophical Quarterly* 84, no. 4 (2010): 651–92.

Hursthouse, Rosalind. *On Virtue Ethics*. Oxford: Oxford University Press, 1999.

Ignatius of Antioch. *Lettres Martyre de Polycarpe: Philadelphians VIII*. In *Sources Chrétiennes* 10 bis, edited by Pierre-Thomas Camelot. Paris: Cerf, 1998.

Ip, Pui Him. "'Back to the Fathers': The Nature of Historical Understanding in 20th-Century Patristic *Ressourcement*." *Reviews in Religion and Theology* 23, no. 1 (2016).

Irenaeus and James R. Payton. *Irenaeus on the Christian Faith: A Condensation of Against Heresies*. Eugene, OR: Pickwick, 2011.

Jerome. *Trois vies de moines: Paul, Malchus, Hilarion*, edited by Pierre Leclerc, Edguardo Martín Morales, and Adalbert de Vogüé. In *Sources Chrétiennes* 508. Paris: Cerf, 2007.

Jersild, Paul T. *Spirit Ethics: Scripture and the Moral Life*. Minneapolis: Fortress Press, 2000.

Johnson, Timothy J. *Franciscans at Prayer: The Medieval Franciscans*. Leiden: Brill, 2007.

Jones, L. Gregory. "Formed and Transformed by Scripture: Character, Community, and Authority in the Biblical Interpretation." In *Character and Scripture: Moral Formation, Community, and Biblical Interpretation*, edited by William Brown. Grand Rapids: Wm. B. Eerdmans, 2002.

Jones, Tony. *Divine Intervention: Encountering God through the Ancient Practice of Lectio Divina*. Colorado Springs: Th1nk Books, 2006.

Julian of Norwich. *Revelations of Divine Love*, translated by Grace Warrack. Grand Rapids: Christian Classics Ethereal Library, 1901.

Justin. "Apologie pour les Chrétiens." In *Sources Chrétiennes* 507, edited by Charles Munier. Paris: Cerf, 2006.

Kalaitzidis, Pantelis. "From the 'Return to the Fathers' to the Need for a Modern Orthodox Theology," edited by Paul Meyendorff. *St. Vladimir's Theological Quarterly* 54, no. 1 (2010): 5–36.

Kavanagh, Aidan. *On Liturgical Theology: The Hale Memorial Lectures of Seabury-Western Theological Seminary*. Collegeville, MN: Liturgical Press, 1984.

Keenan, Mary Emily. "De Professione Christiana and De Perfectione: A Study of the Ascetical Doctrine of Saint Gregory of Nyssa." *Dumbarton Oaks Papers* 5 (1950): 167–207.

Keith, Aimee L. "The Process of Resolving Spiritual Struggle Following Adulthood Trauma." PhD diss., Antioch University, 2017.

Keller, Simon. "Virtue Ethics Is Self-Effacing." *Australasian Journal of Philosophy* 85, no. 2 (2007): 221–32.

Kellner, Hans. "Introduction: Describing Re-Descriptions." In *A New Philosophy of History*, edited by Frank Ankersmit and Hans Kellner. Chicago: University of Chicago Press, 1995.

Khawaja, Irfan. "David Solomon on Egoism and Virtue." In *Beyond the Self: Virtue Ethics and the Problem of Culture*, edited by Raymond Hain. Waco: Baylor University Press, 2019.

Kierkegaard, Søren, and Howard V. Hong. *Søren Kierkegaard: Journals and Papers—Volume 4, S–Z*. Bloomington: Indiana University Press, 1975.

King, Karen L. *What Is Gnosticism?* Cambridge, MA: Belknap Press of Harvard University Press, 2003.

King, Robert H. *Thomas Merton and Thich Nhat Hanh: Engaged Spirituality in an Age of Globalization*. New York: Continuum International, 2001.

Klijn, Albertus Frederik Johannes. *The Acts of Thomas: Introduction, Text, and Commentary—Supplements to Novum Testamentum*, 2nd rev. ed. Leiden: Brill, 2003.

Koltun-Fromm, Naomi. *Hermeneutics of Holiness: Ancient Jewish and Christian Notions of Sexuality and Religious Community*. Oxford: Oxford University Press, 2010.

———. "Sexuality and Holiness: Semitic Christian and Jewish Conceptualizations of Sexual Behavior." *Vigiliae Christianae* 54 (2000): 375–95.

Kotva, Joseph J. *The Christian Case for Virtue Ethics: Moral Traditions and Moral Arguments*. Washington, DC: Georgetown University Press, 1996.

Kreidler, Mary Jane. "Montanism and Monasticism: Charism and the Authority in the Early Church." Paper presented at Oxford Patristics Conference, "Critica, Classica, Ascetica, Liturgica," Leuven, 1983.

Laird, Martin S. *Gregory of Nyssa and the Grasp of Faith: Union, Knowledge, and Divine Presence*. Oxford Early Christian Studies. Oxford: Oxford University Press, 2004.

Lossky, Vladimir. *In the Image and Likeness of God*. Crestwood, NY: St. Vladimir's Seminary Press, 1985.

———. *The Mystical Theology of the Eastern Church*. London: J. Clarke, 1957.

Loughlin, Gerard, and Virginia Burrus. "Queer Father: Gregory of Nyssa and the Subversion of Identity." In *Queer Theology: Rethinking the Western Body*. Oxford: Blackwell, 2007.

Louth, Andrew. *The Origins of the Christian Mystical Tradition: From Plato to Denys*, 2nd ed. Oxford: Oxford University Press, 2007.

Lowther Clarke, W. K. *St. Gregory of Nyssa: The Life of St. Macrina*. London: Society for Promoting Christian Knowledge, 1916.

Ludlow, Morwenna. "Christian Formation and the Body–Soul Relationship in Gregory of Nyssa." In *Exploring Gregory of Nyssa: Philosophical, Theological, and Historical Studies*, edited by Anna Marmodoro and Neil B. McLynn, 160–78. Oxford: Oxford University Press, 2018.

———. "Divine Infinity and Eschatology: The Limits and Dynamics of Human Knowledge, According to Gregory of Nyssa." In *Gregory of Nyssa: Contra Eunomium II*, edited by Lenka Karfíková, Scot Douglass, and Johannes Zachhuber. Leiden: Brill, 2004.

———. *Gregory of Nyssa*. Oxford: Oxford University Press, 2013.

———. *Gregory of Nyssa, Ancient and (Post)Modern*. Oxford: Oxford University Press, 2007.

———. *Universal Salvation: Eschatology in the Thought of Gregory of Nyssa and Karl Rahner*. Oxford: New York, 2000.

Luther, Martin. *Martin Luther's Basic Theological Writings*, edited by Timothy F. Lull. Minneapolis: Fortress Press, 2005.

MacIntyre, Alasdair C. *After Virtue: A Study in Moral Theory*, 3rd ed. Notre Dame, IN: University of Notre Dame Press, 2007.

Maican, Petre. "Holiness and Personal Development: A Balthasarian Approach to Holiness for Eastern Orthodox Use." *Communio Viatorum* 61, no. 1 (2019): 28–39.

———. "Overcoming Exclusion in Eastern Orthodoxy: Human Dignity and Disability from a Christological Perspective." *Studies in Christian Ethics* 33, no. 4 (2019): 496–509.

Marion, Jean-Luc. *The Visible and the Revealed*. New York: Fordham University Press, 2008.

Martinez, Joel. "Is Virtue Ethics Self-Effacing?" *Australasian Journal of Philosophy* 89, no. 2 (2011): 277–88.

Maspero, Giulio. "Deification, Relation (Schesis) and Ontology in Gregory of Nyssa." In *Theosis/Deification Christian Doctrines of Divinization East and West*, edited by John Arblaster and Rob Faesen, 19–34. Leuven: Peeters, 2018.

Matera, Frank J. *New Testament Ethics: The Legacies of Jesus and Paul*, 1st ed. Louisville: Westminster John Knox Press, 1996.

Mattison, William C. *The Sermon on the Mount and Moral Theology: A Virtue Perspective.* Cambridge: Cambridge University Press, 2017.

Maximovitch, John. *Humility and Struggle: The Fundamental Virtues.* Passaic, NJ: Sts. Cosmas and Damian Russian Orthodox Church, 1953. http://passaicrussianchurch.com/books/english/sermons_john_maximovich.htm?fbclid=IwAR1r-O4bk7rFYxygb_wZTxgGY6sLxjEYUdP71I91E45iVQMqXV-XYjiJ8bo#_Toc100019543.

McGowan, Andrew Brian. *Ancient Christian Worship: Early Church Practices in Social, Historical, and Theological Perspective.* Grand Rapids: Baker Academic, 2014.

McGuckin, John Anthony. "St. Gregory of Nyssa: Bishop, Philosopher, Exegete, Theologian." In *Exploring Gregory of Nyssa: Philosophical, Theological, and Historical Studies,* edited by Anna Marmodoro and Neil B. McLynn, 7–28. Oxford: Oxford University Press, 2018.

Meawad, Stephen M. "Liturgy as Ethicizer: Cultivating Ecological Consciousness through a Coptic Orthodox Liturgical Ethos." In *T&T Clark Handbook of Christian Theology and the Modern Sciences,* edited by John P. Slattery, 307–17. London: T&T Clark, 2020.

Meilaender, Gilbert. *The Theory and Practice of Virtue.* Notre Dame, IN: University of Notre Dame Press, 1988.

Mendola, Joseph. *Goodness and Justice: A Consequentialist Moral Theory.* Cambridge Studies in Philosophy. Cambridge: Cambridge University Press, 2006.

Meredith, Anthony. *Gregory of Nyssa.* London: Routledge, 2012.

Méthode D'Olympe. "Le Banquet," edited by Herbert Musurillo and Victor-Henry Debidour. In *Sources Chrétiennes* 95, edited by H. de Lubac, J. Daniélou, and C. Mondésert. Paris: Cerf, 1963.

———. *St. Methodius: The Symposium—A Treatise on Chastity,* edited by Herbert Musurillo. New York: Paulist Press, 1958.

Migne, J. P. "Exegetica in Psalmos." In *Patrologia Graeca Tomus XII,* Origenes, Tomus II. Seu Petit-Montrouge: Venit Apud Editorem, 1857.

———. "Salutate Priscillam." In *Patrologia Graeca Tomus LI.* S.P.A. Joannis Chyrostomi. Seu Petit-Montrouge: Venit Apud Editorem, 1860.

Mignolo, Walter. *The Darker Side of Western Modernity: Global Futures, Decolonial Options.* Durham, NC: Duke University Press, 2011.

Moberly, Jennifer. *The Virtue of Bonhoeffer's Ethics: A Study of Dietrich Bonhoeffer's Ethics in Relation to Virtue Ethics.* Princeton Theological Monograph Series. Eugene, OR: Pickwick, 2013.

Morray-Jones, C. R. A. "The Temple Within: The Embodied Divine Image and Its Worship in the Dead Sea Scrolls and Other Jewish and Christian Sources." *Society of Biblical Literature Seminar Papers* 37 (1998): 400–431.

Moss, Candida R. *The Myth of Persecution: How Early Christians Invented a Story of Martyrdom.* New York: HarperCollins, 2014.

Musurillo, Herbertus. "De Vita Moysis." In *Gregorii Nysseni Opera VII,* edited by Wernerus Jaeger and Hermannus Langerbeck. Leiden: Brill, 1964.

Neusner, Jacob. *Aphrahat and Judaism: The Christian-Jewish Argument in Fourth-Century Iran.* Studia Post-Biblica. Leiden: Brill, 1971.

Nikolakopoulos, Konstantinos. "An Orthodox Critique of Some Radical Approaches in New Testament Studies." *GOTR* 47 (2002): 338–53.

Nietzsche, Friedrich Wilhelm. *Die fröhliche Wissenschaft ["La Gaya Scienza"].* Munich: Wilhelm Goldmann Verlag, 1959.

Oakley, Justin. "Virtue Ethics and Bioethics." In *The Cambridge Companion to Virtue Ethics*, edited by Daniel C. Russell. Cambridge: Cambridge University Press, 2013.

O'Keefe, John J., and Russell R. Reno. *Sanctified Vision: An Introduction to Early Christian Interpretation of the Bible.* Baltimore: Johns Hopkins University Press, 2005.

O'Leary, Joseph S. "Divine Simplicity and the Plurality of Attributes." In *Gregory of Nyssa: Contra Eunomium II*, edited by Lenka Karfikova, Scot Douglass, and Johannes Zachhuber. Leiden: Brill, 2004.

Origen. *Exeg. in Psalm*, I 3 (Migne, *Patrologia Graeca Tomus XII*, 1080C).

———. "Homélies sue le Cantique de Cantiques." In *Sources Chrétiennes* 37 bis, edited by Olivier Rousseau. Reprint of 2nd revised and corrected edition. Paris: Cerf, 2019.

———. "Homélies sur le Lévitique, tome I." In *Sources Chrétiennes* 286, edited by Marcel Borret. Paris: Cerf, 1981.

———. "Traité des Principes, tome IV." In *Sources Chrétiennes* 268, edited by Henri Crouzel and Manlio Simonetti. Paris: Cerf, 1980.

Origen and Gary Wayne Barkley. *Homilies on Leviticus: 1–16*. Fathers of the Church. Washington, DC: Catholic University of America Press, 1990.

Osiek, Carolyn, and Helmut Koester. *Shepherd of Hermas: A Commentary*. Hermeneia—a Critical and Historical Commentary on the Bible. Minneapolis: Fortress Press, 1999.

Paintner, Christine Valters. *Lectio Divina: The Sacred Art—Transforming Words and Images into Heart-Centered Prayer*. Woodstock, VT: SkyLight Paths, 2011.

Paintner, Christine Valters, and Lucy Wynkoop. *Lectio Divina: Contemplative Awakening and Awareness*. New York: Paulist Press, 2008.

Paisios, Elder. *Spiritual Counsels III: Spiritual Struggle*, translated by Peter Chamberas. Patmos, Greece: Monastery of St. John the Theologian, 2010.

Papaconstantinou, Arietta. "Historiography, Hagiography, and the Making of the Coptic 'Church of the Martyrs' in Early Islamic Egypt." *Dumbarton Oaks Papers* 60 (2006): 65–86.

Papanikolaou, Aristotle. "Theosis." In *The Oxford Handbook of Mystical Theology*, edited by Edward Howells and Mark Allen McIntosh, 569–85. Oxford: Oxford University Press, 2020.

———. "Trinity, Virtue, and Violence." In *God and the Moral Life*, edited by Myriam Renaud and Joshua Daniel, 115–34. London: Routledge, 2017.

Parfit, Derek. *Reasons and Persons*. Oxford: Oxford University Press, 1987.

Pargament, Kenneth I., and Julie J. Exline. "Religious and Spiritual Struggles," 2020. www.apa.org/research/action/religious-spiritual-struggles.

Pope Paul VI. *Decree on Priestly Training: Optatam Totius*, no. 16. Vatican City, 1965.

Paulsell, Stephanie. "'The Inscribed Heart: A Spirituality of Intellectual Work': Reading as a Spiritual Practice." *Lexington Theological Quarterly* 36 (Fall 2001): 139–54.

———. "Spiritual Formation and Intellectual Work in Theological Education." *Theology Today* 55 (July 1998): 229–34.

Pettigrove, Glen. "Is Virtue Ethics Self-Effacing?" *Journal of Ethics* 15, no. 3 (2011): 191–207.

Pinckaers, Servais. "Scripture and the Renewal of Moral Theology." In *The Pinckaers Reader: Renewing Thomistic Moral Theology*, edited by John Berkman and Craig Steven Titus, 46–63. Washington, DC: Catholic University of America Press, 2005.

Pincoffs, Edmund L. *Quandaries and Virtues: Against Reductivism in Ethics*. Lawrence: University Press of Kansas, 1986.

Piper, John. *The Justification of God: An Exegetical and Theological Study of Romans 9:1–23*, 2nd ed. Grand Rapids: Baker Books, 1993.

Podmore, Simon D. *Struggling with God: Kierkegaard and the Temptation of Spiritual Trial.* London: James Clarke & Co., 2013.

Ponticus, Evagrius, and Ilaria L. E. Ramelli. *Evagrius, Kephalia Gnostika: A New Translation of the Unreformed Text from the Syriac,* translated by Ilaria L. E. Ramelli. Writings from the Greco-Roman World, edited by Sebastian Brock, vol. 38. Atlanta: SBL Press, 2015.

Porter, Jean. *Nature as Reason: A Thomistic Theory of the Natural Law.* Grand Rapids: Wm. B. Eerdmans, 2005.

———. *The Recovery of Virtue: The Relevance of Aquinas for Christian Ethics.* Louisville: Westminster John Knox Press, 1990.

———. "The Subversion of Virtue: Acquired and Infused Virtues in the *Summa Theologiae.*" *Annual of the Society of Christian Ethics* 12 (1992): 19–41.

Pseudo-Dionysius, Günther Heil, and Adolf Martin Ritter. *De Coelesti Hierarchia; De Ecclesiastica Hierarchia; De Mystica Theologia; and Epistulae* [in Greek, with critical matter in German]. Corpus Dionysiacum 2, überarb. Aufl. ed. Berlin: De Gruyter, 2012.

Pseudo-Macarius. *The Fifty Spiritual Homilies; and the Great Letter.* Classics of Western Spirituality. New York: Paulist Press, 1992.

Quispel, Gilles. "The Study of Encratism: A Historical Survey." In *Gnostica, Judaica, Catholica: Collected Essays of Gilles Quispel,* edited by Johannes Van Oort. Nag Hammadi and Manichaean Studies. Leiden: Brill, 2008.

Ramelli, Ilaria L. E. "Gregory's and Evagrius's Biographical and Theological Relations: Origen's Heritage and Neoplatonism." In *Evagrius between Origen, the Cappadocians, and Neoplatonism,* edited by Ilaria Ramelli. *Studia Patristica* 84: 165–231.

———. "Gregory of Nyssa on the Soul (and the Restoration): From Plato to Origen." In *Exploring Gregory of Nyssa: Philosophical, Theological, and Historical Studies,* edited by Anna Marmodoro and Neil B. McLynn, 110–41. Oxford: Oxford University Press, 2018.

———. "L'inno a Cristo-Logos Nel Simposio Di Metodio Di Olimpo." In *Motivi e forme della poesia cristiana antica tra Scrittura e tradizione classica: Incontro di studiosi dell'antichita cristiana, Roma, Augustinianum, 3–5 Maggio 2007.* Studia Emphemeridis Augustinianum (Rome, 2008), 257–80.

———. "Mysticism, Apocalypticism, and Platonism, in Platonic Pathways." Paper presented at Fourteenth Annual Conference of the International Society for Neoplatonic Studies, Bream, United Kingdom, 2018.

———. "Origen to Evagrius." In *Brill's Companion to the Reception of Plato in Antiquity,* edited by Harold Tarrant, Danil A. Layne, Dirk Baltzly, and François Renaud, 271–91. Leiden: Brill, 2018.

———. *Social Justice and the Legitimacy of Slavery: The Role of Philosophical Asceticism from Ancient Judaism to Late Antiquity.* Oxford Early Christian Studies. Oxford: Oxford University Press, 2016.

———. "Transformations of the Household and Marriage Theory between Neo-Stoicism, Middle Platonism, and Early Christianity." *Rivista di Filosofia Neoscolastica* 100, nos. 2–3 (2008): 369–96.

Ratzinger, Joseph. *Biblical Interpretation in Crisis: The Ratzinger Conference on Bible and Church.* Encounter Series 9, edited by Richard John Neuhaus. Grand Rapids: Wm. B. Eerdmans, 1989.

Roberts, Robert C. "Varieties of Virtue Ethics." In *Varieties of Virtue Ethics,* edited by David Carr, James Arthur, and Kristján Kristjánsson, 17–34. London: Palgrave Macmillan, 2017.

Roskam, Geert. *On the Path to Virtue: The Stoic Doctrine of Moral Progress and Its Reception in (Middle-) Platonism*. Ancient and Medieval Philosophy, Series 1. Leuven: Leuven University Press, 2005.

Rubenson, Samuel. *The Letters of St. Antony: Monasticism and the Making of a Saint*. Studies in Antiquity and Christianity. Minneapolis: Fortress Press, 1995.

Sanders, Jack T. "The Question of the Relevance of Jesus for Ethics Today." In *The Use of Scripture in Moral Theology*, edited by Charles Curran and Richard McCormick. New York: Paulist Press, 1984.

Sandis, Constantine. "Modern Moral Philosophy Before and After Anscombe." *Enrahonar* 64 (2020): 39–62.

Sanford, Jonathan J. *Before Virtue: Assessing Contemporary Virtue Ethics*. Washington, DC: Catholic University of America Press, 2015.

Schmidt, Richard H. *God Seekers: Twenty Centuries of Christian Spiritualities*. Grand Rapids: Wm. B. Eerdmans, 2008.

Schüssler Fiorenza, Elisabeth. "Introduction: Exploring the Intersections of Race, Gender, Status, and Ethnicity in Early Christian Studies." In *Prejudice and Christian Beginnings: Investigating Race, Gender, and Ethnicity in Early Christian Studies*, edited by Laura Salah Nasrallah and Elisabeth Schüssler Fiorenza, 9–18. Minneapolis: Fortress Press, 2010.

Sferlea, Ovidiu. "On the Interpretation of the Theory of Perpetual Progress (Epektasis): Taking into Account the Testimony of Eastern Monastic Tradition." *Revue d'histoire ecclésiastique* 109, nos. 3–4 (2014): 564–87.

Sherwin, Michael. "Infused Virtue and the Effects of Acquired Vice: A Test Case for the Thomistic Theory of Infused Cardinal Virtues." *The Thomist* 73, no. 1 (2009): 29–52.

Siker, Jeffrey S. *Scripture and Ethics: Twentieth-Century Portraits*. Oxford: Oxford University Press, 1997.

Silvas, Anna. *Gregory of Nyssa: The Letters*, translated from the Ancient Greek. Supplements to *Vigiliae Christianae*. Leiden: Brill, 2007.

Sirka, Zdenko S. "The Role of Theoria in Gregory of Nyssa's 'Vita Moysis' and in 'Canticum Canticorum.'" *Communio Viatorum: A Theological Journal* 11 (2012): 142–63.

Slote, Michael. *From Morality to Virtue*. Oxford: Oxford University Press, 1992.

———. *The Impossibility of Perfection: Aristotle, Feminism, and the Complexities of Ethics*. Oxford: Oxford University Press, 2011.

Smith, J. Warren. "John Wesley's Growth in Grace and Gregory of Nyssa's Epectasy: A Conversation in Dynamic Perfection." *Bulletin of the John Rylands University Library of Manchester* 85, nos. 2–3 (2003): 347–57.

———. *Passion and Paradise: Human and Divine Emotion in the Thought of Gregory of Nyssa*. New York: Crossroad, 2004.

Smith, Michael. "Deontological Moral Obligations and Non-Welfarist Agent-Relative Values." In *Developing Deontology: New Essays in Ethical Theory*, edited by Brad Hooker. Malden, MA: Wiley-Blackwell, 2012.

Smith, Trevor William. "Virtue, Oppression, and Resistance Struggles." PhD diss., Marquette University, 2015. http://epublications.marquette.edu/dissertations_mu/551.

Sorabji, Richard. *Emotion and Peace of Mind: From Stoic Agitation to Christian Temptation*. Gifford Lectures. Oxford: Oxford University Press, 2000.

Spinks, Bryan D. *Do This in Remembrance of Me: The Eucharist from the Early Church to the Present Day*. London: SCM Press, 2013.

Spohn, William C. *What Are They Saying About Scripture and Ethics?* Fully rev. and expanded ed. New York: Paulist Press, 1995.

Stefaniw, Blossom. "Exegetical Curricula in Origen, Didymus, and Evagrius." *Studia Patristica* 44 (2010): 281–95.

Sterk, Andrea. *Renouncing the World Yet Leading the Church: The Monk-Bishop in Late Antiquity*. Cambridge, MA: Harvard University Press, 2004.

Stokas, A. G. "A Genealogy of Grit: Education in the New Gilded Age." *Educational Theory* 65 (2015): 513–28.

Stylianopoulos, Theodore. "Perspectives in Orthodox Biblical Interpretation." *GOTR* 47 (2002): 325–36.

———. *The New Testament: An Orthodox Perspective*. Brookline, MA: Holy Cross Orthodox Press, 1997.

Sue, Derald Wing, Jennifer Bucceri, Annie I. Lin, Kevin L. Nadal, and Gina C. Torino. "Racial Microaggressions and the Asian American Experience." *Asian American Journal of Psychology* 8, no. 1 (2009): 88.

Swanton, Christine. "Practical Virtue Ethics." In *International Encyclopedia of Ethics*. New York: Wiley Online Library, 2013.

Tadros, Samuel. *Motherland Lost: The Egyptian and Coptic Quest for Modernity*. Stanford, CA: Hoover Institution, 2013.

Teresa of Avila. *The Life of Saint Teresa of Avila by Herself*, edited by J. M. Cohen. London: Penguin Classics, 1988.

Tessman, Lisa. *Burdened Virtues: Virtue Ethics for Liberatory Struggles*. Studies in Feminist Philosophy. Oxford: Oxford University Press, 2005.

Tholfsen, Trygve R. "Postmodern Theory of History: A Critique." In *Memoria y Civilización* 2 (1999): 203–22.

Tough, Paul. *Helping Children Succeed: What Works and Why*. Boston: Houghton Mifflin Harcourt, 2016.

Tracy, David. *The Analogical Imagination: Christian Theology and the Culture of Pluralism*. New York: Crossroad, 1981.

Trimble, Walter. "First Philosophy in a 'Post-Christian' World." *Sankt-Peterburgskoi Dukhovnoi Akademii* 1, no. 3 (2019): 27.

Truscott, Derek, and Kenneth H. Crook. *Ethics for the Practice of Psychology in Canada, Revised and Expanded Edition*. Edmonton: University of Alberta Press, 2013.

Vardy, Peter, and Charlotte Vardy. *Ethics Matters*. Norwich: SCM Press, 2012.

Verhey, Allen. *Remembering Jesus: Christian Community, Scripture, and the Moral Life*. Grand Rapids: Wm. B. Eerdmans, 2002.

———. "The Use of Scripture in Ethics." In *The Use of Scripture in Moral Theology*, edited by Charles Curran and Richard McCormick. New York: Paulist Press, 1984.

Vigorelli, Ilaria. "Soul's Dance in Clement, Plotinus and Gregory of Nyssa." In *Evagrius between Origen, the Cappadocians, and Neoplatonism*, edited by Ilaria Ramelli. Leuven: Peeters, 2017.

Ware, Kallistos. *The Orthodox Way*. Classics Series. Crestwood, NY: St. Vladimir's Seminary Press, 2018.

Williams, Rowan. *The Wound of Knowledge: Christian Spirituality from the New Testament to St. John of the Cross*, 2nd rev. ed. Cambridge, MA: Cowley Publications, 1991.

Weil, Simone. *Attente De Dieu [Lettres Écrites Du 19 Janvier Au 26 Mai 1942.]*. Paris: Éditions Fayard, 1966.

Wetzel, James. *Augustine and the Limits of Virtue*. Cambridge: Cambridge University Press, 1992.

Williams, Bernard. *Ethics and the Limits of Philosophy*. London: Routledge, 2011.

Wogaman, J. Philip. *Christian Ethics: A Historical Introduction*, 2nd ed. Louisville: Westminster John Knox Press, 2011.

Woodill, Joseph. *The Fellowship of Life: Virtue Ethics and Orthodox Christianity*. Moral Traditions and Moral Arguments Series. Washington, DC: Georgetown University Press, 1998.

Wright, Brian J. *Communal Reading in the Time of Jesus: A Window into Early Christian Reading Practices*. Minneapolis: Fortress Press, 2017.

Xia, Hui. "From Light to Darkness: The Progress of the Spiritual Journey According to Gregory of Nyssa's 'De Vita Moysis.'" In *Gregory of Nyssa: Contra Eunomium II*, edited by Johan Leemans and Matthieu Cassin, 540–51. Leiden: Brill, 2010.

Yu, Jiyuan. "The Practicality of Ancient Virtue Ethics: Greece and China." *Dao: A Journal of Comparative Philosophy* 9, no. 3 (September 2010): 289–302.

Zachhuber, Johannes. "The Soul as Dynamis in Gregory of Nyssa's 'On the Soul and Resurrection.'" In *Exploring Gregory of Nyssa: Philosophical, Theological, and Historical Studies*, edited by Anna Marmodoro and Neil B. McLynn, 142–59. Oxford: Oxford University Press, 2018.

Zizioulas, John D. *Communion and Otherness: Further Studies in Personhood and the Church*, edited by Paul MacPartlan. London: T&T Clark, 2009.

Παϊσίου Ἁγιορείτου. ΠΝΕΥΜΑΤΙΚΟΣ ΑΓΩΝΑΣ. ΣΟΥΡΩΤΗ ΘΕΣΣΑΛΟΝΙΚΗΣ: Ἱερὸν Ἡσυχαστήριον Μοναζουσῶν «Εὐαγγελιστὴς Ἰωάννης ὁ Θεολόγος», 2001.

INDEX

Tables and notes are indicated by "t" and "n" following the page numbers.

acquired vs. infused virtues, 48–50, 62–63n38, 63n39

Acts of Thomas, 138, 142

Adam and Eve, 150, 162–63n48. *See also* fallen and risen human nature

Adams, Robert Merrihew, 39–40, 44, 63nn57–58, 64n59

adiastema and *diastema*, 130n156

adverse virtue, 88

agency: in antinomianism, 52; Aquinas on, 57–58; grace and divine-human co-agency, 46–50, 54, 55, 57–59, 83–84, 93, 101; Gregory of Nyssa on, 101; in Pelagianism, 47

Aimilianos, Father, 157

Alfeyev, Hilarion, 22–23n26, 188n7

allegory in sacred reading, 156, 170–71, 176, 184, 187, 189nn12–13

altruism, 44–45

Ambrose of Milan, 16

Amphilochius of Iconium, 25n62

anagogy: body as instrument in, 136; *epektasis* and, 9; Godward progress through, 44, 61n9, 86, 100, 108–15, 129n142; Gregory of Nyssa's theory of, 16, 18, 19, 22n22, 25n58, 100, 108–15, 182; purification and, 118–19

angelification and restoration, 20, 135, 136, 143–49, 158

angels, 143–44

Annas, Julia, 33, 62–63n38, 65n77

Anscombe, G. E. M., 4–6, 11, 22n7

anthropology: in Aristotelian ethics, 32; ethics inquiry and, 5–7, 50, 60, 99–100; fallen and risen nature of humanity in, 7–8, 46; in Gregory of Nyssa's theory of progress, 110, 115, 124, 132n196; Luther and, 51, 60; structural oppression and, 85

antinomianism, 45, 46, 50–55

Antony the Great: Athanasius and, 14, 80–81, 84, 145–46, 164n64; consecration ritual and, 163n63; on taking that which is edifying from all we encounter, 18; transformational relationship with Scripture of, 185–86

apatheia (passionlessness), 120–21, 131–32n186

Aphrahat, 139–42, 150, 166n139

apocalypticism and apocalyptic literature, 144, 150–52, 155–56, 160

apophaticism and cataphaticism, 29, 61n9, 63n58, 107–8, 115, 124

Aquinas, Thomas, 30–31, 42, 45, 48–49, 57–58; *Summa Theologica*, 57. *See also* Aristotle and Aristotelian-Thomistic ethics

aretaic life. *See* anagogy; *epektasis*; good life

Aristotle and Aristotelian-Thomistic ethics, 30–31; God as orienting principle in, 93; Gregory of Nyssa compared to, 104, 113; habits and habituation in, 32, 37, 45–46, 76; moral luck and moral effort in, 39–43, 64n71; oppression and, 87–88; perfectionism and (un)attainability in, 32–38, 77; struggle in, 74, 76–77, 83; universalism and appeal of, 193; virtuous agents and unity of virtues in, 32–35, 37, 62n30
asceticism: angelic restoration and, 135, 143–49; bodily passions and, 20, 75, 147, 160–61, 195–96; cultures of, 162n47; divine indwelling and, 14, 135–36, 149–58; ethics context for, 10, 19–20; grace and, 81, 96n56; Gregory of Nyssa on, 110; inequality and, 195–96; liturgical transformation and, 149–58; love and, 89; marriage and, 158; among nonmonastics, 159–60; Orthodox Christianity and roots of, 24n43; sexual purity and, 135–43; spiritual struggle compared to, 75; struggle against base desires and, 80, 141–42
Athanasius of Alexandria (saint), 24n39, 25n62; marginalization of women and, 16–17; spiritual struggle of, 14; *Vita Antonii*, 80–81, 84, 145–47, 164n64, 185, 196
Athanassoulis, Nafsika, 22n17, 39
Augustine, 44–45, 47–48, 55–57, 67n145, 67n148

Baker, Jennifer, 98n120, 132n197
Balás, David, 112
Balthasar, Han Urs van, 101, 121
baptism, 150, 163n48
Barnabas, 34
Barnes, Patrick, 65n91
Basil of Caesarea, 18, 25n62, 101, 147, 182–83
beatific visions, 62n10, 100
Beatitudes, Gregory of Nyssa's commentary on, 105–6, 110–12, 116, 120
Beeley, Christopher A., 24n39
Behr, John, 158–59
Benedict XVI (pope), 190n22
Berkhof, Kendrikus, 58
Biblical Ethics in the 21st Century (Chan), 181
Biermann, Joel, 51–52
bodies and bodily passions: asceticism and, 20, 75, 147, 160–61, 195–96; demonic struggles compared to, 84; denigration of, 41; divine indwelling and, 135–36, 150–53, 155; in Gregory of Nyssa's *epektasis* theory, 19, 101, 102, 108, 110, 118–21, 124; in Luther's theology, 51, 66n116; pleasure and, 36, 140–42; purification of, 136, 143, 149; sacred reading and, 182; souls' development with, 81, 124, 196; spirituality and, 29–30; spiritual struggle against desires of, 79–85, 117–21, 196; temptation and, 84–85, 87. *See also* sexuality and sexual continence
Body of Christ. *See* Church; Jesus Christ
Boersma, Hans, 17, 47, 58–59, 99–100, 128n127, 148, 188n7
Bohm, Thomas, 116
Bradshaw, Paul F., 165n107
Breck, John, 170–71, 174, 189–90n18, 190n21, 191n41
Brock, Brian, 169, 175, 181
Brock, Sebastian P., 162–63n48
Brown, Peter, 138, 140
Bucur, Bogdan, 144–45, 173, 189n12
Burrows, Mark, 157
Burrus, Virginia, 16–17, 24–25n58

Cadenhead, Raphael, 130n161
Cahill, Lisa, 88, 166n144, 191n59, 196
Cappadocian fathers. *See* Basil of Caesarea; Church Fathers; Gregory of Nazianzus; Gregory of Nyssa
Caputo, John, 21n2
Cartwright, Sophie, 97n102
Cassien, Jean, 96n56
cataphaticism and apophaticism, 29, 61n9, 63n58, 107–8, 115, 124
Catholicism, 8, 60n2, 61n9, 167
Chan, Lucas: *Biblical Ethics in the 21st Century*, 181

character: action from state of good character, 64n62; asceticism and, 75; assessment of, 76; deontology and, 11; Godward progression and, 119, 168; grace and works and, 62, 63n39; moral effort and, 45; sacred reading and, 181–82; submission to God and, 45; virtue as emanation of, 33, 36, 37

charity and self-sacrifice, 75, 195

chastity, 137, 141, 160, 166n148. *See also* monasticism; sexuality and sexual continence

children and childhood, 41–42, 198–99

Christocentrism, 168, 171–75, 180

Christology, 165n109

Chrysostom, Saint John, 154, 175, 190n21

Church: communal scriptural exegesis in, 169, 176–77, 191n41; dogma and doctrine of, 44; Holy Spirit in, 60n3, 156; martyrdom and, 86, 97n91; Patristic scholarship grounded in, 9, 22–23n26, 24n43, 101; sacred reading and, 20; spiritual struggle in, 19, 85, 86

Church Fathers: asceticism and, 136, 142–43; Christocentricity and, 172, 174–75; context of, 22–23n26; defending reliance on, 12–18, 22–23n26, 23n29, 198, 199; Orthodox Christianity and, 24n43, 99, 101; philosophical currents contemporary with, 102, 109; pluralism of scriptural interpretation among, 188n7; sacred reading and, 170–72, 176–77, 182–83; teleological framework of, 10; on Trinity, 85; typology and allegory of, 172–73, 189n12; virtue and heritage of, 30. *See also specific Church Fathers*

Cicero: *De Finibus*, 77–78

circumstantial differences. *See* inequality; moral luck and moral effort

Clairmont, David, 94n1

Clement of Alexandria, 129n142, 140–45, 147, 159, 163n53, 163n62, 189n12

clothing metaphors, 163n48

Coakley, Sarah, 101, 102, 107, 124, 125n21

Cochran, Elizabeth, 95n28

community: liturgy and, 154–55; methodology from experience of, 192n75; monasticism and, 157; sacred reading and, 94n7, 168, 169, 175–78, 182; spiritual struggle in, 84–90, 93, 99, 145

Constantine's edict, 10, 14

conversion, 49–50

cooperation/synergy, 145, 164n65

Coptic Orthodox Church, 97n91

Crook, Kenneth H., 98n120, 132n197

Daley, Brian, 124

Daniélou, Jean, 101, 103, 116, 131n184, 189n12

David (king), 122

Dawson, David, 189n12

deconstructionism, 3–4

deification, 61n9, 130n156

deontology, 4, 5, 10, 11, 20, 157

desert spirituality, 84, 153

diastema and *adiastema*, 130n156

disability, 89–90

discipleship, 144–45, 152–53, 197

divine indwelling. *See* unity with God

dogma and doctrine: Church Fathers and, 101, 172; in early Church, 44; *epektasis* and, 103, 107; humans in image of God, 8; irresistibility, 96n56; moral theology and, 119; mystical theology and, 131n182; Origen on, 183; pluralism and, 188n7; Scripture and, 172; spiritual struggle and, 79; Stoicism and, 78–79, 131n186, 140; truth claims to power and, 14

double predestination, 54, 66n116

Duckworth, Angela, 40, 64n65

Eastern Orthodox Christianity, 61n9, 65n91, 127n56, 131nn182–83, 166n138

economy of salvation, 8, 47, 50, 65n89, 66n116, 77, 83–84

Edwards, Mark, 125n25

egoism. *See* self-centeredness and self-effacement

eldership and discipleship, 144–45, 152–53, 197

Encratitic Gnostics, 140–41

Enlightenment, 7–8, 21n4, 172

epektasis (perpetual progress): Aristotelian ethics compared to, 32, 37; asceticism

epektasis (*continued*)
and, 145; Clement and, 143–44, 163n62; coined in *Vita Macrinae*, 16; defined, 9, 22n22; as Godward spiritual struggle, 61n9, 93–94, 100, 102–9, 114, 129n142; grace and works in, 58–59; liturgy and, 154–55; love of God and neighbor and, 44; Luther and, 52–53; mysticism and, 120; nonlinear spectrum of, 120–21; Orthodox Christian ethics grounded in, 28; Platonic and biblical conceptions fused in, 102; self-centeredness and, 43; souls in theory of, 116–17; spiritual struggle elevated in, 38, 86, 114; unattainability of virtue and, 57; unity of virtues and, 35–36. *See also* anagogy; Godward orientation and progression
Epictetus, 78, 79–80, 95n28
Erickson, Milliard J., 58
eschatology: denominational approaches to, 63n48; *epektasis* and, 105–7; Godward spiritual struggle and, 123; in Patristic theology, 13, 16–18, 99, 101, 105; perfection and, 37; temples in, 150
ethics: development of field of, 23n28; Nietzschean shift in, 3–4, 21n4; *politeia* describing, 27; role of Scripture in, 167; as subset of spiritual life, 9, 10, 26. *See also* Orthodox Christian ethics; virtue ethics
Eucharist, 150, 152, 153–56, 176–77
Eudemian and *Nicomachean* ethics, 32, 36. *See also* Aristotle
Eunomius, 126n39
Evagrius of Pontus, 129n142, 144, 151, 152
Evdokimov, Paul, 159–60
evil and demonic forces, 73*t*, 84–90, 93, 99, 108, 121

faith: community from, 86; Godward spiritual struggle and, 110; grace and works in, 52–53, 56, 80; Luther on, 50–53; proof-texting and, 175; purity and, 110; sacred reading and, 181, 188n7, 190n22. *See also* dogma and doctrine; grace and works
fallen and risen human nature: angelification and restoration of, 143–49; base desires and, 79, 147; bodily passions and, 79; communal spiritual struggle and, 86; fulfilled in virtue, 77, 80–81, 113, 123, 146–47; God as fulfillment of, 8–9, 30; Godward progress and, 102, 106–8, 200; in Gregory of Nyssa's works, 101; reason and, 22n20; sexuality and, 140–41, 159; shared anthropology of, 6–8
fasting, 51, 85, 97n83, 137, 183, 195. *See also* asceticism
fidelity, 141, 184
First Temple literature, 151
flow, Julia Annas on concept of, 33
Foot, Philippa, 40, 64n59
Fortuin, Robert, 127n56
Fowl, Stephen E., 178, 183–84
friendship with God, 113–14

Garden of Eden. *See* fallen and risen human nature
God: deification and, 61n9; as fulfillment of human nature, 8–9, 30; goodness in unity with, 8, 43–44, 111–12; humans as image of, 8, 22n21, 143–45, 150–51; infinite/unknowable nature of, 104–5, 107–8, 112–13, 117, 127n56; modern philosophy omitting, 9; as paragon of virtue, 112–14, 119, 123, 128–29n130; Platonic thought on, 103; spiritual struggle with/toward, 90–93, 98n109, 115, 119; submission to, 81–84, 93; unity of virtues and, 35. *See also* grace and works
Godward orientation and progression: anagogy and, 108–14; angelification and restoration in, 143–49; detachment from bodily desires and, 135–37, 143, 144; *epektasis* and perpetual nature of, 102–8; Gregory of Nyssa's theological integration of, 101–2, 125n14; nonlinear spectrum of, 120–23, 195; prayer and, 194–95; sexuality and, 159; spiritual struggle and, 93–94, 99, 114–15, 118–19, 135, 187; stages of, 114–23, 135–36, 149, 158, 168, 195; virtue from,

104. *See also* asceticism; sacred reading; spiritual struggle
Golden Patristics. *See* Church Fathers; Patristic theology
Golitzin, Alexander, 151–52, 156, 157, 166n134
good life: in Aristotelian-Thomistic ethics, 30–31, 34, 45–46, 87; human nature fulfilled in, 45–46; oppression and, 87–88; perpetual progress in, 104, 113; practice's transformation in, 9; in pursuit of God-likeness, 43; self-centeredness and, 34; spiritual struggle in, 43, 118; unity with God in, 27; universality/particularity of, 36; virtue as byproduct of, 11
grace and works, 45–46; antinomianism and, 50–55; Aristotelian perfectionism vs., 37–38; in Athanasius's account of Antony, 145–46; as attribute of God, 63n57; contemporary consensus between, 55–59; in Eastern Orthodoxy, 65n91; in Orthodox Christianity, 47, 50, 65n89, 96n56; perfectionism and, 37–38; perpetual progress and, 43–44, 116, 117; prayer and, 91; spiritual struggle and, 46–50, 55–59, 80–85, 96n56, 99; virtue and, 37, 39, 46–50
Greer, Rowan J., 94n8, 125n14
Gregory of Nazianzus, 18, 25n62, 182
Gregory of Nyssa: anagogy and, 16, 18, 19, 22n22, 25n58, 100, 108–15, 182; angelification and, 144, 147–48; asceticism of, 147–48, 166n148, 196; beatific visions of God and, 62n10; Burrus on, 24–25n58; Clement and, 145; *epektasis* theory of, 28, 38, 43–44, 93–94, 102–8, 115, 125nn13–15, 145, 148, 182; grace and works and, 47, 58–59; lower/higher categorization by, 95n32, 110, 119; Origen and, 104–5, 125n25, 126n37, 126n39, 131n184; Orthodox Christianity and, 99; Platonism and, 102–5, 125n25, 126n42, 129n142; self-determination in works of, 97n102; stages of Godward spiritual struggle and, 114–23, 129n142; theological integration of, 101–2, 127n56; on unity of virtues, 128–29n130; women's marginalization and, 16–18
Gregory of Nyssa, works of: Beatitudes commentary, 105–6, 110–12, 116, 120; *Contra Eunomium I*, 112; *De perfectione*, 102, 104; *De virginitate*, 148; "De vita moysis," 105, 108, 109, 111–12, 116, 120–22, 124–25n11; "In Canticum Canticorum," 106, 108–9, 118; Psalms commentary, 108, 110, 116, 117, 120; Song of Songs commentary, 102, 117; *Vita Macrinae*, 16–18, 147
grit, 40, 64n65, 195
Guigo II, 168
Guroian, Vigen, 26, 60n2, 60n4
Gustafson, James, 178

habits and habituation: in Aristotelian ethics, 32, 37, 45–46, 76; asceticism and, 195; Augustine on, 48; Godward orientation of, 31, 46; grace and, 48; to likeness with God, 144, 151; Paisios on, 79–80; sexuality and, 142; in Thomistic ethics, 49; of thoughts, 79–80; virtue from, 30, 45
Haldane, John, 10
Hamilton, William, 193
Hampson, Daphne, 53
Harakas, Stanley, 60n2
Harper, Demetrios, 6, 21n4
Harrington, Daniel, 58
Hauerwas, Stanley, 86, 178
Hays, Richard, 177–78, 180
Heine, Ronald, 117, 126n37, 126n39
Herdt, Jennifer, 48–49, 54, 55, 61n7
heresy, 13–14
Hermas, 141
hermits, 85, 97n85, 153
Holy Spirit: Church guided by, 60n3, 156; ethics and, 27; grace and, 22n21; in Gregory of Nyssa's theological integration, 102; human nature redeemed in, 27; interiorization and, 151–52; sacred reading and, 174, 176, 178, 180, 183, 197; sexual continence and, 95n42; suffering and, 191n67
hubris and pride, 43, 44, 48, 55, 108

Hughes, Amy Brown, 138
human nature. *See* fallen and risen human nature
humility, 14, 28, 38, 81, 150, 160, 169, 180, 184
Hursthouse, Rosalind, 64n62

Ignatius of Antioch, 174
imperfection. *See* perfectionism and (un)attainability
impulse control, 136–43
individualism, 39, 61n9, 85–87, 131n182
inequality, 40–42, 195
infused vs. acquired virtues, 48–50, 62–63n38, 63n39
injustice or oppression, 40, 41, 84–90, 97n91, 196
interiorization, 150–58, 160, 197
intimacy, 87, 93, 114, 117, 157. *See also* sexuality and sexual continence; unity with God
Ip, Pui Him, 23n34
Irenaeus, 174, 176
irresistibility, doctrine of, 96n56
Isaiah (prophet), 119

Jersild, Paul, 177
Jesus Christ: ethics grounded in, 197; imitation of, 103–4, 111, 118, 150–51; on marriage in afterlife, 140; personal distinctness in, 166n137; Peter's denial of, 122; risen human nature and, 7, 8; sacred reading and, 168, 171–76, 179, 185, 197; servitude and, 15; spiritual struggle and belief in, 76–77; as temple, 155; temptation of, 84–85; typology and, 172–73; virginity and, 138. *See also* God; Holy Spirit; unity with God
Job, 83
John of the Cross, 92–93
Jonah (prophet), 34
Jones, L. Gregory, 178, 183–84
Judaism, 139–40, 144, 151
Julian of Norwich, 82–83, 91
justice, 54, 105, 179. *See also* injustice or oppression
Justin Martyr, 176–77

Kalaitzidis, Pantelis, 23n36
Kant, Immanuel, 6, 21n4
Keenan, James, 58
Keenan, Mary Emily, 101
Khawaja, Irfan, 43
Kierkegaard, Søren, 71, 76, 90, 91, 94n1, 119
King, Robert H., 166n138
Koltun-Fromm, Naomi, 139–40
Kotva, Joseph J., 58
Kreidler, Mary Jane, 185–86
Kyrillos VI (pope of Coptic Orthodox Church), 186

Lazarus, 83
lectio divina, 167–68, 191n41. *See also* sacred reading
likeness with God. *See* God; unity with God
liturgy: Christian identity in, 153, 165n107, 165n109; Christology and, 165n109; divine indwelling and, 149–53; as interiorizer, 153–56; as locus of person's holistic ascent to God and virtue, 55; regional variation in, 165n107
Lossky, Vladimir, 29, 131n182
Louth, Andrew, 116–17, 120, 126n42
love of God and neighbor: asceticism and, 136–37, 160–61, 196; Church and community and, 86–87, 93; *epektasis* and, 42–45; grace and, 63n57; sacred reading and, 171, 179; virtue as perfection of, 55, 89
luck. *See* moral luck and moral effort
Ludlow, Morwenna, 12, 16, 17, 101, 102, 114, 130n165
Luther, Martin, 50–54, 66n116, 76, 80, 81, 87

MacIntyre, Alasdair, 6, 11, 22n7, 23n28, 35–36
Macquarrie, John, 58
Macrina of Nyssa, 16–18, 147
Maican, Petre, 166n137
Malaty, Tadros Yacoub, 186
Marion, Jean-Luc, 131n183
marriage, 137–42, 158–59, 162n39. *See also* sexuality and sexual continence
Martens, Peter W., 189n12

martyrs and martyrdom, 13–14, 24n37, 97n91
Matera, Frank, 173
Mattison, William, 181
Maximovich, John, 38
Maximus the Confessor, 62n18, 64n75
McGowan, Andrew, 153
meditation, 51, 75, 168, 175, 185–87, 195
Meilaender, Gilbert, 52
Meredith, Anthony, 103, 126n42, 131n184
Methodius of Olympus, 95n42, 137–39
Moberly, Jennifer, 47
modern moral philosophy: absence of spiritual struggle in, 19, 31, 71–72, 100, 198; fragmentation in, 27; God omitted from, 9; Orthodox Christian praxis and, 11, 59–60, 198
monasticism: Antony and, 14, 145–46, 185–86; decline in, 158; Eastern Christian, 166n138; *epektatic* ascent and, 145; Gospel's role in, 163n63; interior transformation and, 152, 157; lay origins of, 137, 145, 166n139; Orthodox Christianity and roots of, 24n43; Pachomius and, 157; poverty and obedience vows of, 166n148; sacred reading and, 186; servitude and, 15; sexual continence and, 141; struggle against base desires and, 80
moral injury, 88–89
moral luck and moral effort, 39–43, 89
Morray-Jones, C. R. A., 149, 157
mortification. *See* purification and purgation
Moses (prophet): celibacy of, 139–40; "De vita moysis" and, 124–25n11; disobedience at Meribah, 122; *epektasis* and, 102–3, 105, 111; as example of divine-human cooperation, 34, 84; Pachomius as image of, 157
Musurillo, Herbert, 117
mysticism and mystical theology, 101, 116–17, 120, 127n84, 131n184, 131nn182–84, 166n138. *See also* unity with God

Nag Hammadi manuscripts, 12
narrative quests/journeys, 12, 13, 35–36, 50, 51
negative theology, 29–30
neighbor, love of. *See* love of God and neighbor
Nicaean-Constantinopolitan Creed, 14
Nicomachean and *Eudemian* ethics, 32, 36. *See also* Aristotle
Nietzsche, Friedrich, 3, 6, 21n4
Niketas Stethatos, 152–53, 155

obedience, monastic vow of, 160, 166n148
O'Keefe, John J., 17, 174, 183, 189n12
O' Leary, Joseph, 107
oppression. *See* injustice or oppression
Origen: on angelification, 144; Gregory of Nyssa and, 104–5, 125n25, 126n37, 131n184; Louth on, 116; sacred reading and, 167, 168, 171, 174–76, 183, 190n35; typology and allegory and, 189nn12–13
Orthodox Christian ethics: Aristotelian-Thomistic ethics compared to, 30–38, 40, 60; asceticism in, 75; as category, 60nn1–2, 61n8; context for, 26–32; efficacy of, 198–99; *epektasis* in, 28; God as *telos* of, 27–28, 30; Godward progress in, 100, 103–4, 114–15, 120, 123–24, 136, 194, 198–200; grace and works in, 45–46; moral luck and effort in, 40–43; perfectionism and, 36–38; perpetual progress in, 99; sacred reading and, 167; self-centeredness and self-effacement, 43–45; spiritual struggle and, 93–94; unity with God in, 27–28, 30, 31, 32–33; universalism and particularism of, 193–94, 196–97; virtue ethics in conversation with, 30–32, 59–60, 61n8, 62n18, 119, 197–98. *See also* Orthodox Christianity
Orthodox Christianity: anthropology of, 7–8, 46, 132n196; asceticism and, 136–37; Church Fathers and, 24n43, 99, 101; communal scriptural reading in, 191n41; context for analysis, 8–10, 24n43; deification and, 61n9; Godward spiritual struggle in, 93–94, 101–2; grace and works in, 47, 50, 65n89, 96n56; Gregory of Nyssa's influence in, 99;

Orthodox Christianity (*continued*)
integrative nature of, 28–30; mysticism and, 120; resistance to systematization, 60n4; uniting with God, 27–28; unity of virtues in, 35

Pachomius, 157
pagans and paganism, 47–48, 55–56, 76–77, 79
Paisios of Mount Athos (elder), 79, 80, 81, 82
Papanikolaou, Aristotle, 29–30, 88–89
Parfit, Derek, 3, 4
patriarchy, 12, 15
Patristic theology, 9–10; defense of reliance on, 12–18, 22–23n26; divine indwelling in, 149; sacred reading and, 168, 171–72, 174–75, 197; servitude in, 13, 15–16. *See also specific Patristic authors*
Paul (apostle), 34, 38, 74, 83, 94n8, 97n85, 106, 121–22, 140
Paul of Thebes, 97n85
Paulsell, Stephanie, 179
Pelagianism, 45–47, 50, 51, 55, 56, 59, 81
penance, 75, 83
perfectionism and (un)attainability: in Aristotelian ethics, 32–38, 77; grace and, 37–38; in Orthodox Christian ethics, 36–38; saints of Scripture and, 34–35; spiritual struggle and, 38, 42, 104, 108–14, 123
perpetual progress. *See epektasis*
persecution narratives, 23–24n37, 24n43
personhood vs. individualism, 85–86
Peter (apostle), 34, 122
Pincoffs, Edmund, 22n7
Plato and Platonism, 102–5, 125n25, 126n42, 129n142
Plutarch, 78
Podmore, Simon, 76, 94n1
politeia, 27. *See also* Orthodox Christian ethics
Porphyrius, 138
Porter, Jean, 33, 49, 57, 62n29, 64n63
postmodernism, 12, 15, 21n4
poverty, 41–42, 160, 166n148
praxis: contemplation and, 29; ethical framework from, 9, 28, 135, 193; habituation to good action through, 46; sincerity in, 197; spiritual struggle and, 45–46, 77, 135. *See also* asceticism; sacred reading
prayer: asceticism and, 160; Christian identity in, 181; habituation to good action through, 46; Luther on, 51; sacred reading and, 179–81; spiritual struggle through, 74, 75, 82, 85, 91–92, 194–95; Teresa of Avila and, 82, 91–92
predestination, 52, 54, 66n116
pride and hubris, 43, 44, 48, 55, 108
primordial nature. *See* angelification and restoration; fallen and risen human nature
procreation, 137, 139, 141, 159. *See also* sexuality and sexual continence
proof-texting, 55, 173, 175, 185
Protestantism, 8, 60n2, 61n9, 131n186
prudence, 49
Psalms, Gregory of Nyssa's commentary on, 110, 116, 117, 120
Pseudo-Dionysius the Areopagite, 129n142
Pseudo-Macarius, 151–52, 154–55
psychology and spiritual struggle, 71–72, 73*t*, 98n120, 132n197
purification and purgation: of bodily temple, 136, 143, 149; in Gregory of Nyssa's theory of perpetual progress, 110, 115–19, 129n142; liturgy and, 153–54; Paisios's model for, 79–80; sacred reading and, 180, 182–85; sexual continence and, 136, 138, 142–43, 145, 148–49, 158; spiritual struggle and, 83, 90–93, 98n109, 99, 119, 158

quandary ethics, 22n7
queerness, 24–25n58

Raasch, Juana, 151
Ramelli, Ilaria L. E., 17, 140–41, 166n148
rationalism, 22n20
Ratzinger, Joseph Cardinal (later Pope Benedict XVI), 190n22

real presence, 153
Reno, Russell, 17, 174, 183, 189n12
ressourcement theology, 13, 23n34, 59–60
restoration. *See* angelification and restoration; fallen and risen human nature; unity with God
Roberts, Robert C., 10
Roskam, Geert, 78

Sabbath songs of Qumran, 150
sacred reading: Christocentricity and, 171–75, 197; communal exegesis and, 94n7, 175–78; ethics context for, 10, 19; habituation to good action through, 46; prayerful embodiment and, 179–81; spiritual struggle and, 20–21, 171, 179, 183; as transformative practice, 20, 21, 167–69, 178, 179, 184, 189n9; unity with God and, 184–88; virtue and, 181–84; vulnerability and, 169–72, 180
salvation, 47, 49, 53, 54, 58, 76, 125n14, 149, 190n18
sanctification, 58–59. *See also* angelification and restoration; purification and purgation; unity with God
Sandis, Constantine, 5–6
Sanford, Jonathan, 4, 5, 10, 11, 22n7, 30–31
Schmidt, Richard, 28, 93
Scholasticism, 21n4
Scriptural citations: Leviticus 7:9, 176; Numbers 20, 122; Deuteronomy, 185; Psalms 17:12, 107; Psalms 43:1, 112; Matthew 19:21, 185; Matthew 25:14–30, 42; Luke 20:34–36, 140; John 17:3, 107; Romans 2, 42; Romans 9:22–23, 54; 1 Corinthians 7:1–9,32–35, 140; 2 Corinthians 5:6–10, 135; Philippians 3:13, 121; James, 84; James 2:19, 185
Scripture: Saint Athanasius and, 14; contemporary ethics and, 167, 177–78; Godward progress and, 122; Old and New Testaments as unity in, 173–74; Origen on, 167; pluralism in interpreting, 168, 188n7; spiritual reality of, 170; spiritual struggle and codification of, 74, 99, 174. *See also* sacred reading
Second Temple literature, 136, 149–50, 160
self-centeredness and self-effacement, 43–45, 64n71, 86–87
Sermon on the Mount, 161, 169
servitude in Patristic theology, 13, 15–16
sexuality and sexual continence: addictive quality of, 142–43, 159; angelification and, 148; asceticism in early church and, 137–43, 145; Clement of Alexandria on, 140–45, 159; in Godward spiritual struggle, 20, 95n42, 137; Gregory of Nyssa on, 148; pleasure and, 140–42; purification and, 136, 138, 142–43, 145, 148–49, 158; queerness and, 24–25n58. *See also* asceticism; bodies and bodily passions
Shenouda III (pope of Coptic Orthodox Church), 186–87
Shepherd of Hermas, 141, 180, 191n67
Sherwin, Michael, 49–50
Shonkoff, Jack, 41
sin and vices: in antinomianism, 52, 53; in Aristotelian ethics, 34, 43; Gregory of Nyssa on, 109; Luther on, 51; sacred reading and, 184; spiritual struggle and, 38, 57–58, 80–85, 98n109; temptation of Christ and, 84–85; in Thomistic ethics, 49. *See also* sexuality and sexual continence
sincerity, 197
Sirka, Zdenko, 124n9
slavery, 87, 166n148
Smith, J. Warren, 94n8, 116, 124, 125n14, 126n42
Song of Songs: Gregory of Nyssa's commentary on, 102, 117; Origen's commentary on, 171; Shenouda III's commentary on, 187
souls: anagogy and, 109, 110, 114, 118; asceticism and transformation of, 143, 149, 151, 155, 158, 159, 195–96; bodies and development of, 81, 124, 196; in Gregory of Nyssa's *epektasis* theory, 19, 101, 103, 105–7, 117, 122, 124, 125n21; liturgy and, 156; in Luther's theology, 51, 80; sacred reading and transformation

souls (*continued*)
of, 181–87; terminological considerations, 200n2
Spinks, Bryan D., 165n109
spirituality: bodies and, 29–30; consequences for absence of God in, 100; dogma and doctrine and, 131n182; in Gregory of Nyssa's works, 101–2; premodern and modern notions of, 28–29
spiritual struggle, 8; Aristotelian-Thomistic ethics and, 74, 76–77, 83; Athanasius and, 14; against base desires, 79–84, 95n42; as Christian worldview, 75; community and, 84–90, 93, 99, 145; defining elements of, 9, 27–28, 73–75, 83; embodied, 94n8; Godward orientation of, 93–94, 99, 114–15, 118–19, 135, 187; grace and, 46–50, 55–59, 80–85, 96n56, 99; inherent goodness of, 57; interiorization and, 156; lower/higher categorization in, 90–91, 95n32, 115, 119; Luther and, 51; moral luck and effort in, 40–43; perfection and, 38, 42; as purgative, virtuous encounter with God, 90–93, 119; as pursuit of virtue, 36, 38; sacred reading and, 20–21, 171, 179, 183; Scriptural roots of, 74; self-centeredness and, 45; sincerity in, 197; stages of, 114–23; Stoicism and, 74, 77–79, 83; submission to God enabled by, 83; types of, 72–74, 73*t*; unity with God and, 57, 60, 76–77, 93–94; universality of, 64n63; virtue through, 11, 19, 25n63, 32, 76, 80–81, 87–89, 111; as worldview for Christian life, 75. *See also* asceticism; Godward orientation and progression; praxis; sacred reading
Sterk, Andrea, 15
Stoicism: *apatheia* in, 131–32n186, 140; Clement of Alexandria and, 140; Gregory of Nyssa's departure from, 113; intimations of God in, 93, 95n28; struggle in, 74, 77–79, 83
Stokas, A. G., 64n65
Symeon the New Theologian, 152, 156
teleological frameworks, 6, 22n17; in Aristotelian vs. Orthodox ethics, 30, 32–33, 35, 76–77; clothing metaphors and, 163n48; community and, 85–87, 93; disabilities and, 89–90; in Gregory of Nyssa's works, 99–100, 104, 113; lower/higher categorizations in, 95n32; sacred reading and, 184; sanctification in, 182, 199–200; universality and particularity of, 196–97
temples and temple imagery, 136, 138, 149–53, 159–60
temptation, 84–85, 87, 90, 108
Teresa of Avila, 82, 91–92
Tertullian, 24n38
Tessman, Lisa, 87–88
theosis, 130n156, 166n134
Thomistic ethics. *See* Aquinas, Thomas; Aristotle and Aristotelian-Thomistic ethics
Tough, Paul, 41
Tracy, David, 178
transformation: asceticism and, 75; in embodying Godward spiritual struggle, 9, 76–77, 115, 119–20, 123, 129n130, 130n161, 136; *epektasis* and, 104; in eschaton, 63n48, 105; grace and, 46, 57; liturgical, 149–58; monasticism and, 152, 157; perfection and, 38; sacred reading and, 21, 167, 168, 169, 178, 179, 184, 189n9; through truth, 13; in unity with God, 31–32, 45, 102, 119–20. *See also* angelification and restoration; purification and purgation
Trinity, 85, 114. *See also specific aspects*
Truscott, Derek, 98n120, 132n197
typology, 170, 172–73, 176, 180, 184, 186–89, 189n12

unity of virtues, 32–35, 62n30, 128–29n130
unity with God: asceticism and, 14, 135–36, 149–58; beatific visions of God and, 62n10; *epektasis* and, 103–5; eschatology and, 99; grace and, 47–48, 55–56; Gregory of Nyssa's theory of perpetual

progress and, 16, 19, 115–20, 123–24; habituation in the good and, 79–80; interiorization and, 156–58; liturgical transformation and, 149–58; negative theology and, 29–30; in Orthodox Christian ethics, 27–28, 30, 31, 32–33; prayer and, 92; sacred reading and, 184–88; spirituality and, 29; spiritual struggle and, 45, 57, 60, 76–77, 82–83, 93–94; terminological considerations, 61n9, 130n156; virtue from, 27, 31–32, 44, 55, 92–93, 108, 112–14. *See also* Godward orientation and progression

Verhey, Allen, 173, 177, 180, 184
vices. *See* sin and vices
Vigorelli, Ilaria, 148
virginity, 137–42, 147–48, 158. *See also* sexuality and sexual continence
virtue: acquired vs. infused, 48–50, 62–63n38, 63n39; adverse, 88; anagogy/perpetual ascent and, 108–14; angelification and, 145–47; God as paragon of, 112–14, 119, 123, 128–29n130; grace and works and, 37, 39, 46–53, 91; moral luck and, 39–43; oppression and, 87–89; in Orthodox Christian ethics, 30–33, 35, 193; perfectionism and (un)attainability of, 35–38, 42–43; possession of, 63n39; sacred reading and, 20–21, 168, 181–84; self-centeredness and self-effacement and, 43–45; sexual continence and, 138; spiritual struggle enabling, 11, 19, 25n63, 32, 76, 80–81, 87–89, 111; unity of virtues, 32–35, 62n30; virtue ethics subverting, 31
virtue ethics, 4–5, 10–11; grace and agency in, 47–50, 58–59; imitation of Christ and, 103–4; Orthodoxy in contemporary discussion with, 30–32, 59–60, 61n8, 62n18, 119, 197–98; practicality and applicability of, 98n120, 123, 132n197, 193–94; Scripture and, 170, 178, 181–82; self-centeredness and self-effacement in, 44, 64–65n77; spiritual struggle absent in contemporary, 19, 31, 71–72, 100, 198; spiritual struggle as pathway to, 93–94; unity of virtues and, 62n30
virtuous agents: acquired vs. infused virtues in, 49–50; in Aristotelian-Thomistic ethics, 32–35, 37, 62n30; communal orientation of, 86; grace orienting, 46; inequality and, 42; knowledge of God and, 44; moral luck and, 39; perfectionism and, 37; salvation and, 58
vulnerability in sacred reading, 169–72, 184–85

Ware, Kallistos, 61n9
weaknesses and base desires, 79–84, 91, 92, 141–42. *See also* sexuality and sexual continence; vices
Weil, Simone, 87
Wetzel, James, 67n148
Williams, Bernard, 6
women, marginalization of, 16–18
Woodill, Joseph, 62n18
works. *See* grace and works; spiritual struggle

Xia, Hui, 116

Yu, Jiyuan, 98n120, 132n197

Zachhuber, Johannes, 125n25
Zizioulas, John, 85

ABOUT THE AUTHOR

STEPHEN M. MEAWAD is an assistant professor of theology at Caldwell University. He received his BA in religious studies from New York University; his MTS from Holy Cross School of Theology; and his PhD in theology from Duquesne University. His continued research lies at the intersection of theology, spirituality, and moral philosophy.

www.ingramcontent.com/pod-product-compliance
Lightning Source LLC
LaVergne TN
LVHW040158080826
844660LV00001B/20

* 9 7 8 1 6 4 7 1 2 3 1 1 6 *